THE PENGUIN ENGLISH GRAMMAR A–Z

for Advanced Students

Geoffrey Broughton

ELT

PENGUIN BOOKS

Published by the Penguin Group
27 Wrights Lane, London W8 5TZ, England
Viking Penguin Inc., 40 West 23rd Street, New York, New York 10010, USA
Penguin Books Australia Ltd, Ringwood, Victoria, Australia
Penguin Books Canada Ltd, 2801 John Street, Markham, Ontario, Canada L3R 1B4
Penguin Books (NZ) Ltd, 182–190 Wairau Road, Auckland 10, New Zealand

Penguin Books Ltd, Registered Offices: Harmondsworth, Middlesex, England

Published in Penguin Books 1990

Designed by Jacky Wedgwood

Filmset in Malaysia

Made and printed in Great Britain by
BPCC Hazell Books Ltd
Member of BPCC Ltd
Aylesbury, Bucks, England

Acknowledgements

It would be impossible to write about English grammar today without acknowledging a debt to Sir Randolph Quirk and his collaborators at University College, London, both in the monumental *Survey of English Usage* and in the series of scholarly grammars which culminated in their definitive *Comprehensive Grammar of the English Language* (Longman, 1985). To Professors Quirk, Greenbaum, Leech and Svartvik my homage, admiration and gratitude. This book would also have been impossible without the generous and expert advice of my former colleague, C. P. Hill, of London Institute of Education, the tolerant guidance of Joy McKellen of Penguin Books and the unfailing support and practical skills of my wife, Pamela.

Geoffrey Broughton Lima, Trivandrum, Gaucin

Introduction

This book is designed to help advanced students and teachers to come to grips with a modern, mainstream, description of the grammar of British English. The material is organised into a number of separate entries, arranged alphabetically. The basic arguments for this are that grammar needs to be presented and studied in digestible chunks, and that these need to be readily accessible.

Grammar is a major system of any language (alongside phonology and lexis). But most frequently we turn to a reference book for information on one particular item. The alphabetical arrangement and full index of this book are designed to ease such inquiries. Yet each item is part of a larger system: grammar is a system of systems no less than the human body, a motor-car engine or any other mechanism. For this reason, each entry ends with references to other, related, entries. By following these sign-posts the inquirer is helped to appreciate how the system and its parts inter-relate.

The arrangement of the book, therefore, means that an entry into the study of grammar can be made at almost any point, and where that point of study is decided by personal choice or need, the motivation is strong to explore connecting parts of the system.

Another benefit of the A to Z organisation is that we have been able to produce entries on features of grammar which cross the boundaries of traditional categories: for example, assertion/non-assertion, dynamic/stative use, gradable/non-gradable.

Wherever possible – in about three-quarters of the entries – the grammar points are exemplified by authentic language, taken from a broad spectrum of English writers. (See page 312 for the sources of citations.) In addition, many entries include a final quotation, chosen as a witty, wise or otherwise memorable example of the particular point of grammar. Let us not forget that:

> *'The fundamental thing about languages is that they can and should be used to describe something; and this something is, somehow, the world. To be constantly and almost exclusively interested in the medium – in spectacle cleaning – is a result of a philosophical mistake.'*
>
> Karl Popper

Symbols and abbreviations used in this book

~ corresponds to

* not acceptable English

= has the same meaning as

> becomes

→ produces

△ omitted word(s) or zero form

[ ] square brackets enclose communicative functions

/ / slants enclose phonemic transcription

ˈ stressed syllable

ˋ stressed syllable with high falling intonation

ˎ stressed syllable with low falling intonation

ˊ stressed syllable with high rising intonation

ˏ stressed syllable with low rising intonation

ˇ stressed syllable starting an intonation pattern which falls then rises

adj.	Adjective
adv.	Adverb/Adverbial
aux.	Auxiliary verb
C.	Complement
conj.	Conjunction
D.O.	Direct Object
intrans.	Intransitive
I.O.	Indirect Object
N.	Noun
N.P.	Noun Phrase
op.	Operator
P.P.	Prepositional Phrase
pred.	Predication
prep.	Preposition
pron.	Pronoun
S.	Subject
trans.	Transitive
V.	Verb
V.P.	Verb Phrase

Pronunciation table

Consonants		Vowels	
Voiceless	*Voiced*	/iː/	leap
/p/ pat	/b/ bat	/ɪ/	lip
/t/ toe	/d/ doe	/e/	bend
/k/ cot	/g/ got	/æ/	band
/f/ few	/v/ view	/ɑː/	hard
/θ/ think	/ð/ this	/ɒ/	not
/s/ sue	/z/ zoo	/ɔː/	nought
/ʃ/ shoe	/ʒ/ pleasure	/ʊ/	book
/tʃ/ cheap	/dʒ/ jeep	/uː/	boot
/h/ hat	/m/ hem	/ʌ/	much
	/n/ hen	/ɜː/	bird
	/ŋ/ ring	/ə/	among
	/l/ light	/eɪ/	lay
	/r/ right	/əʊ/	low
	/j/ yes	/aɪ/	lie
	/w/ west	/aʊ/	cow
		/ɔɪ/	coy
		/ɪə/	here
		/eə/	hair
		/ʊə/	poor
		/eɪə/	layer
		/əʊə/	lower
		/aɪə/	liar
		/aʊə/	power
		/ɔɪə/	employer

1

a – series adjectives and adverbs

This small group of words like *away*, all starting with *a-*, do not fit neatly into any one word class. All can follow linking verbs (*become*, *remain* etc.). Some are more like adjectives (*asleep*), some are usually called adverbs (*away*) and others may be both. Even dictionaries still disagree about some *a-* words.

Though many *a-* words are non-gradable, two have all four qualities we use to identify central adjectives; *aloof* and *alert* are used attributively (***aloof** men*, ***alert** women*) and predicatively (*they grew* **aloof**, *they became* **alert**); they follow intensifiers (*extremely* **aloof**, *very* **alert**) and they have comparative and superlative forms (*more* **aloof**, *most* **alert**). These two words also have -ly forms as adverbs: *aloofly*, *alertly*. *Aloof* and *alert* are certainly adjectives.

But we cannot distinguish adjectives from adverbs by using intensifiers and comparatives. These demonstrate gradability, which is shared by both adjectives and adverbs. However, *a-* adjectives typically take the predicative position:

The house was **ablaze** Never **the* **ablaze** *house*

a- adjectives mean something to do with temporary states, and they only follow verbs of motion in their idiomatic sense: e.g. *to come alive*.

a- adverbs less readily follow linking verbs and then often in fixed verb phrases:

to remain afloat *to stand aloof* *to go aground*

a- adverbs have a meaning of direction after verbs of motion except in idiomatic fixed phrases like *to fall asleep*, *to fall askew*.

The commonest *a-* adjectives are:

ablaze	*ajar*	*aloof#*	*awake*
adrift	*alert#*	*ashamed (of)*	*aware (of)*
afloat	*alike*	*asleep*	*awash*
afraid (of)	*alight*	*astir*	*away#* (as in *an* ***away** game*)
aghast	*alive*	*averse (to)*	

(# may be used attributively)

The commonest *a-* adverbs are:

aboard	*abroad*	*apart*	*aside*
abreast	*ahead*	*ashore*	*astride*

The commonest *a-* words which we use as both adjectives and adverbs are:

adrift	*aground*	*alone*	*askew*
afloat	*aloof*	*amiss*	*astray*

GUIDELINES

Except for *alert* and *aloof*, we do not use *a-* adjectives in attributive position:

**afraid* children **alive* men **asleep* babies

When do absolute clauses often open spoken sentences?

Use *too* and *very* only with *afraid*, *alike* and *ashamed*. Other *a*- adjectives have fixed intensifiers:

all alone   *fast asleep*   *wide awake*   *fully aware*

'An ambassador is an honest man sent to lie abroad for the good of his country.'

Sir Henry Wotton, written in a friend's album

▸ see

4	Adjectives, general	4	Central adjectives
5	Adjectives, position	105	Gradability
6	Adjectives & adverbs	141	Linking verbs
12	Adverbs	203	Predicative adjectives

2

Absolute participle clauses

Sometimes we include a subject in an *-ing* or *-en* clause different from that of the main clause. This is known as an absolute clause:

Main clause

He looked menacing in the hood, **only the eyes showing**.

(Ile de Roc) *was well named*, **massive cliffs rising out of the sea**.

He stood, **silver hair swept back, arm raised in salute**.

Nothing could have been more elegant than the woman . . . **blonde hair perfectly groomed**.

Notice that none of these absolutes starts with a subordinator, though we could use 'with' in all of them.

Absolute clauses are most common in descriptive writing, though they can function as sentence adverbials in conversation, when they frequently take front position:

Everything considered . . .   *God willing . . .*   *Weather permitting . . .*

'Here we are again, with both feet firmly planted in the air.'

Hugh Scanlon (trade union leader), *Observer* newspaper, 'Sayings of the Year', 1973

▸ see

94	*-en* participle	185	Participles
123	*-ing* form	257	Sentence adverbials
127	*-ing* clauses	262	Subordinators

3

Active and passive voice

Most transitive verbs have active and passive forms – this difference is known as voice. Compare

He **had done** *his duty.* *His duty* **had been done**.

Notice how the subject of the active form – the doer, or agent – may be dropped in the passive, also how the object of the active form becomes the subject of the passive. Active and passive sentences are not, however, two ways of saying the same thing. See how Conrad selects the passive when the agent is unknown, unimportant or to be disguised:

Not a shot **was fired**.

That evening – ***I was informed*** *– Abdullah landed . . .*

He must **be killed**.

At other times the author uses the passive to front a phrase he wishes to emphasise:

His will, all his sensations, his personality – all this	– fronting

seemed to be lost.

Occasionally the passive is the only way of expressing a complex thought without awkwardness:

He **was carried** *away by a flood of hate, disgust and contempt . . . for that blood which was not his blood, for that race which was not his race . . . for the hearts false like the sea, blacker than night.*

▶ GUIDELINES

A small number of transitive verbs in stative use do not appear in the passive. These are verbs like *to belong, to cost, to have.* We can say:

Conrad had a Polish surname. But not **A Polish surname was had by Conrad.*

(A number of prepositional verbs are not used in the passive voice. Examples are: *to agree with, to arrive at (a place), to look for, to turn to.*)

Interestingly, there are two common verbs which we usually use in the passive: *to be born, to be/get married:*

Conrad was born in the Ukraine.
He was married in 1895.

▶ **see**

98 Fronting
222 Prepositional verbs
87 Stative verbs
270 Transitivity
271 Verbs

4

Adjectives: general

Some formal features

Adjectives are a major class of words which tell us more about (modify) a noun or a pronoun:

. . . the ***silent*** *sea and its* ***endless*** *patience*

In the word *endless*, the suffix *-less* tells us that it is an adjective. Some other adjectival suffixes are: *-ful*, *-ish* and *-y*. But, outside their context, most common adjectives have no particular form or ending to show they are adjectives. *Right* and *wrong* are adjectives only when used as adjectives: we also use them as verbs and nouns. So how do we know when *good* and *bad* are adjectives?

We use most adjectives in four patterns:

before a noun (the attributive position, pre-modifying the noun): *the* ***unmistakeable*** *white shape*

after a linking verb (the predicative position, complementing the verb): *the forest was* ***dark***

after intensifiers like *very*, *so* etc.: *very* ***grateful***
with comparative and superlative forms: *her face seemed* ***softer, simpler***

Adjectives which are used in all four of these ways are called central adjectives.

Other adjectives are restricted to attributive position only or predicative position, and some are used in post-position, after their noun. When several adjectives are used together, we tend to place them in a fixed order:

a ***small black*** *shape* Never **a* ***black small*** *shape*

Adjectives overlap with adverbs, and participles. They have a close relationship with nouns and verbs, and often have fixed complements.

Some semantic features

Adjectives help us to talk and think about things which are identified by nouns and pronouns. When we add an adjective to a noun it enables us to think, speak or write more accurately and deeply. *The* ***silent*** *sea*, *the* ***dark*** *forest* and *the* ***unmistakable white*** *shape* are all more exact phrases than *the sea*, *the forest* or *the shape*.

Most languages have a useful number of pairs of adjectives with opposite meanings: *good bad*; *kind unkind*; *comfortable uncomfortable*. These are paired opposites. Some of these stand at each end or pole of a scale of meaning and are polar adjectives, like *open shut*; *high low*; *full empty*.

Adjectives like these give points of reference to our thinking and communication. But we also need to identify points in between the extreme poles: ***fairly*** *good*, ***pretty*** *bad*, *kind****er***, ***most*** *unkind*, ***extremely*** *uncomfortable*, ***rather*** *uncomfortable*, ***nearly*** *open*, ***almost*** *shut*, ***quite*** *high*, *low****ish***, *full* ***to the brim***, ***getting*** *empty*.

These examples show that many adjectives, like adverbs and nouns, can be gradable or non-gradable. Some groups of adjectives with similar meanings help us to be more accurate about points on the scale between two extremes. Here is a common series of adjectives: *cold*, *cool*, *warm*, hot. We say that *cold*, *cool*, *warm* and *hot* are in serial relationship. Adjectives, like adverbs, nouns and verbs, can stand in serial relationship.

Most adjectives appear in defining use; that is, they give added definition to their noun phrase. But when applied to nouns naming unique entities they are non-defining. In

the ***silver*** *moon*
our ***respected*** *Member of Parliament*
dear *mother*,

the adjectives are not singling out one moon/MP/mother from several but adding attributes in the same way as non-defining clauses:

~ *the moon, which is silver*
~ *our MP, whom we all respect*
~ *mother, who is dear to me*

Similarly, when we modify a noun, particularly in post-position, by way of adding information rather than defining, that post-modification is non-defining. Consider:

He rose, ***pale and feeble,*** *from his sickbed.*

Even more commonly, when nouns are already defined in some way that gives them common focus, any additional adjective is often non-defining: *the* ***honourable*** *gentleman opposite*, *in England's* ***green and pleasant*** *land*, *Homer's* ***wine-dark*** *sea*.

▶ see

6 Adjectives and adverbs
7 Adjectives and nouns
8 Adjectives and participles
9 Adjectives and verbs
10 Adjectives with suffixes
11 Adjective order
47 Attributive adjectives
64 Comparison with adjectives
65 Complementation
82 Defining/non-defining
105 Gradable/non-gradable
130 Intensifiers
141 Linking verbs
201 Post-position adjectives
203 Predicative adjectives
204 Pre-modifiers
276 Word classes

5

Adjectives: position, general

Central adjectives can stand in two positions:

before the noun, the attributive position, as premodifiers:

a ***happy*** *man*   *a* ***strange*** *event*   ***different*** *noises*.

after linking verbs, the predicative position:

he is ***happy***   *it seemed* ***strange***   *they sound* ***different***.

Sometimes adjectives can stand in a third position – after the noun or pronoun as post-modifiers: *'something* ***old,*** *something* ***new,*** *something* ***borrowed,*** *something* ***blue'*** (traditional advice on what an English bride should wear for good luck).

Some adjectives are only used attributively. Other adjectives appear only in the predicative position (*she seemed* **awake** but not **the* ***awake*** *girl*). Some appear in both positions, but with a change of meaning. (Compare: a ***firm*** *friend* and *my friend is* ***firm***). Others appear both before and after nouns, but with a changed meaning. (Compare: ***present*** *friends* ~ current friends; *friends* ***present*** ~ friends here now.)

▶ **see**
47 Attributive adjectives
201 Post-position adjectives
203 Predicative adjectives

6

Adjectives and adverbs

Adjectives and adverbs have common features and are closely related both in form and meaning. There are some adjective/adverb lookalikes which are identical in form. There are also certain adjectives which look like adverbs.

In general, it is true to say that adjectives are used in close connection with (modify) nouns and pronouns: adverbs are used in close connection with (modify) verbs and other word classes.

Common features of adjectives and adverbs

Adjectives and adverbs can be gradable and non-gradable, although in each case most are gradable. It follows that all gradable adjectives and adverbs have comparative and superlative forms and are modified by intensifiers. So:

Adjective: *heavy* *heavier* *heaviest* *very heavy*
Adverb: *heavily* *more heavily* *most heavily* *very heavily*

Semantic relationships of adjectives and adverbs

The largest group of adverbs is formed by adding *-ly* to common adjectives. This produces adjective/adverb pairs in which the meanings are very similar. The pairs are well illustrated in definitions:

a ***slow*** *train is one that travels* ***slowly***
a ***clever*** *boxer is a man who boxes* ***cleverly***
an ***obvious*** *genius is someone who is* ***obviously*** *a genius*

Adjective and adverb lookalikes

Some words ending in *-ly* can be both adjective and adverb. Most mean something to do with time: *early*, *daily*, *fortnightly*, *hourly*, *monthly*, *nightly*, *quarterly*, *weekly*, *yearly*. So *early* (adj.) risers get up *early* (adv.); *daily* (adj.) papers are on sale *daily* (adv.) etc.

GUIDELINE

Watch out for adjectives in *-ly* which are not used as adverbs and have no corresponding adverb:

cowardly	*kindly*	*lonely*	*masterly*
deadly	*kingly*	*lovely*	*ugly*
friendly	*lively*	*manly*	

Other common words have the same form (without *-ly*) as both adjective and adverb: *fast, long, straight, still.*

Adjectives: ***fast*** *cars* *a* ***long*** *time* ***straight*** *lines*

Adverbs: *to travel* ***fast*** *can't stay* ***long*** *to go* ***straight***

Others also have a second adverbial form in *-ly*. In the following examples, both adverbs have a similar meaning:

Adjective	Adverb	-ly Adverb
a ***deep*** *river*	*to sink* ***deep***	*to sleep* ***deeply***
an ***easy*** *climb*	*to go* ***easy***	*to climb* ***easily***
a ***fair*** *game*	*to play* ***fair***	*to play* ***fairly***
a ***quick*** *answer*	*to come* ***quick***	*to come* ***quickly***
a ***slow*** *journey*	*to go* ***slow***	*to drive* ***slowly***

Other common words have the same form (without *-ly*) for both adjective and adverb, with a second adverbial form in *-ly* having a different meaning.

Adjective	Adverb	Adverb
clean *hands*	*get* ***clean*** *away*	*cut it* ***cleanly***
clear *skies*	*stand* ***clear***	*write* ***clearly***
a ***close*** *relative*	*stand* ***close***	*watch* ***closely***

Other pairs include:

dead/ly	*free/ly*	*late/ly*	*sharp/ly*
dear/ly	*hard/ly*	*light/ly*	*short/ly*
direct/ly	*high/ly*	*pretty/prettily*	*wide/ly*
fine/ly	*just/ly*	*right/ly*	*wrong/ly*

GUIDELINE

We are here in the border country between adjectives and adverbs. Remember that, like other word classes, adjectives and adverbs are abstract grammatical categories and many words can operate as members of more than one category.

When the same form can be used as both adjective and adverb, and when both word classes can complement certain verbs, how can we identify *right* in:

Do it right next time?

The best test is to substitute other adjective/adverb pairs: *correct/ly proper/ly*. The *-ly* forms fit, so *right* in the sentence above is being used as an adverb.

Does **eccentric** mean the same as adjective and noun?

'Power tends to corrupt, and absolute power corrupts absolutely.'

Lord Acton, *Historical Essays*

▶ **see**

12 Adverbs
19 Adverbs as modifiers
64 Comparison with adjectives
105 Gradable/non-gradable
130 Intensifiers

7

Adjectives and nouns

Adjectives have a close relationship with nouns as modifiers and many adjectives are formed from nouns. There are a number of adjective/noun lookalikes, like *chief* and *square*; nouns frequently operate as adjectives, both attributively (as in ***women** priests*) and – less commonly – predicatively (as in *The book is **copyright***) and we often use some adjectives as nouns (*taking the **rough** with the **smooth***). Watch out for adjectives used as plural nouns like this no-nonsense medical use of ***sharp:***

DANGER **Contaminated** **SHARPS**

Adjective/noun lookalikes

Words like *square* are both adjectives and nouns: *square* is an adjective when it is used attributively and predicatively – ***square** tables*, *it looks **square***. It also follows intensifiers – *very **square***, *completely **square***; and has comparative and superlative forms – ***squarer***, ***squarest***.

Square is a noun when it follows a determiner: ***the square***; and has a plural form: ***squares***. As a noun it stands as the subject and object of verbs:

> *Trafalgar **Square** contains Nelson's Column.*
> *Cross Parliament **Square** by the underpass.*

There are certain nouns whose suffixes make them look like adjectives: *adhes**ive***, *adolesc**ent***, *circul**ar***, *eccent**ric***, *origin**al***. But they all have regular plural forms, follow determiners and stand as subject or object of verbs. Despite their suffixes, they are established in the language as both adjectives and nouns and are usually given separate entries in dictionaries, often with slight changes of meaning. National labels ending in -ese, like *Chinese*, *Japanese* and *Portuguese* are equally adjectives and nouns:

> *The **Portuguese** laurel* *Christina Rossetti's 'Sonnets from the **Portuguese**'*

Nouns used as adjectives in attributive position. Nouns are often used as attributive adjectives to pre-modify another noun: *Salisbury is a **cathedral** city*. But we cannot say **Salisbury is **cathedral***, or **Salisbury is a very*

***cathedral** city*. So *cathedral* is not an adjective but a noun used as an adjective, an adjectival.

Usually a pre-modifying noun is singular, although the meaning may be plural. Someone who collects *tickets* is a ***ticket** collector* and we exhibit *dogs* in a ***dog** show*.

Some nouns normally have a plural form only. But even they are usually made singular when used as adjectives. So *a* ***trouser** pocket*, *a* ***pyjama** jacket* and *a* ***spectacle** case* (but *a* ***glasses** case*).

Notice a number of exceptions, which remain plural –

nouns ending -ics which are the names of subjects:

an ***athletics** meeting* *a* ***classics** degree* *an* ***economics** course*

the names of some illnesses:

***measles** spots*, ***mumps** infection*, ***shingles** rash*.

news: a ***news** agent*, *a* ***news** boy*.

clothes: a ***clothes** basket*, *a* ***clothes** horse*, ***clothes** hangers*.

goods: ***goods** train*, ***goods** wagon*, ***goods** yard*.

sport: the ***sports** page*, ***sports** shop*.

Man and *woman* are used as adjectives in both singular and plural forms. We talk about – ***man**-eaters* and ***man** haters*, but ***men** drivers*, ***men** friends* and ***men** teachers*. ***Woman** chasers*, ***woman** haters* and ***woman** trouble*, but ***women** drivers*, ***women** priests* and ***women** teachers*. The plural forms *men* and *women* are used as attributive adjectives when *men* and *women* are the subject of the underlying verb:

***men/women** drivers* ~ *the men/women drive*
but ***man/woman** haters* ~ *they hate men/women*
Consider ***woman** killers/*
***women** killers/*

GUIDELINES

We use the singular form of nouns as adjectives unless the phrase is ambiguous. See how both forms are needed in these examples to avoid ambiguity and notice the stress differences:

a ***'classics** failure* and *a* ***'classic'** failure*
an ***ath'letics** meeting* and *an* ***ath'letic'** meeting*
a ***'news** letter* and *a* ***'new'** letter*
a ***'goods** vehicle* and *a* ***'good'** vehicle*.

Watch for new attributive uses of nouns. Phrases like *a* ***comfort** person*, *a* ***fun** person*, *a* ***jewellery** lady*, *a* ***whisky** man* are recent (and are stressed on the first noun).

Nouns as adjectives in predicative position

A few nouns are used both attributively and in predicative position – the names of some materials that things are made of:

a ***slate/thatch/tile** roof* *the roof is* ***slate/thatch/tile***
a ***cotton/nylon/wool** shirt* *the shirt looks* ***cotton/nylon/wool***
a ***brick/concrete/stone** house* *the house looks* ***brick/concrete/stone***.

the names of famous artists, craftsmen, etc.

a ***Wren*** *church* *the church is* ***Wren***
a ***Holbein*** *painting* *the painting looks* ***Holbein***

the names of well-known places/influences which show provenance:

her ***Yorkshire*** *accent* *her accent sounds* ***Yorkshire***
her ***county*** *manners* *her manners seem very* ***county***

with the verb *to be*, familiar nouns can take conversational short-cuts:

They were neither **church**△ *nor* **chapel**△.
Are you **club**△ *or* **tourist**△?

Adjectives as nominals

Some adjectives are used in noun positions. We order beer by asking for a pint of *bitter/mild* or *draught*. Our newspaper may be a *daily* or a *weekly*. These are really a short way of saying a phrase from which we have dropped the noun. Both speaker and listener understand what noun has been left out. A motorist may say, '*It's an automatic* △.' or, '*I'm afraid I've got a flat* △.'

Doctors informally use several adjectives in this way:
They give us *a medical* or *a physical*; they administer *an anaesthetic* with *a hypodermic*; they refer to patients as *an alcoholic*, *an arthritic*, *an asthmatic* or *a coronary*.
And how about this adventurous counter sign from Boots the Chemists?

Aftersuns
Suntans
Sunglasses

▶ GUIDELINE

This use of adjectives is not as common in English as it is in other languages. Even talking to another motorist and pointing to your shattered car window you still cannot say *'*I've got a broken*△.'

Sometimes we use adjectives with generic meaning after *the*:
the ***old*** *and the* ***young*** ~ all old people and all young people.

The adjectives are usually those to describe people and always refer to the whole group or class.

> *'The young have aspirations that never come to pass,*
> *the old have reminiscences of what never happened.'*
> Saki, 'Reginald at the Carlton'

We talk about a small group of nationalities in the same way. They all end in /ʃ/ or /tʃ/ and cannot follow *a/an*. We can't say **a British* etc., but we do say

the British *the Danish* *the Spanish* *the Dutch* *the French*

Another use of *the* is with a few abstract adjectives used as nouns, often in fixed phrases: *take the rough with the smooth*, *work from the known to the unknown*, *go from the sublime to the ridiculous*.

> *'The difficult takes a little time; the impossible takes a little longer.'*
>
> F. Nansen, attrib.

A third use of *the* + adjective is a very small group using *-en* forms. Legal language includes *the accused* and *the deceased*. Church language includes *the betrothed* and *the bereaved*.

Adjectives ending in *-able* and *-ible* are sometimes used as nominals: *perishables*, *submersibles* and *untouchables*.

GUIDELINE

Adjectives used as nouns are far less common than nouns used as adjectives. If in doubt about usage, consult a good dictionary.

> *'The English country gentleman galloping after a fox – the unspeakable in full pursuit of the uneatable.'*
>
> Oscar Wilde, *A Woman of No Importance*

see

10 Adjectives with suffixes
94 *-en* participle
130 Intensifiers
172 Nouns, plural only
204 Premodifiers

8

Adjectives and participles

Many adjectives have the same form as the *-ing* and *-en* participles. These adjectives are called participial adjectives. Some of the commonest are:

-ing *amazing* *amusing* *exciting* *frightening* *interesting* *shocking* *surprising* *tiring* *worrying*

-en *amazed* *amused* *excited* *frightened* *interested* *shocked* *surprised* *tired* *worried*

Here the *-ing* is active and the *-en* is passive.

The thing that ***interests*** *you is* ***interesting****.*
The result is that you become ***interested****.*

When is an *-ing* or an *-en* form adjectival and when verbal? We must remember that we use both as adjectives and in finite verb forms and as non-finites:

adjectives *It's an* ***amusing*** *game.*
The baby seems ***amused****.*

finites	*She's* ***amusing*** *the baby.*
	It is ***amused*** *by the game.*
non-finites	*She's happy* ***amusing*** *it.*
	When ***amused*** *it laughs.*

We can say that any *-ing* or *-en* form is fully adjectival if it can take attributive and predicative position, follow intensifiers like *very* and *so*, and have comparative and superlative forms. These are all participial adjectives.

We can say that an *-ing* or *-en* form is in adjectival use when

it follows a linking verb other than *to be*.

He seems ***tired***.

it follows an intensifier.

It was so ***disappointing***.

it is made into a compound:

*home-***made**, *fair-***haired**, etc.

We can also say that any *-ing* form is in verbal use when it has a direct object: *You're* ***frightening*** *me*. Likewise any *-en* form with *by* + agent is verbal:

I was ***frightened*** *by the dog*.

Ambiguity can arise, however, when adjectival and verbal uses take the same form:
She's ***entertaining*** can mean both –

She's an ***entertaining*** *person* and *She's* ***entertaining*** *guests*.

Notice that a few verbs have two participial forms, one for verbal use, one for adjectives.

Participial	**Adjectival**
He has ***drunk*** *it*	*a* ***drunken*** *driver*
He has ***shaved***	*a* ***shaven*** *head*
It has ***shrunk***	*a* ***shrunken*** *head*
It has ***struck***	*a* ***stricken*** *family*
It has ***sunk***	*a* ***sunken*** *ship*

Some participial adjectives in attributive position refer not to the following noun, but to a connected subject. So *a bored look* is not *a look which is bored*. It is *the look of a bored person*. In cases like this the participial adjective cannot take a predicative position.

a ***bored*** *woman*	*the woman is* ***bored***
a ***bored*** *look*	**the look is* ***bored***

So we can say:	but we can't say:
a ***waiting*** *game*	*the game is ***waiting***
a ***losing*** *hand*	**the hand is* ***losing***
a ***satisfied*** *smile*	**the smile is* ***satisfied***
a ***pleased*** *expression*	**the expression is* ***pleased***

Which two kinds of verbs commonly have adjective complements?

GUIDELINES

Some *-en* participles of intransitive verbs, which have an active meaning, are used in the attributive position only. We can say:

*the **departed** visitors* *an **escaped** lion* *an **exiled** king* *an **exploded** theory* *a **fallen** tree* *a **returned** soldier* *the **vanished** treasure*

But we cannot say **the visitors are* ***departed***, etc. (though we can say *have departed*).

Some *-en* suffixes are pronounced /ɪd/ when used as adjectives:

beloved *crooked* *ragged* *wicked*

'A schoolgirl answered the question, "In what countries are elephants found?" Elephants are very large and intelligent animals, and are seldom lost.'

James Agate, *Ego, 9*

---

see

4	Central adjectives	130	Intensifiers
69	Compound adjectives	141	Linking verbs
94	*-en* participle	157	Non-finite verbs
96	Finite verbs	185	Participles
124	*-ing* participle	204	Pre-modifiers

9

Adjectives and verbs

The commonest way in which adjectives are used with verbs is as a complement to linking verbs and complex transitive verbs.

Edward VI died young. They found Wilde guilty.

Otherwise some adjectives are used as verbs and some become verbs by taking verb suffixes.

Adjectives used as transitive verbs

Here we have adjective/verb lookalikes, with the verb meaning *to make adjective*. So

clean (verb) the windows ~ make the windows clean (adj.)

In the same way you can:

***calm** your nerves* ***dry** your face*
***clear** your throat* ***empty** your pockets*
***cool** your temper* ***lower** your voice*
***dirty** your hands*

Some transitive phrasal verbs consist of an adjective with a particle; the verb meaning *to make something adjective*. So

*to **tidy** a place up ~ to make a place **tidy***

Is **to darken** transitive or intransitive?

In the same way you can:
blank *a notice out*
calm *someone down*
dry *things out*
smooth *things away*

Adjectives used as intransitive verbs

There are rather fewer lookalikes for adjective/intransitive verbs. Here the verb means *to become adjective*. So

the clothes were ***drying*** ~ *the clothes were becoming* ***dry***

Similarly, sometimes as we grow old, *our hair* ***greys*** *and* ***thins****, our complexions* ***pale****, our skin* ***yellows*** *and our arteries* ***narrow***! Some intransitive phrasal verbs consist of an adjective with a particle, the verb meaning *to become adj*.

So when you ***cool*** *down* or *off* you *become* ***cool***. In the same way you can ***calm*** *down*, ***dry*** *up*, ***sober*** *up*, and ***warm*** *up*.

Verbs formed from adjectives

Adj. + *-en* forms verbs meaning *become adj*. or *to make adj*. So, when our faces ***redden*** they *become* ***red*** and when we ***sweeten*** coffee we *make* it ***sweet***.

Notice that these verbs are both transitive and intransitive. Several come from polar adjectives and are paired opposites: *the sky* ***lightened/ darkened***. Sometimes the *-en* verb is complementary to a lookalike verb: *his eyes* ***narrowed/widened***.

The following pairs are used both transitively and intransitively:

blacken/whiten *tauten/slacken*
darken/lighten *tighten/loosen*
harden/soften *shorten/lengthen* (from the noun)
sadden/gladden

Other *-en* verbs include:

broaden *flatten* *quicken* *stiffen*
deafen *gladden* *quieten* *straighten*
deepen *heighten* *ripen* *weaken*
fasten *moisten* *sharpen* *widen*
fatten

'All the things I really like to do are either immoral, illegal or fattening.'

Alexander Woollcott, *Wit's End*

Adj. + *-ise* form transitive verbs meaning *to make adj*. So, when we ***publicise*** something we make it ***public***. In the same way we *familiarise, immunise, legalise, localise, modernise, nationalise, specialise* and *tenderise*.

▶ GUIDELINE

Adjective/verb lookalikes should be learnt together. Verbs formed from adjectives should be learnt in relationship to the adjectives (*short/shorten*).

Paired opposites should be learnt together (*darken/lighten*). So should common particles and objects with their verbs (*cool down, cool off, cool your temper*).

▶ **see**
141 Linking verbs
195 Phrasal verbs, transitive
268 Transitive verbs, complex
271 Verbs

10

Adjectives formed with suffixes

The following suffixes form adjectives from many nouns or verbs, and each has a clear meaning:

-able/-ible -al -ed -en -ese -ful -(i)an
-ic -ical -ish -ive -less -like -ly -ous -y

We add suffixes to the base form of the noun or verb:

to do with an editor ~ **editori**al
(weather) *that might change* ~ **change**able

New adjectives ending in *-y* continue to appear, but they tend to be colloquial: *comfy*, *dishy*, *dicey*, *fishy*, *gutsy*, *handy*, *nervy*, *toothy*, *trendy*, *whiffy*.

'I may never have been very pretty but I was jolly larky and that's what counts in the theatre.'

Dame Edith Evans, *Radio Times*

The use of *larky* above is an example of a word invented for the occasion, and therefore slightly humorous. *Larky* is readily interpreted as *full of larks, full of fun*

-y, together with *-able*, *-ish*, *-less* and *-ful* are the most productive of adjective suffixes. All are found in new forms, often with humorous intent. Part of the delightful, gentle humour of A. A. Milne's children's stories about Winnie the Pooh, a Bear of very little Brain, is Pooh's adventurous use of adjective suffixes. When Pooh is at peace with the world, it's *a hummy sort of day* and he and Piglet can meet at the *Thoughtful spot* to do nothing. When, however, it's *a very Blusterous day outside* Pooh's thoughts readily turn to his honey pots and he begins to *feel a little eleven o'clockish*. And once Piglet had a brain-wave:

'Courage,' he said. 'There's always hope.
I want a thinnish piece of rope.
Or, if there isn't any, bring
A thickish piece of string.'

A. A. Milne, *The House at Pooh Corner*

The same suffixes are used by serious authors in creating new, artificial languages. When Orwell designed the simple futuristic language, Newspeak, for his novel, *1984*, he decided that all adjectival meanings could be expressed by adding *-ful* to the noun/verb form, giving *speedful* = rapid, *plusful* = many, more and *goodthinkful* = orthodox, incapable of thinking a bad thought. Anthony Burgess's more colourful nightmare in *A Clockwork Orange* needs a more adventurous new vocabulary. Burgess selects the suffixes *-ful*, *-ish*, *-less* and *-y*:

insulting and hurtful veck *so very appetitish*
a domeless wonderboy *a warm vibraty feeling*

(As in two of these examples, the addition of suffixes often involves minor changes of spelling and pronunciation.)

Of the suffixes listed above, the most productive is *-y*.

11

Adjectives: order in attributive position

When two or more adjectives premodify a noun there is usually an accepted order. We say: *brown hair*, *light brown hair*, *straight light brown hair*, *long straight light brown hair* and *beautiful long straight light brown hair*. Any other order would sound and feel odd.

Adjectives placed after the noun and in predicative position are usually fewer in number and have more freedom in their order.

Notice that the ordering of adjectives is part of a larger grouping. Adjectives in a noun phrase come between determiners and the noun head:

All her (dets.) *beautiful long straight light brown hair* (head).

Here we are considering adjectives only.

Central adjectives always follow intensifiers:

a rather ***cursory*** *sense*, *such* ***cruel*** *things*,
a quite ***good-looking*** *boy*.

Within the class of central adjectives, the preferred sequence is as follows:

evaluation *size* *age* *shape* *colour* *participle* *noun-derived*

Here are some examples:

a funny little girl *nice square teeth* *a tiresome old husband*
a big powerful girl *the small, calm radiant unsmiling face*
an awkward affectionate animal *with short pale bobbed hair*
my little caged bird *her tough defeated acceptance*
her innocent little palpitating heart *a long white shelf*
tiny scarlet veins *the high white wall*

In the final position before the noun head we place nouns in adjectival use:

Such nice sleek ***animal*** *ears*
a valuable ***London*** *property*
the warm powdery dirty ***London*** *air*

GUIDELINE

This is a complicated area and the order described above is not always followed by English writers. In speech we do not often use more than three or four adjectives together.

▶ see

47 Attributive adjectives
4 Central adjectives
84 Determiners
178 Noun phrases
204 Premodifiers

12

Adverbs: general

Adverb is a label which has been applied to a wide range of words. Modern grammar is still in the process of refining this traditional rag-bag. The central type of adverb ends in *-ly* and is usually derived from an adjective:

happy (adj.) → *happily (adv.)* *beautiful (adj.)* → *beautifully (adv.)*

But other adverbs, usually one-syllable words, have no particular form to show their word class. In fact a number are identical with adjectives:

I've known him a long (adj.) time. Have you known him long (adv.)?

Like adjectives, many adverbs have comparative and superlative forms: *long, longer, longest.*

We use adverbs for two main purposes, as modifiers and as adverbials. As modifiers, e.g. ***very*** *big*, they modify several other word classes. As adverbials, they have the same relationships and sentence positions as a variety of phrases and clauses.

Carefully
With great care } *he took the porcelain.*
Taking great care

Adverbs have a choice of three positions in a sentence: front- mid- and end-position. Choice of position is sometimes fixed but often depends on meaning and emphasis. When two or more adverbs stand together their order is not entirely free. We classify adverbs by meaning. The traditional categories of place, manner and time remain valid.

What used to be called adverbs of degree have been divided into focusing adverbs and intensifiers, added to which it is useful to identify sentence adverbs and linking adverbs.

▶ see

6 Adjectives and adverbs
13 Adverbs: comparison
14 Adverbs: focusing
16, 17 Adverbs: intensifying
18 Adverbs of manner
19 Adverbs as modifiers
20 Adverbs of place
21 Adverbs: position
22 Adverbs of time
23 Adverbials
36 Adverbials: sequence
140 Linking adverbials
257 Sentence adverbials
276 Word classes

13

Adverbs: comparison of adverbs

The comparison of gradable adverbs is similar to that of adjectives. Regular adverb comparison consists of adding *-er/-est* to adverbs of one syllable, and using *more/most* with others:

late, later, latest *early, earlier, earliest*
fully, more fully, most fully *quickly, more quickly, most quickly*

The commonest adverbs with irregular comparison are:

well	*better*	*best*
badly	*worse*	*worst*
little	*less*	*least*
much	*more*	*most*
far	*farther/further*	*farthest/furthest*

The alternative *farther/further* forms refer to distance and mean the same. Otherwise, *further/furthest* = later, additional.

For equal comparison of adverbs, as with adjectives, we use *(not) as . . . as*:

He can swim as well as you.

▸ **see**
64 Comparison of adjectives
105 Gradable/non-gradable

14

Adverbs: focusing adverbs

We use focusing adverbs to focus attention on part of a sentence. The adverb usually precedes the word, phrase or clause:

Stephen ***absolutely*** *and* ***utterly*** *forbade her.* [word]
She had wished ***only*** *for the belt.* [phrase]
It is astounding . . . the effect of a natty little domestic apron suddenly put on over an elaborate and costly frock . . . ***especially*** *when the apron is smoothed out by jewelled fingers.* [clause]

Most focusing adverbs are simple *-ly* words. Common examples are: *alone, also, chiefly, even, exactly, just, mainly, mostly, only, particularly, principally, purely, simply, solely.*

Alone is unusual in following the noun or pronoun it focuses:

She dressed to please him ***alone****.*

▸ GUIDELINE

We can also use *also, even, just* and *only* in mid-position so that occasionally it may not be clear whether they are focusing part or the whole of what follows:

She ***only*** *writes letters in English.*

In fact, in speech, we avoid any possible ambiguity by stress and intonation patterns. The same solution avoids spoken ambiguities with *too* and *either*, focusing adverbs which prefer end-position:

He writes novels in German ***too****.*

▶ **see**
21 Adverbs: position
97 Focus

15

Adverbs: intensifying adverbs

Intensifiers express some kind of degree. It is useful to identify two main kinds of intensifiers, both modifying mainly verbs, adjectives and other adverbs:
Amplifiers which intensify upwards:

to love ***completely*** ***highly*** *original* ***really*** *quickly*

and downtoners which scale downwards:

to ***almost*** *agree* ***slightly*** *warm* ***somewhat*** *hastily*

▶ **see**
16 Amplifiers
17 Downtoners
19 Adverbs as modifiers
130 Intensifiers

16

Intensifying adverbs: amplifiers

Amplifiers usually stand in mid-position when modifying verbs, but end-position is possible and usual in non-assertive and imperative sentences:

There were occasions when his deafness was ***extremely*** *pronounced.*

He regretted it ***profoundly****.*

Had Ella recovered her speech ***perfectly****?*

When modifying adjectives or other adverbs, amplifiers usually precede them:

His gratitude was ***slightly*** *premature.*

They came ***extra-specially*** *dressed.*

His invalid brother, whom he had ***so*** *deeply harmed . . .*

Common amplifiers are:

absolutely	*indeed*	*so*
awfully (informal)	*immensely*	*strongly*
completely	*intensely*	*terribly* (informal)
deeply	*more*	*thoroughly*
entirely	*most*	*too*
fully	*much*	*totally*
generally	*perfectly*	*utterly*
heartily	*really*	*well*
highly	*right*	
	simply	

We use intensifiers only with gradable verbs – you can't **kill someone completely*, but we can (metaphorically) ***totally** kill an idea*.

Some amplifiers are in common use with certain verbs, almost to the extent of being fixed phrases:

I entirely agree/ deeply regret/ utterly despise/ strongly approve/ fully understand.

In daily conversation we each tend to have our own current set of amplifiers.

GUIDELINE

Informal amplifiers have lost much of their meaning. With adjectives we use them to give emphasis, rather than to convey their literal meaning:

*That's **awfully** kind She's **terribly** sweet*
*They're **frightfully** rich*

see
17 Downtoners
19 Adverbs as modifiers
130 Intensifiers

17

Intensifying adverbs: downtoners

Downtoners usually modify verbs, adjectives and other adverbs, scaling down their meaning:

*I **little** thought that I would be returning.*	[verb]
***Almost** as unknown as in the days of Balboa.*	[adjective]
*He drove me **rather*** erratically back to the hotel.	[adverb]

When modifying, downtoners take mid-position, although we can use them in end-position:

*The guerrilla war, which **in a way** he desired, had begun.*

*The guerrilla war, which he had desired **in a way**, had begun.*

When we use them with an adjective, another adverb, or a noun, they precede the word.

*. . . not **nearly** so simple as he made out.*

*My happiness was **only a little** diminished.*

*It must have taken **nearly** two hours.*

Common adverbial downtoners include:

a bit	*hardly*	*nearly*	*rather*
a little	*kind of*	*not so*	*scarcely*
all but	*least*	*only*	*simply*
as good as	*less*	*partly*	*slightly*
at all	*little*	*practically*	*somewhat*
barely	*merely*	*pretty*	*sort of*
enough	*more or less*	*quite*	*virtually*

Notice that *quite* has meanings both as amplifier with non-gradables and as a downtoner (with gradables).

I have **quite** *finished.* *I* **quite** *enjoyed myself.*

GUIDELINE

a bit, *at all* and *enough* are usually placed in end-position after verbs; and the following adverbials can take front-position: *partly*, *to some extent*, *in some respects*.

'All the world's a stage
And all the men and women merely players.'
William Shakespeare, *As You Like It*

see

11	Adjectives: order	16	Amplifiers
47	Adjectives: intensifiers	105	Gradable/non-gradable
19	Adverbs as modifiers	130	Intensifiers
21	Adverb position	204	Premodifiers

18

Adverbs of manner

Manner adverbs answer the question *how?*, telling us how actions and events take place.

Horace left ***quietly.***

This category has sometimes included means (by + noun) and instrument (with + noun), though modern grammarians often call them adjuncts since they are usually fully integrated into their sentences.

Manner adverbs normally modify verbs and most often take end-position, though mid-position is possible, particularly when expressing value judgement and with passives:

Horace related his misfortunes ***airily.***
Horace was ***jocularly*** *ushered into the nursery.*
He was ***solemnly*** *exhorted not to apply himself to business.*

As with all types of adverb, we can only generalise about their position. Manner adverbs have to take front-position as sentence adverbs.

Unhappily *his health was not good.* [sentence adverb]

And note the effect of changing the position of a manner adverb with a negative verb:

He didn't do it ***deliberately.*** He did it.
He ***deliberately*** *didn't do it.* He didn't do it!

(This is an example of what we call scope of negation.) Notice that we use manner adverbs with verbs in dynamic use.)

Compare:

* *The material feels roughly.* [stative]
He felt it roughly. [dynamic]

Common adverbs of manner include: *beautifully*, *dishonestly*, *fearfully*, *gratefully*, *loudly* and many other *-ly* words.
Also *hard*, *fast*, *slow*, *still*, *well*, etc.

GUIDELINE

Many adverbs have cognate adjectives and abstract nouns (*happy*, *happily*, *happiness*) which offer three adverbial ways of expressing the same meaning.

He paid the bill promptly.
in a prompt manner.
with promptness.

The single-word adverb is usually the least formal, and most direct, form of expression.

see
21 Adverbs: position
30 Adverbials of manner
87 Dynamic/stative use
204 Premodifiers
257 Sentence adverbials

19

Adverbs as modifiers

Traditional grammar taught that adverbs modified verbs, adjectives and other adverbs:

He can walk ***quite well***
Side-splittingly *funny*
Somewhat *flat features*
Not ***long*** *afterwards*

Modern grammar also acknowledges sentence adverbials which modify the whole sentence:

Unhappily, *his health was not good.*

In addition we use certain adverbs, many formerly called degree adverbs, to modify a range of word classes and phrases:

Adverbs modifying nouns

A few time and place adverbs postmodify certain nouns with time or place meanings:

A few months ***later***
His return ***home*** *was a shock.*
They were in the nursery ***upstairs.***

Adverbs modifying adjectives

Usually the adverb stands before the adjective:

A smile and a scowl that were ***equally*** *effective*

Only *enough* follows its adjective:

It was a noble act, rare ***enough*** *in the Five Towns.*

GUIDELINE

When we use *too* and *so* to premodify an adjective in a noun phrase, we use the indefinite article after the adjective:

Horace was ***too*** *perfect a man.*

In the same way, *How* in exclamations and questions requires the indefinite article before single count nouns:

How *perfect a man!* ***How*** *serious an invalid was he?*

Adverbs modifying other adverbs

These are always intensifiers. The modifying adverb comes first, with the exception of *enough*.

Horace had behaved not ***quite*** *nicely.*
Strangely ***enough****, inexplicably* ***enough****, Horace did not feel like a prodigal.*

Adverbs modifying determiners, pronouns and numerals

Horace had ***scarcely*** *any friends.*	[determiner]
He learnt ***practically*** *nothing.*	[pronoun]
. . . ***about*** *fifty . . .* ***over*** *twenty*	[numerals]

Else postmodifies *who*, *what*, *where* and *how*, and pronouns ending *-body*, *-one*, *-thing*; also *much* and *little*.

What ***else*** *could Horace do?*
Ella had eyes for no one ***else****.*
Sidney played the banjo and did little ***else****.*

Adverbs modifying noun phrases

This small group includes: *almost*, *quite*, *rather*, *such* and *what* (in exclamations). The adverb always stands before any determiners.

These were ***nearly*** *the last words.*
Sidney was ***quite*** *a different story.*
What *a shame!*

Adverbs modifying prepositional phrases

Many *-ly* intensifying adverbs premodify prepositional phrases. They include:

completely *utterly*
entirely *rather*
perfectly *quite*
thoroughly *somewhat*
totally

His health was ***steadily*** *on the up grade.*
Ella was ***completely*** *in her confidence.*

see
16 Adverbs: intensifiers
204 Premodifiers
200 Postmodifiers
257 Sentence adverbials

20

Adverbs of place

Place adverbs answer the question *Where?*, telling us where the action of the verb takes place. Place includes both location (simple *where?*) and direction (*where to?*).

I'm in a hostile country **here.** [location]
Did you have a comfortable journey **down***?* [direction]

Some place adverbs have recognisable adverbial suffixes:

inward(s) *onward(s)* *forward(s)* *backward(s)* etc.
somewhere *nowhere* *anywhere* *elsewhere*

Other common place adverbs include:

about	*back*	*home*	*off*
above	*behind*	*in*	*out*
abroad	*down*	*inside*	*outside*
away	*far*	*on*	*round*

He simply bore irresistibly **downwards.**

'Now, you see this girder?' he said, looking **upwards.**

The house seemed much larger **inside** *than* **out.**

Most place adverbs take end-position. But *Here* and *There* commonly take front-position, with inversion of subject/verb when the subject is not a pronoun.

Here *we are.* **There** *they go.*

Here *was the attitude of the woman whose soul was like crystal.*

Other place adverbs only take front-position in formal or literary language. Compare:

He flew **off** *to escape my thanks.*
Off *he flew to escape my thanks.*

Compared with the infinite number of place adverbials the closed class of single-word place adverbs is small.

PETER SELLERS: *In South America.*
HARRY SECOMBE: *That's abroad, isn't it?*
PETER SELLERS: *It all depends where you're standing.*

The Goon Show

▶ **see**
31 Adverbials of place
98 Fronting
138 Inversion with place adverbials

21

Adverbs: position

There are three positions which adverbs take in sentences.

front-position – at the very beginning:

__Neither__ can I

mid-position – before a simple lexical verb (except *to be*) or a single auxiliary:

He __quickly__ worked his way up.
He __always__ did.

after the operator or *to be*:

He was __fast__ reaching the conclusion . . .
He was __still__ chairman of the largest private company.

end-position – at the very end:

The corporal smiled __nervously__.

We cannot use all adverbs in all positions, though most can stand in mid- or end-positions.

He ate his meal __quickly__ ~ *He __quickly__ ate his meal.*

Front-position

The following kinds of adverb can be used in front-position:

sentence adverb

__Perhaps__ they always managed to lose.

linking adverbs

__After all__, Eduardo had never collected the rent.

most time adverbs

__Again__ Eduardo waved a languid hand.

some frequency adverbs

__Normally__, an assistant would have put it on for him.

some place adverbs

__In the corner of the lift__ stood a stubby, balding, overweight man.

some manner adverbs

__Tentatively__, they had come to the conclusion that . . .

Mid-position

Most adverbs can stand in mid-position. Special cases include:

emphatic sentences, in which the adverb stands before the operator:

You'll __never__ find one . . . but emphatic
You __never__ will.

negative sentences, in which the position before or after *not* varies with the adverb and with the meaning:

*He had not **yet** received it.*
*He had **still** not appeared.*
*He **really** did not say. He didn't **really** say.*

The following avoid mid-position so as not to be stylistically awkward:

time adverbs of definite time and definite frequency

*They were reporting **daily**.*
They were ~~daily**~~ reporting.*

place adverbs

*Eduardo went **downstairs**.*
**Eduardo ~~downstairs~~ went.*

evaluative manner adverbs

*The driver hoped he had done **well**.*
The driver hoped he had ~~well**~~ done.*

(Notice, however, that with passive verb forms, these adverbs often precede the main verb:

*The passenger steps had been **hurriedly** pushed into place . . .*)

long adverbials

*Manuel wore a shirt **for the first time in years**.*

End-position

Many adverbs can take end-position. Those which normally DO NOT without change of meaning and intonation include:

sentence adverbs

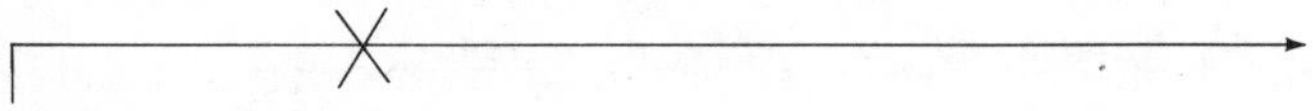

***Regretfully**, Mr de Silveira would have to eat in the main dining room.*

linking adverbs

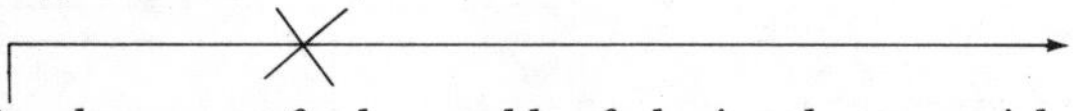

***So**, they are perfectly capable of playing the same trick.*

focusing adverbs

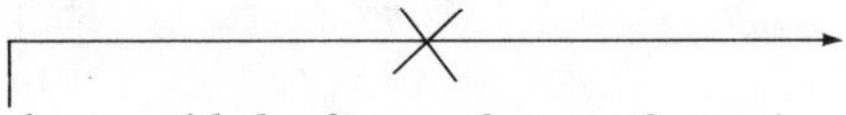

*He **only just** avoided a face-to-face confrontation.*

intensifiers

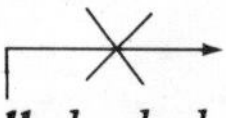

*His calendar was **fully** booked.*

GUIDELINE

These indications are not hard-and-fast rules. Adverbs may be moved from regular positions for emphasis and slight shifts of meaning, and to avoid bunching.

For more detail and exceptions see the sections on the different classes of adverb.

▶ **see**

18	Adverbs of manner	98	Fronting
20	Adverbs of place	16	Intensifiers
22	Adverbs of time	140	Linking adverbials
14	Focusing adverbs	184	Operator
22	Frequency adverbs	257	Sentence adverbials

22

Adverbs of time

Any form of time expression in English is complex. Even restricting ourselves to single-word adverbs, it is useful to identify three main categories, all of which modify verbs. These categories are adverbs of

fixed time, answering the question *When?* e.g. *today*.
duration, answering the question *How long?* e.g. *always*.
frequency, answering the question *How often?* e.g. *often*.

But the time we have in mind may be either definite or indefinite. Compare: *tomorrow/later* – both adverbs of fixed time. It is this dimension which largely determines the position in a sentence of any time adverb. But note that several time adverbs have more than one meaning.

Adverbs of definite fixed time usually have end-position:

I'm engaged **tonight**.
He emerged on the platform **again**.
I can't fancy my food **nowadays**.

Other adverbs are:

first *next* *then* *tomorrow*
late *now* *today* *yesterday*

Adverbs of indefinite fixed time may stand in front-, mid- or end-position:

Afterwards *there was a discussion.*
I perceived **instantly** *that she was excited.*
He said nothing to Lady Dain **immediately**.

Other adverbs are:

afterwards *first* *presently*
earlier *lately* *soon*
eventually *next* *sometimes*
finally *since*

Adverbs of duration usually take mid-position:

Priscilla had **always** *been quiet and self-reliant.*
She had been **only too briefly** *married to Toby Hall.*

Other adverbs are:

long *permanently* *temporarily* *lately* *recently*

Notice that these are less definite and less common than noun phrases and prepositional phrases used as time adverbials: *all day long*, *throughout the night*, *since Monday*, *until midday*, *for ten days*.

Adverbs of definite frequency usually have end-position:

Philip wrote to his mother ***weekly****.*
The doorbell rang ***twice****.*

Other adverbs are:

annually	*hourly*	*yearly*
daily	*monthly*	*once*
fortnightly		

Adverbs of indefinite frequency usually stand in mid-position:

My mother ***never*** *came to meet me.*
I have ***frequently*** *mentioned Agnes in my letters.*

Other adverbs are:

always	*ever*	*#occasionally*	*seldom*
constantly	*forever*	*#often*	*#sometimes*
continually	*#generally*	*rarely*	*#usually*
continuously	*#normally*	*#regularly*	

(notice that *ever* is non-assertive)

Often and other adverbs marked # above are also used in front- and end-position to change the meaning or emphasis of a sentence. Compare:

He was ***usually*** *jolly. ~ It was his habit to be jolly.*
Usually *he was jolly ~ but not on this occasion.*

GUIDELINE

When we use adverbs of indefinite frequency with a single auxiliary we place them immediately after the subject as comments on someone else's words.

You'd better wash your hands. *I* ***always*** *do.*
He can't join us tonight. *He* ***rarely*** *can.*

Other indefinite time adverbs indicate relationships of time. Most can have mid-position, but are used in other positions for subtle changes of meaning. Compare:

Later*, Stephen was coming home.*
Stephen was coming home ***later****.*
He visited Child Row ***last****. ~ finally*
He ***last*** *visited Child Row about twenty-four years ago.*

Other adverbs are:

already, *just*, *still* (mid-position);
since, *yet* (usually end-position);
early, *late* (end-position).

GUIDELINE

Still usually stands in mid-position:

Are you ***still*** *listening? There's* ***still*** *time.*

But, meaning *and yet*, it can be used in front-position:

Still*, it may not happen.*

But, in negative sentences, to emphasise concern/ surprise, it is placed immediately after the subject:

*You **still** haven't told me everything!*

> *'Love is like the measles – all the worse when it comes late in life.'*
>
> Douglas Jerrold, *Wit and Opinions*

▶ **see**
21 Adverbs: position
34 Adverbials of time
46 Assertion/non-assertion

23

Adverbials

We use the term adverbial as an umbrella term for those structures which have the same function, meaning and position in sentences as simple adverbs, as well as adverbs themselves. Adverbials can be finite clauses

*He fell, **just as his mother had feared.***

non-finite clauses

(infinitive)

*Women turned **to look at him** in the street.*

(*-ing* participle)

***School being impossible,** he had instruction at home.*

(*-en* participle)

***When asked where his wife was,** Sidney replied she was lying down.*

prepositional phrases

*It began **in the little house of Mrs Carpole.***

verbless clauses

*The poor little convalescent lay **moveless and insensible.***

noun phrases

***One afternoon** . . . Horace came home.*

noun phrases and *ago*, etc.

A few months later . . .

Longer adverbials can carry all the meanings common to simple adverbs (time, place, manner, etc.) but adverbial clauses also have further categories (condition, comparison, etc.).

Adverbials appear in front-, mid- and end-positions. When two or more adverbials appear together, we usually place them in a certain order.

▶ GUIDELINE

Arnold Bennett's style, exemplified above, is bland and literary. Longer adverbials are more typical of this type of written prose than of speech. Several popular writers today, aiming at a brisker style, tend to avoid finite clauses in favour of shorter adverbials, which they may even separate off as individual 'sentences':

> *I glowered at the Admiral and repeated the question. Savagely. He looked frail and worn right then. But only for a moment.*
>
> Brian Callison, *A Frenzy of Merchantmen*

▸ **see**

24	Adverbial clauses	96	Finite/non-finite
35	Adverbials: position	125	*-ing* clauses
36	Adverbials: sequence	178	Noun phrases
94	*-en* participle	218	Prepositional phrases

24

Adverbial clauses

Finite clauses and their reduced forms are a major category of adverbials. They are usually introduced by subordinating conjunctions, and stand in front- or end-position. We classify adverbial clauses by meaning into the following groups:

cause/reason

As he was a contemporary of my father*, Eric must have been nearly seventy.*

comparison

(He) is more interested in 'up front' ***than posterity****.*

concession/contrast

Although he was hard of hearing*. . . he was always amusing.*

condition

You would be backing a loser ***if you depend on that****.*

manner

They proceeded ***as though nothing had happened****.*

place

He met Eric ***where he had met Shrimpton****.*

proportion

The later *it got,* ***the more restless*** *they became.*

purpose/result

They brought the score to 20 all, ***so that everything would depend on the final game****.*

time

As he left the locker room*, I went over to the mirror.*

> *'Be wiser than other people, if you can, but do not tell them so.'*
>
> Lord Chesterfield in a letter to his son, 19 November 1745

▶ **see**

23 Adverbials
26 Adverbials of cause/reason
27 Adverbials of comparison
28 Adverbials of concession/contrast
29 Adverbials of condition
30 Adverbials of manner
31 Adverbials of place
32 Adverbials of proportion
33 Adverbials of purpose /result
25 Adverbial reduced clauses
34 Adverbials of time
76 Conjunctions

25

Adverbial reduced clauses

These are of two kinds, non-finite and verbless:

They shook hands, ***to seal the bargain.***
Although nearly bald, *he had a remarkable physique.*

They are often introduced by the same subordinators as those for full clauses, though two (absolute clauses and participle clauses) have no subordinating conjunction.

Reduced adverbials may fulfil the same functions and have the same sentence positions as full clauses:

cause/reason
(There was) no conflict of interest **because of their different tasks.**

comparison
He looked **less than his thirty-five years.**

concession/contrast
. . . they differed, **although only on points of detail.**

condition
He briefed her on cheap trips to the States **when accompanying your husband.**

manner
Harry strolled in, **looking very dapper.**

place
Wherever possible, *he chose a corner seat.*

proportion
As well as *can be expected.*

purpose/result
Adrian was invited to Los Angeles **to address a Media Conference.**

time
After exchanging greetings *they took the lift to the second floor.*

Additionally they may express meanings which finite clauses do not:

circumstance
Without asking, *Debbie poured two whiskies.*

consequence
Michael downed his coffee in two gulps, **scalding his mouth slightly.**

preference
She chose to have coffee **rather than drink brandy.**

Which cause/reason adverbials have no subordinators?

GUIDELINE

This use of the bare infinitive after *rather than/sooner than* is unique in reduced clauses. But it is parallel with *would rather/would sooner* + bare infinitive as in: *I would sooner die.*

> *'It seems to be the habit to elect presidents for their lack of evident vices, instead of for their possession of evident virtues. The existence of vices is allowed to become apparent during the incumbency.'*
>
> Peter Ustinov, *Dear Me*

see

2 Absolute clauses
26 Adverbials of cause/reason
27 Adverbials of comparison
28 Adverbials of concession/contrast
29 Adverbials of condition
30 Adverbials of manner
31 Adverbials of place
32 Adverbials of proportion
33 Adverbials of purpose/result
34 Adverbials of time
185 Participles

26

Adverbials of cause/reason

A subordinate adverbial of cause or reason usually refers to a situation which is earlier in time than that of the main clause.

He had not been eligible for National Service **on account of his flat feet.**

The relationships between the two situations may be:

cause and effect

Owing to this gross lack of consideration, *he did not manage to get away.*

motivation and result

Henry left the room empty **because he disliked the thought of unknown persons splashing in the sunken marble bath.**

circumstances and consequence

Everyone left the field, **drenched by a thunderstorm.**

Common clause subordinators include: *as, because, for, since, seeing (that).*

Prepositional phrases may start with *because of, due to, on account of, owing to.*

-ing and *-en* clauses are not introduced by subordinators.

for- clauses of cause/reason always take end-position and so usually do *because-* clauses.

His name in England was a household word, **for he had captained Oxford and India at cricket.**

It worried him, **because even he realised that he had no qualifications.**

Clauses with *as* and *since* may take front- or end-position.

As he had no interest in graduating, he by-passed tradition.

He wore evening dress, ***since he wanted to impress his guest.***

GUIDELINE

The commonest subordinator for cause/reason clauses is *because*. But we never use it with reduced clauses. It is also unique in being the only subordinator which we use in short answers to *Why?* questions.

'Because it's there.'

G. H. Mallory, in answer to the question why he wanted to climb Everest.

see

35 Adverbials: position
94 *-en* clauses
125 *-ing* clauses
218 Prepositional phrases
261 Subordination

27

Adverbials of comparison

Clauses of comparison are rather different from other adverbials because the main clause, which must come first, is often incomplete without the subordinate comparison clause, and at best cannot stand alone without change of meaning. Consider:

We must get him something that looks ***as if it belongs to him.***

These clauses are sometimes classified as adverbials of similarity and comparison because they can make comparisons of equal and comparative degree:

It was going to be as hot a day ***as the day before.***

There was more wind . . . ***than there had been.***

The main clause often contains elements like *as*, *not as*, *more*, *less*, *fewer*. The comparison clause is introduced by *as*, *as if*, *as though*, *than*, etc. Non-finite and verbless clauses are usually introduced by *as*, *as if*, *as though*:

I felt ***as though my eyes were full of oil.*** [finite]

He stood there ***as though deafened.*** [non-finite]

GUIDELINE

Comparison clauses raise the problem of subject/object pronoun with incomplete clauses.

Do we say *She was older than he*, or *She was older than him*? Traditional grammar taught that *than*, as a subordinator, must be followed by the subject pronoun, whether omission has taken place or not:

Maddison was worse than I (was).

Yet in current English, the object pronouns, *me*, *him*, *her*, *them* are acceptable and preferred nine times out of ten. Modern grammar accounts for this by viewing *than*, in such positions, as a preposition. And prepositions are followed by object pronouns.

see
79 Correlatives   183 Objects
98 Fronting   205 Prepositions

28
Adverbials of concession/contrast

In these adverbials the meaning of the main clause is seen to be somewhat contrary or in contrast to the meaning of the concession clause:

At a corner table . . . sat a woman who, ***although not young,*** *was elegant.*

I would have liked to reply . . . ***whereas I actually discussed my ideas for another novel.***

Subordinators include: *although*, *even if*, *even though*, *however*, *no matter what/who*, *though*, *whatever*, *whereas*, *while*, *whilst*, *whoever*.

For concession the commonest is *(al)though*.

For contrast, *whereas*, *while* and *whilst*.

There is a certain overlap in meaning between clauses of concession and condition, especially with *even if*:

Critics had been complimentary, ***even if the cheques from my publishers were less so.***

All subordinators except *when/whereas* can introduce both finite and non-finite clauses.

GUIDELINE

With *though* we sometimes use inversion, and with *as* in this meaning the inversion is obligatory:

Prepared though he was, *the meeting proved a shock.*

Try as you will, *you'll never catch him out.*

see
29 Adverbials of condition   136 Inversion
96, 157 Finite/non-finite   261 Subordination

29
Adverbials of condition

Here, the truth of the main clause depends on the situation of the conditional clause: it may precede or follow the main clause:

If the authorities wanted to get rid of her, *she would have to be assassinated.*

My methods cannot be condemned ***unless they can be proved to be . . . improper.***

Common subordinates include:

as long as   *if*   *on condition (that)*   *provided (that)*   *providing (that)*
so long as   *suppose (that)*   *supposing (that)*   *unless*   *whether . . . or*

GUIDELINES

Only *if*, *unless*, *whether . . . not* may introduce reduced clauses.

***If found**, please return to the address below.*
*The fruit should not be picked, **whether ripe or not**.*

> **INSTANT CREDIT**
> **for all customers over ninety, if accompanied by both parents.**

(Notice in Indian emporium)

see
72–5   Conditional sentences

30

Adverbials of manner

Manner clauses are sometimes included with clauses of comparison since they always have a sense of comparison in their meaning (in a way that manner prepositional phrases and simple adverbs do not).

However, they usually answer the questions *How?* and *In what way?* and can take front-position which comparison clauses cannot.

*. . . with the ache of Mr Crutwell's solitude within me, **as though I too were old**.*

The common manner clause subordinators are: *as*, *as if*, *as though*.

*Not that I knew him **as she did**.*
*He read Shakespeare **as if he were reading a brief**.*

Prepositional phrases are common as manner adverbials, which include means (*by* + noun) and instrument (*with* + noun). They can take front- but more usually end-positions.

***With a determined step**, I went to the mirror.*
*He gave me confidence **by having such unswerving confidence in himself**.*
*The spring air . . . would close behind me . . . **like the sea in the wake of a ship**.*

GUIDELINE

In everyday conversation we may hear *like* and *how(ever)* as clause subordinators:

He shook like he was afraid.
Dress how(ever) you wish.

But these are not strictly acceptable, especially in writing.

▶ **see**
18 Adverbs of manner
27 Adverbials of comparison
35 Adverbials: position
218 Prepositional phrases
261 Subordination

31

Adverbials of place

These answer the question *Where?*

Clause adverbials are uncommon: introduced by *where/wherever* they can precede or follow their main clause:

> ***Where Farthing Hill flattened out**, the open gates . . . appeared on my right.*
>
> *To David, Rose was always a princess in a tower, **wherever they were together**.*

Noun phrases + *away/back/below/further* etc. provide another small group of place adverbials:

> *Two paces **up the stairs**, he had come to a standstill.*

Other examples:

> *a mile away* *two blocks back* *five fathoms below*

The most common place adverbials are prepositional phrases:

> ***At the end of the school drive**, we turned down . . . the Private Road. **On one side of it**, over the hedge, were the empty playing-fields and **beyond them on higher ground** the school building.*

The wealth of prepositions available for adverbials of place is suggested by the entries on prepositional types.

▶ **see**
20 Adverbs of place
178 Noun phrases
218–20 Prepositional phrases

32

Adverbials of proportion

This is a small group. The situations in the two clauses are compared, drawing a parallel between them of a balanced plus/minus difference. One of the two forms for adverbials of proportion is introduced by *as . . .* followed by an optional correlative, *so*:

> ***As** light and darkness cannot co-exist, **so** there is a faith that puts away doubt.*

The other proportion pattern uses *the* + comparative . . . *the* comparative.

***The least** said **the better**.*

The balanced, formulaic ease of the structure lends itself to the expression of folk wisdom:

The sooner the better. *The more the merrier.*
The nearer the bone, the sweeter the meat.

'The bigger they come, the harder they fall.'

Bob Fitzsimmons, nineteenth-century world heavyweight boxing champion

---

see
13 Comparison of adverbs
79 Correlatives

33

Adverbials of purpose/result

There is an overlap in these two related categories. Not only do they have subordinators in common, but their meanings are relative to one another (successful purpose = result).

The major difference is that purpose clauses are usually tentative or hypothetical (expressed by modals) whereas result clauses are factual (expressed by ordinary tenses). Consider:

He slept with the key under his pillow ***so that no one should steal it.*** [purpose]
He slept with the key under his pillow ***so that no one stole it.*** [result]

Purpose adverbials

Finite clause subordinators include: *in case, in order that, lest, so that/such that.*

He moved forward ***so that he could help Mr Letterby.***
She added, ***lest she should overstep the boundary of politeness,*** *'But it works the other way.'*

The more common non-finite clauses of purpose may be introduced by: *for . . . to, in order to . . ., in order for . . . to, in the hope of, for the sake of*:

In the hope of warding this off, *I was taking refuge behind Rose's hat.*

Commonest purpose adverbial of all is the *to*-infinitive:

I opened my mouth ***to speak.***
We parted, ***to busy ourselves in aloof detachment.***

Occasionally prepositional phrases, especially with *for*, can express purpose:

I had pasted (the chess problem) on the card ***for later attack.***

The door was locked so that he didn't escape. Where's the ambiguity?

Result adverbials

Finite clause subordinators include: *so, so that, such that.*

I would remake myself . . . **so that I didn't feel half-false**, *whatever I did.*

Additionally the constructions *so + adj./adv. + that, such +* N.P. *+ that* are used in literary forms, sometimes with inversion:

The hall had been **so** *quiet* **that a bluebottle made a tearing sound.**

Such *had been their inattentiveness* **that it had enabled them to behave as if I had not been there.**

The *only + to*-infinitive pattern is a rare non-finite adverbial of result:

I crawled in, **only to reflect that I must certainly be the first to enter on hands and knees.**

Otherwise non-finite and verbless clauses follow linking adverbials or connectors like *accordingly, as a result, consequently, hence, and so, therefore, thus*:

The gates were never used, **the hinges consequently clogged with rust.**

▶ GUIDELINE

Given the close relationship of these two adverbial types, it is not surprising that ambiguity can arise:

David took extra classics lessons **so that he missed cricket.**
Purpose? Result?

Yet avoidance is simple: select specific purpose and result adverbials:

He took extra lessons (in order) to avoid cricket. [purpose]

He took extra lessons, so avoiding cricket. [result]

▶ **see**

96, 157 Finite/non-finite
120 *to*-infinitive clauses
136 Inversion
140 Linking adverbials
261 Subordination

34

Adverbials of time

Adverbials in this large group express meanings of fixed time, duration and frequency. Each of these may refer to definite and indefinite time:

fixed time
A month ago [definite]
When she said this [indefinite]

duration
. . . while I set my chess-table [definite]
as long as I can remember [indefinite]

frequency
every day [definite]
now and again [indefinite]

Clause conjunctions include: *as often as*, *as long as*, *as soon as*, *before*, *immediately*, *no sooner than*, *once*, *since*, *till*, *until*, *when(ever)*, *while*.

The sound was almost as thin as it had been **when I was in the park**.

... nowhere else to live **while he made his way as a barrister**.

Reduced clauses may be introduced by *when*, *whenever*, *while*, *-ing* clauses by *after*, *before*, *on*, *since*, *when*.

When abruptly launched into excitement, *he could find nothing to say*.

It was my custom, **on arriving there** *... to knock on the window*.

We use a number of noun phrases as adverbials of fixed time:

A month ago *This evening*
One evening *Some day*

Other noun phrases are:

that moment/night/day, *those days*, *every night*, *about this time*, *most days/times/weekends*.

Prepositional phrases can express all time meanings.

In the eighteenth century (fixed time)
for a week (duration)
on certain days (frequency)

All positions in a sentence can be occupied by time adverbials, but there are some limitations. Finite clauses can either precede or follow their main clause:

Since she came back, *she's always tinkling*.

I thought it best not to go into the morning-room **until I had washed**.

Shorter adverbials of fixed point in time usually take end-position, though *since*- or *when*-clauses occasionally take front- and mid-positions:

She was always there **at that hour**.

She had run the house, **since my mother's death**.

Adverbials of definite frequency and of duration tend to take end-position:

She doesn't even come to church **on Sunday mornings**.

She hadn't collected stamps **for years**.

Phrases of indefinite frequency take front- or end-position. Occasionally we find a time phrase embedded in a finite clause:

When, **for a little while**, *one is inside the room of another's life, one is still, so ridiculously, a face at the window*.

See how Charles Morgan's opening sentences to a chapter of reminiscence are loaded with time adverbials:

The evening which singles itself out as a point of departure must have been **towards the end of an Easter term**. **Across the gulf of more than forty years**, *only feeling lives, and even the feeling of that hour,* **as I came away from school between daylight and dark**, *may be tempered in recollection. By the knowledge which I have* **now** *of what was to happen to me* **before I reached home** *and of what I should find* **when I came there**.

Which of two final adverbials can be fronted?

▶ **see**

22 Adverbs of time
76 Conjunctions
178 Noun phrases
218–20 Prepositional phrases

35

Adverbials: position

The position in clauses of single-word adverbs is discussed in 21, since adverb position is more complex than that of other adverbials. The two entries should be read in conjunction. The same three positions in a clause or sentence are available to longer adverbials: front-position, mid-position and end-position. Choice of adverbial position depends on structure and length, partly on meaning and any special emphasis required. The adverb sequence of manner/place/time is generally true for all adverbials:

The black Mercedes drove **slowly through the gates.** [M + P]

He was expecting to have an audience **with the President on Friday***.* [P + T]

He sat **alone in his room for the rest of the day***.* [M + P + T]

But we usually place longer adverbials after shorter ones; clauses after phrases:

He was prepared to return **to Brazil if Rodriguez turned out to be involved***.*

He studied . . . the proposal sent to him **a week later, after the general had returned***.*

Longer adverbials usually stand in end-position, though front-position is sometimes necessary:

Remind me of this conversation **five minutes before I see the Minister***.*

While these thoughts were going through Eduardo's mind, *the Mercedes drew up.*

▶ GUIDELINE

When two time or place adverbials occur in end-position we usually put the 'larger' one last; as with single-word adverbs:

He wouldn't move himself or his staff **one centimetre out of Brazil***.*

But only this 'larger' adverbial can be fronted:

You have an appointment with him **at nine o'clock on Thursday morning***.*

On Thursday morning, *you have an appointment with him* **at nine o'clock***.*

At nine o'clock,** *you have an appointment with him* **on Thursday morning.*

His private plane sat idly **on the tarmac only a few miles away***.*

Only a few miles away, *his private plane sat idly* **on the tarmac***.*

On the tarmac,** *his private plane sat idly,* **only a few miles away.*

▶ **see**
21 Adverbs: position
97 End-weight
98 Fronting

36

Adverbials, sequence

When we use two or more adverbials together, particularly in end-position, the usual order is manner, place, time (Remember M, P, T – in alphabetical order).

The Mayor strode ***with great assurance, through the door.*** [M + T]
His wife met him ***at the front door at seven-thirty.*** [P + T]
He ceased breathing ***hard while in the water.*** [M + T]
She bathed the baby ***routinely in the bedroom each evening.*** [M + P + T]

We can change this order to avoid breaking up fixed phrases:

Mr Blackshaw went ***home quickly.*** [P + M]

to give emphasis, end focus, to a particular element:

She could always end an argument ***when she chose,*** *and* ***in her own favour.*** [T + M]

and when, for reasons of style, we place the longest adverbial last:

He arrived ***at his residence in the very nick of time*** *and* ***full to overflowing with innocent paternal glee.*** [P + T + M]

▶ GUIDELINES

In fact we usually try to avoid putting too many adverbials in end-position, transferring time or place adverbials to front-position:

Then, ***at a quarter to five*** *. . . he saw a burly shadow* ***behind the glass door.***

When two place adverbials have end-position, the 'larger' place comes last:

He worked ***at the Electricity Works in Bursley.***

When two time adverbials have end-position we put the shorter or the more precise one first:

The bath took place ***at five o'clock in the evening.***

'This is my final word. It is time for me to become an apprentice once more. Somewhere, sometime, soon.'
Lord Beaverbrook's last public speech, given on his eighty-fifth birthday

see
35 Adverbials: position
97 Focus

37

Apposition

Noun phrases in apposition are of equal rank, stand next to each other and refer to the same person or thing:

... ***his third and last wife, Livia Augusta***

Appositive clauses are nominal clauses marked off by commas, which have a similar relationship to the preceding noun head. They may be *that*-clauses, *wh*-clauses, or *to*-infinitive clauses. The head of an appositive clause is always an abstract noun like: *appeal*, *belief*, *decision*, *idea*, *news*, *opinion*, *promise*, *question*, *reply*, *rumour*, *threat*.

... *news came* ... **that Caius had been sent to the East**

... *she sent a message* **that Castor would be out** ...

Tiberius' promise **to take care of the regiments**

Notice that appositive clauses may be defining and non-defining, although either kind may be deleted without the sentence losing meaning:

Augustus had a shrewd notion ***that Livia intended Aemilia's husband to be no other than myself.*** [defining]

Cato's often-stated opinion, ***that Carthage should be destroyed,*** *resulted in popular nervousness.* [non-defining]

GUIDELINES

Here is an easy way of distinguishing appositive clauses from relative clauses. Both may start with *that*. But appositive clauses may not start with *which*, as relatives can. So where *which* can alternate with *that*, the clause is likely to be relative and not appositive.

appositive

The premature news ***that this battle was lost*** ... *caused consternation.*

relative

The premature news {***that*** / ***which***} ***said the battle was lost*** ... *caused consternation.*

▸ see

82	Defining/non-defining	247	Relative clauses
156	Nominal clauses	119	*to*-infinitive clauses
178	Noun phrases	273	*wh*-clauses

38

Articles: general

There are two articles in English, the definite article *the*, and the indefinite article *a* or *an*. The articles are members of the class of words called determiners, which stand before nouns. We often use articles with common nouns, very rarely with proper nouns and occasionally with adjectives. For certain meanings we use the noun without an article, zero article.

The is usually pronounced /ðə/ and *a* is usually pronounced /ə/ We say:

ðə ə
The moon's a balloon.

This always happens when the following sound is a consonant: the (m)oon, a (b)alloon. But in English we rarely say /ə/before a vowel sound. So, before a vowel sound, *the* is pronounced /ði/ and we change *a* to *an*.

ði ən
The actor, David Niven, was an Englishman.

Notice that it is the sound, not the spelling, of the word after the article which decides its pronunciation:

ə
a usual time – ***an*** *unusual time*

A few words are spelt with an initial silent *h*. We treat them as though they start with a vowel:

an hour   *an honest man*   *the heir*   *the honour*

The, *a* and *an* have stressed forms, pronounced /ði/ ei/ and æn/ These are usually used to emphasise some unique quality. In print they are often shown in italics:

ei ði
I said I'd met a Tom Jones. Not the Tom Jones.

▸ GUIDELINES

Don't be caught out by abbreviations. Some consonant letters are pronounced with an initial vowel:

F ~ /ef/   L ~ /el/   M ~ /em/   etc. So:

the European Economic Community	*the EEC*
a Heavy Goods Vehicle Licence	*an HGV licence*
a Member of Parliament	*an MP*

Also: *an X-ray*

When do we use proper nouns with generic meaning?

> *'A man in a queue is as much the image of a true Briton as a man in a bull-ring is the image of a Spaniard or a man with a two-foot cigar of an American.'*
>
> George Mikes, *How to be Inimitable*

▶ **see**

39 Articles with proper nouns
40 Articles with common nouns
41 Articles: the definite article
42 Articles: indefinite & zero
43 Articles: fixed phrases
44 Articles & class meaning
84 Determiners
158 Nouns
277 Zero forms

39

Articles with proper nouns

The articles are not normally used with proper nouns. The main exceptions are personal and family names.

Some literary characters are remembered for certain qualities and their names are used to mean a person with those qualities. So if we say a man is *a Scrooge*, we mean he's a miser; *a Romeo* is a young romantic lover; and someone wanting to be *a Sherlock Holmes* is ambitious to be a detective. This use has generic meaning. More commonly we refer to a family in the plural, using the; *the Watsons*, *the Doones*, *the Borgias*: we also use *a* with the family name, meaning a member of . . . *The Montagues* and *the Capulets* were bitter enemies – Romeo was *a Montagu* and Juliet *a Capulet*.

> *'Keeping up with the Joneses was a full-time job with my mother and father. It was not until many years later when I lived alone that I realised how much cheaper it was to drag the Joneses down to my level.'*
>
> Quentin Crisp, *The Naked Civil Servant*

Other plural names which follow *the* include:

Countries and areas
the Netherlands   *the United States*   *the Home Counties*   *the Tropics*

Groups of islands
the Bahamas   *the British Isles*   *the Canaries*   *the Philippines*
the Shetlands   *the West Indies*

Ranges of mountains and hills
the Cotswolds   *the Pennines*   *the Alps*   *the Andes*   *the Himalayas*
the Pyrenees   *the Rockies*

Singular proper nouns which follow *the* include:

Countries and areas
the German Federal Republic   *the United Kingdom*   *the Arctic*
the Far East   *the Middle East*   *the West*

Rivers
the Avon *the Thames* *the Amazon* *the Danube* *the Mississippi* *the Nile*

Seas and oceans
the Aegean *the Atlantic* *the Baltic*

Canals and sea passages
the Kiel/Panama/Suez Canal *the Bosphorus* *the English Channel* *the Straits of Dover/Gibraltar/Magellan*

Museums, theatres, libraries
the Bolshoi *the British Museum* *the Louvre* *the Prado*

Unique buildings
the Acropolis *the Kremlin* *the Taj Mahal*

Names of newspapers
the Guardian *the Observer* *the Telegraph*

GUIDELINE

The articles are not often used with proper nouns, but when they are used there is nothing difficult or surprising. The indefinite article, *a*, is used meaning a member of a group, a representative, *a Romeo*, *a Borgia*. The definite article, *the*, as a signal of common focus, shows the uniqueness of the noun – *the Thames*, *the Times* – there is only one and we have heard of it before.

'*The* Times *is read by the people who run the country.*
The Guardian *is read by the people who would like to run the country.*
The Financial Times *is read by the people who own the country.*
The Daily Telegraph *is read by the people who remember the country as it used to be.*
The Daily Express *is read by the people who think the country is still like that.*
The Daily Mail *is read by the wives of the men who run the country.*
The Daily Mirror *(which once tried to run the country) is read by the people who think they run the country.*
The Morning Star *is read by the people who would like another country to run the country.'*

Advertisement

---

see
160 Proper nouns

40

Articles with common nouns

The use of the articles with nouns depends on three things. These are: the difference between count and non-count nouns; the difference between individual and class meaning; and the difference between definite and indefinite meaning.

All common nouns are either count nouns or non-count nouns. Singular count nouns name individual objects and plural count nouns a number of individual objects: *a finger/fingers*. Count nouns can be counted and have plural forms: *five fingers*. Non-count nouns name substances which exist in the mass which we cannot count. Therefore non-count nouns have no plural forms: *milk*, *wood*, *metal*, *gold*, *hair*, *furniture*. Count and non-count nouns have different patterns with the articles and other determiners.

Nouns have either individual or class meaning. If we read about Dick Whittington and his cat we are thinking about a particular individual animal. Here *cat* has individual meaning referring to one member of the cat class, which is by far the commoner of the two meanings. But in the following sentences we are referring to the class of cats generally, or to an unspecified individual representing the species:

Golfing for **Cats**. (Title of book by Alan Coren)
A cat *may look at a king*. (Proverb)

In these sentences *cat(s)* has class or generic meaning.

Nouns with individual meaning can have either definite or indefinite meaning. So, when we are talking about particular, known things, in common focus to speaker and listener, the nouns have definite meaning. The same nouns have indefinite meaning if our listener cannot identify them. Compare:

A man first stood on ***the moon*** *on 20 June 1969*. [definite]
Saturn has several ***moons***. [indefinite]

The indefinite article, *a/an*, is singular in meaning and is only used with singular count nouns. It expresses indefinite meaning. To express indefinite meaning with plural nouns and non-count nouns we use zero article.

The definite article *the* is used with all kinds of common nouns and has definite meaning. So:

	definite meaning	indefinite meaning
Singular count	*the chair*	*a chair*
Plural count	*the chairs*	*chairs*
Non-count	*the furniture*	*furniture*

> *'In practical life the woman is judged by man's law, as if she were a man, not a woman.'*
>
> Henrik Ibsen, *Hedda Gabler*

▶ **see**
80 Count/non-count nouns
84 Determiners
160 Common nouns
277 Zero forms

41

Articles: the definite article and definite meaning

We use the definite article with nouns when both speaker and listener know what is being talked about. This common focus may arise from:

the uniqueness of the thing spoken about

the sky *the government* *the (family) car* *the children*

familiarity in the situation

the college *the town* *the baby* *the supermarket*

familiarity in the culture

the radio *the newspaper* *the train* *the post/mail*

the fact that it has been recently mentioned

Place ingredients in a large pan of cold water; cover ***the*** *pan and bring* ***the*** *water to the boil.*

(This is called back-pointing or anaphoric use of *the*.)

what follows the noun (post-modification)

the House that Jack built *the Woman in White*

(This is called the forward-pointing or cataphoric use of *the*.)

▶ **see**
200 Postmodifiers

42

Articles: the indefinite article and zero article with indefinite meaning

We use the indefinite article with singular count nouns to introduce a new topic or one unfamiliar to the speaker and/or hearer:

There was ***a*** *table set out under* ***a*** *tree.*

With plural count nouns and non-count nouns we use zero article or unstressed *some* for indefinite meaning:

There were △ cups and △ saucers and a tea-pot.
'Have ***some*** *wine,' the March Hare said.*

Common examples of individual but indefinite meaning are heard when we are shopping:

*I'd like **a** melon, please. May I have **some** apples?*
What△ vegetables have you got?
*We had△ sprouts yesterday. I'll take **a** cabbage.*

In each case we are not thinking of individual melons, cabbages, etc., but representatives of the species.

GUIDELINE

Use *some* when you are thinking of an indefinite amount of an agreed thing or substance. Use zero article when you are thinking of the category itself. So if you are choosing between categories, zero article is necessary:

Shall we have△ beer or△ wine? Oh, let's have△ wine.

If you know the category and leave the amount indefinite, use *some*:

*Alice helped herself to **some** tea and **some** bread and butter.*

We also use noun phrases starting with *a/an* as complements, when *a/an* means 'one of the following class'.

*'I'm **a** poor man, your Majesty,' he began.*
*'You're **a** very poor speaker,' said the King.*

GUIDELINE

Always put an article before the names of jobs and professions in English:

*Keats qualified as **a** surgeon before he became **a** full-time poet.*

see
178 Noun phrases
277 Zero forms

43

Articles: common fixed phrases with zero article

The following groups of common nouns with zero article have become idiomatic and fixed. The meaning of the noun is indefinite:

to go to△ sea ~ to become a sailor
to enter△ prison ~ to become a prisoner
to go by△ rail ~ to choose a train and no other vehicle

Institutions
at church college university home in bed hospital town

Transport
by bicycle car plane etc.

Fixed times of day/night
at dawn midday sunset etc.

Meals
after breakfast dinner supper etc.

Binomials
arm in arm end to end in sickness and in health etc.

see
160 Common nouns
277 Zero forms

44

Articles and class meaning

To express class meaning we can use all forms of the article.

	a	*the*	Zero article
Sing. count n.	*a man*	*the man*	
Pl. count n.			*men*
Non-count n.			*man (kind)*

Shakespeare uses all four in the same play.

a 'He was a man .'

b 'The apparel proclaims the man .'

c ' Man delights not me.'

d 'I have thought some of nature's journeymen have made men and not made them well.'

a/an + count noun names an indefinite member of a class or species to stand for its qualities.

the + singular count noun names the typical member of a class or species standing for the whole.
This is rather formal.

zero article + non-count noun names the class as an undivided whole.

zero article + plural count noun names all members of the class.

Notice how zero article is used for species meaning with some names of animals and diseases:

hunting △ *lion* ~ that species of animal
having △ *polio* ~ that species of disease

Interestingly we can use *the* as a signal of common focus with those less dangerous diseases which are so familiar as to be almost cultural institutions:

. . . *having the chicken-pox, flu, measles, mumps*

Less common and more serious diseases take zero article:

. . . *suffering from* △ *tuberculosis/lung cancer*

GUIDELINES

To be safe, use a plural count noun or a non-count noun when speaking generally: *Men are selfish*. Always use an article (or a determiner) with a single count noun: *a book, the book, my book*, but not **book*.

Which tenses are not marked for aspect?

> *'That's one small step for a man, one giant step for mankind.'*
>
> Neil Armstrong, on first setting foot on the moon

▶ **see**
80 Count/non-count nouns
84 Determiners
277 Zero forms

45

Aspect

Aspect is the characteristic of verbs which shows whether the action of the verb is complete or still in progress. English has two aspects: the progressive, marked by *-ing*, indicating that the event is regarded as still in progress, and the perfective, marked by *-en*, indicating that the event occurred in the period up to a given point in time – before-now or before-then.

Both finite and non-finite verb forms may be marked for aspect. Finite verb phrases are marked for aspect in complex active tense forms (the simple tenses are marked for time only):

Present progressive	*I am sleep**ing*** (is in progress)
Present perfect	*I have* **slept** (occurred before now)
Present perfect progressive	*I have* **been** *sleep**ing*** (was in progress before now)
Past progressive	*I* **was** *sleeping* (was in progress then)
Past perfect	*I had* **slept** (occurred before then)
Past perfect progressive	*I had* **been** sleep***ing*** (was in progress before then)

In addition to these active tenses, all passive tenses include the *-en* form and are therefore marked for perfective aspect:

> *That fact . . . was nowhere better* **understood** *than in out-of-the-way nooks of the world.*

Verbs in catenative use may select *-ing* or *-en* and thereby mark the verb group for aspect:

> *Nobody had ever seen Lingard* **unwilling** *to act; Lingard* **puzzled,** *because* **confronted** *with a situation that discomposed him.*

Non-finites which are marked for aspect are the *-ing* and *-en* participles. Both function as nominals and adjectivals, which accordingly carry the relevant aspectual signals. See how in one sentence Conrad writes a cameo of Aissa saving her lover Willems from murder by her blind old father, Omar. As Willems regains consciousness, he perceives three actions still in progress (*-ing* forms) and three which have already occurred (*-en* forms):

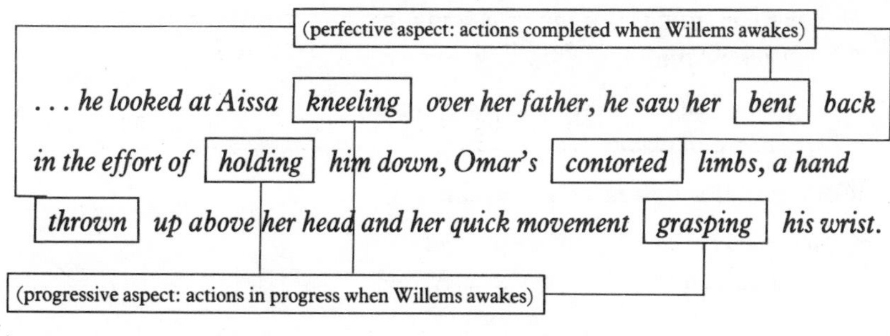

▶ **see**

51	Catenative verbs	142	Marked/unmarked
94	*-en* participle	264	Tenses
96, 157	Finite/non-finite	271	Verbs: characteristics
124	*-ing* participle		

46

Assertion/non-assertion

This is a useful minor concept in modern grammar which brings together forms which traditional grammar could not so comfortably handle.

Positive statements usually make assertions: most questions and negative statements do not.

Other non-assertive contexts include conditional clauses (including tentative *should*-clauses) and comparative clauses.

Those words and phrases which we do not use for making assertions are in non-assertive use. Consider:

***Do you mind** spiders? I **don't mind** spiders.* But not * ***I mind** spiders.*

The verb *to mind* with this meaning, then, is non-assertive. Other non-assertive verbs:

***Would you care** to dance? I **wouldn't care** to dance.*
Not * *I **would care** to dance.*

***Can't she help** it? She **can't help** it.*
Not * *She **can help** it.*
(also *can't abide/bear/stand*)
***Need they** stay? No, **they needn't** stay.*
Not * *But **you need** stay.*

Notice also that the modal *can* in its theoretical possibility meaning is non-assertive:

***Can** this **be** yours? It **can't be** mine.*
Not * *It **can be** yours.*

But the assertive form is acceptable when we include a semi-negative:

*It **can hardly/scarcely** be yours.*

Other items that tend to be limited to non-assertive contexts:

*Has he spoken **yet**? He hasn't spoken **yet**.*
* *He has spoken **yet**.*

What meaning is carried by the assertive use of **to bear**?

Do you swim ***much****? We don't swim* ***much****.*
★ Yes we swim ***much****.*

Is there ***much*** *sugar? There isn't* ***much*** *sugar.*
★ There is ***much*** *sugar.*

Was it ***far****? It wasn't* ***far****. ★ It was* ***far****.*

Also *such . . . as* is usually non-assertive:

Is he/He isn't ***such*** *a clever boy* ***as*** *they are?*
★ He is ***such*** *a clever boy* ***as*** *they are.*

The semi-negative intensifiers *at all*, *barely*, *hardly*, *scarcely*, *almost* and *nearly* are used only with the non-assertive determiners and pronouns (*any-* and *no-* series words).

He'll tell you ***barely*** *anything – nothing* ***at all****.* ★ ***something at all*** etc.

GUIDELINE

It is with the *some-/any-/no-* series that the assertion/non-assertion concept comes into its own and accounts for an area which traditional grammar could only explain with many exceptions.

See how Dorothy Parker built a witty remark round assertive and non-assertive use of the verb *to bear*:

> *Dorothy Parker's haughty escort to a party refused to join in the light-hearted games.*
> *'I can't, I'm afraid,' he said, 'I simply can't bear fools.'*
> *'How odd,' Dorothy Parker said, 'Apparently your mother could.'*

see

27	Comparative clauses	144	Modal *can*
29	Conditional clauses	73, 150	Tentative *should*
72–5	Conditional sentences	258	*Some-any-no-* series
130	Intensifiers		

47

Attributive adjectives

We can say someone is a *light* or a *heavy sleeper*, but we are not thinking about their weight. Similarly we are not thinking about someone's size when we call them a *small* or a *big eater*. These adjectives do not refer to the person: the qualities of lightness and heaviness are not inherent in the sleeper: but they are inherent when we talk about *light* and *heavy rain*. Consider:

Inherent qualities

hard *wood ~ the wood is* ***hard***

married *women* ~ *they are* ***married***
perfect *manners* ~ *the manners are* ***perfect***

Non-inherent qualities
a ***hard*** *worker* ~ *one who works* ***hard***
the worker is* ***hard*
married *life* ~ *life during* ***marriage***
the life is* ***married*
a ***perfect*** *stranger* ~ *one who is* ***perfectly*** *strange*
the stranger is* ***perfect*

Inherent adjectives are used both attributively and predicatively: non-inherent adjectives have an adverbial meaning (*hard*, *perfectly*) and are only used attributively.

Other examples:

a certain/sure/possible winner ~ *it will certainly/surely/possibly win*
a heavy/modest drinker ~ *he drinks heavily/modestly*
a real/firm friend ~ *she is really/firmly a friend*
the present/late chairman ~ *he is/was presently/lately the chairman*
a regular/occasional performer ~ *she performs regularly/occasionally*

> *'The best part of married life is the fights.'*
> Thornton Wilder, *The Matchmaker*

GUIDELINES

Think of non-inherent adjectives as having adverbial meaning. You can safely use the above examples of non-inherent adjectives as fixed phrases. Interestingly we do not care to mix inherent and non-inherent adjectives. So where a non-inherent adjective premodifies a noun, we place any inherent adjectives in post-position:

a ***firm*** *friend* *a* ***loyal and true*** *friend* but *a* ***firm*** *friend*, ***loyal and true***
NEVER * ***a loyal, true*** *and* ***firm*** *friend* or * *a* ***firm, loyal*** *and* ***true*** *friend*

When we want to stress or heighten the meaning of a noun, we can use an adjective as an intensifier. Most adjectival intensifiers are used in attributive position only. Consider:

He's a ***complete/total*** *idiot* ~ ***completely/totally*** *an idiot*
* *the idiot is* ***complete/total***
It's an ***absolute/utter*** *lie* ~ ***absolutely/utterly*** *a lie*
* *the lie is* ***absolute/utter***

Notice again that these adjectives have an adverbial meaning and cannot be used predicatively.
Other examples:

a ***complete*** *accident* ***downright*** *nonsense* *the* ***entire*** *family*
a ***mere*** *child* ***out-and-out*** *honesty* ***pure*** *imagination* ***sheer*** *agony*
the ***pure and simple*** *truth*

Adjectives in intensifying use often contribute to clichés as here. When the same component nouns and adjectives are manipulated by a creative writer out of intensifying use, the result can be witty.

> *'Truth is rarely pure and never simple.'*
> Oscar Wilde, *The Importance of Being Earnest*

GUIDELINE

This is a small group of adjectives which should be used cautiously. If we always use heightened language we become over-dramatic and people think we exaggerate everything. *Complete accidents* are as rare as *true heroes* and *sheer agony*. Think of these intensifiers as having adverbial meaning.

We use certain adjectives to restrict the meaning of a following noun: *the **main** argument, the **chief** reason, the **principal** excuse*. These are restrictive adjectives and they are not used in the predicative position with this same meaning. We cannot say:

the argument is **main*   **the reason is **chief***
the excuse is **principal*

Other examples:

*a **particular/specific** person ~ particularly/specifically that person*
*that **exact/precise** moment ~ exactly/precisely at that moment*
*the **sole/only** occasion ~ solely/only that occasion*

Notice the difference between *a **certain** person* (where *certain* is restrictive) and a ***certain** winner* (where *certain* is an intensifier).

Some of the adjectives formed from Latin or Greek roots with suffixes are non-gradable, for example *social, cosmic*. Some are commonly used attributively but not predicatively. So:

social** services*   **the services are **social
cosmic** dust*   **the dust is **cosmic

Many of these adjectives are technical. Other examples:

***atomic** physics*   ***legal** aid*   ***musical** comedy*   ***cardiac** arrest*
***lunar** vehicles*   ***optic** nerves*   ***cellular** telephones*   ***marine** engineering*
***physical** education*   ***solar** energy*

GUIDELINE

The adjectives which are only used attributively are a very small group. They are best regarded as being used in fixed phrases.

see
5 Adjectives: position
10 Adjectives with suffixes
105 Gradable/non-gradable
130 Intensifiers
201 Postposition adjectives
203 Predicative adjectives
204 Premodifiers

48

Auxiliary verbs

Auxiliary verbs combine with lexical verbs, either in the formation of tenses in the case of *be*, *do* and *have*, the primary auxiliaries:

They ***were*** *approaching*
Do *you understand?*
I ***have*** *promised*

or to express modality, in the case of the modal auxiliaries *can*, *could*, *must* etc.

He ***could*** *see them.*
He ***must*** *be perfectly safe.*

Notice that modal auxiliaries have only a base form (e.g. *can*) and none of the other forms listed for lexical verbs. Nor can modals complete the sentence patterns which lexical verbs can.

GUIDELINES

be, *do* and *have* are special verbs which can be both lexical and auxiliary verbs:

be	(lexical)	*They* ***were*** *a numerous and unclean crowd.*
	(auxiliary)	*Willems* ***was*** *helping.*
do	(lexical)	*He* ***did*** *nothing.*
	(auxiliary)	*She* ***did*** *not complain.*
have	(lexical)	*Willems* ***had*** *the street to himself.*
	(auxiliary)	*He* ***had*** *not talked enough about himself.*

see
50 *be*
86 *do*
88 Ellipsis
106 *have*
139 Lexical verbs
143 Modality
184 Operator
272 Sentence patterns
276 Word classes

49

Back-shift

This is the change of tense we make between the verbs in two corresponding sentences, which involve a change in time reference. We use it most often in indirect speech.

'I [*don't*] *care,' declared Frances.*	[direct – present tense]
Frances said she [*didn't*] *care.*	[indirect – past tense]

In indirect speech a direct-speech verb is often reported in a tense one step back into the past.

So:

present / future tenses	>	past tenses
past tenses	>	past or perfect tenses
present perfect tense	>	past perfect tense
past perfect tense	>	past perfect tense

'Let her know that Bertie [*won't*] *be home tonight.'* ~ *Asked me to let you know that Bertie* [*wouldn't*] *be home tonight.*

'You [*can*] *hang up pillow slips tonight.'* ~ *You said we* [*could*] *hang* [*up pillow*] *slips tonight.*

'I' [*ve*] *been a bit clumsy,' he said. 'My tool slipped.'* ~ *He said he* [*had*] *been a bit clumsy. His tool had slipped.*

Back-shift also occurs in hypothetical conditions, where present and future reference is expressed by the simple past tense and past reference by the past perfect:

If I [*handed*] *you over to the police, you* [*would get*] *what you deserve.* ~ *Perhaps I* [*shall hand*] *you over . . . and you* [*will get*] *what you deserve.*

If I [*hadn't caught*] *you . . . you* [*would have eaten*] *that cake.* ~ *I* [*caught*] *you before you* [*ate*] *the cake.*

A third familiar occurrence of back-shift is with *to wish* where the tenses are similar to those in *if-* clauses of hypothetical conditions:

'I wish you [*had*] *a braver mother.'* ~ *I'm sorry you* [*haven't*] *a braver mother.*

If only their men-folk [*could have been*] *with them.* ~ *It was a pity their men-folk* [*could*] *not* [*be*] *with them.*

Minor uses of back-shift occur in the three following areas:

After *It's time* we use the simple past or past perfect to give a hypothetical meaning to an observation/instruction

It's time you ***thought*** *about other people instead of yourself.*

Similarly we use back-shift after *It's the first/ second time* . . . etc.

It isn't the first time ***I've slept*** *downstairs.*

The modal idioms *Would rather/would sooner* . . . show their meaning of unreality by being followed by past tenses

Stephen would rather **have had** *a watch for Christmas.*

This is a kind of hypothetical meaning.

GUIDELINES

Interestingly this same back-shift for hypothetical meaning can be used in two different functions. When old Mrs Berry found a midnight intruder in her house, instead of the direct questions (below left), she had available the back-shifted alternatives below right, which carry a cool, distant sense of superiority:

Who are you?	*Who might you be?*
What are you doing?	*What might you be doing?*
What do you want?	*What did you want?*
Are you looking for something?	*Were you looking for something?*

Yet we can use the same (back-shifted) forms in other situations to carry the sense of polite – though distant – interest.

WE WOULD PREFER YOU
NOT TO SMOKE
IN THE GARDEN ROOM

A politely distant hotel notice

see
85 Direct/indirect speech
74 Hypothetical conditions
111 Indirect speech
275 Wishing

50

to be

We use *to be* as an auxiliary verb in forming tenses. But we also use it as a lexical verb with a range of meanings. As a linking verb it can be followed by nouns, adjectives and adverbs and, unusually, a combination of these:

He **was** *a distinctive figure.* [noun phrase: *a distinctive figure*]

London **was** *very cold (adj.) and crowded (adj.).*

The road to Olokomeji **was** *quiet (adj.) and through thick rain forest.* [adverbial: *through thick rain forest*]

We also use *to be* in existential sentences, which make statements about the idea of being, or existence. These often start with unstressed *There*:

In the background **was** *a small loch.*
There **was** *a sudden whirr.*

We rarely use progressive tenses of lexical *to be*, and then only to describe temporary or non-typical states.

You ***are*** *being very foolish.*

Auxiliary *do* is only used with *to be* in imperatives:

'Don't *be silly,' she said.*
Do *be quiet.*

and in informal suggestions using the fixed phrase *Why* ***don't*** *you be . . . ?*

Why ***don't*** *you be more careful?*

▶ **see**
48 Auxiliary verbs
135 Introductory *there*
141 Linking verbs

51

Catenative verbs: general

Catenative means chain-like or linking. Ordinary verbs which are followed by non-finite forms of other ordinary verbs are called catenative. For example:

The cars [*began*] [*climbing*] *though wooded countryside.*
(*began*: catenative verb; *climbing*: linked *-ing* form)

In this case the non-finite form is the *-ing* form, one of the four non-finite forms which catenative verbs link with. Examples here are with intransitive verbs:

the bare infinitive	*I dare* ***say***
the *to*- infinitive	*Vogel had agreed* ***to appear***.
the *-ing* form	*He started* ***running***.
the *-en* form	*He became* ***infected*** *with the isolation.*

The same non-finites can follow transitive verbs and their objects:

the bare infinitive	*frustration . . . made his skin* ***prickle***.
the *to*- infinitive	*I want you to do* ***something***.
the *-ing* form	*Aubrey heard the Mercedes' engine* ***retreating***.
the *-en* form	*I want this* ***explained***.

The eight patterns are examined in the following sections. The selection of the non-finite form to link up with a catenative verb in a particular context depends on the meaning: the non-finite forms carry meaning no less than the verbs which select them. As we might expect, those ordinary, lexical verbs which have a precise meaning (reflected in fewer dictionary meanings) always select the same non-finite form. *To struggle*, for example, when we use it as a catenative, always selects the *to*- infinitive:

The driver was struggling ***to retain*** *control.*

Other verbs with broader ranges of meaning may be used in more than one catenative pattern. Consider:

I wanted **to negotiate** *with the Chinese.* [v. + *to*- inf.]
Why did he want **his visitor to leave***?* [v. + o. + *to*- inf.]
I want **them all eliminated***.* [v. + o. + *-en*]

GUIDELINE

Do not confuse the non-finite form in catenative use with the object in transitive use. Compare:

He chose to go. (catenative + *to*- inf.)
He chose tea. (transitive + object)

The transitive sentence has corresponding patterns with the passive and introductory *it*:

Tea was chosen. It was tea that he chose.

Neither is possible with the catenative verb.

see

52–60	Catenative patterns	157	Non-finites
134	Introductory *it*	270	Transitivity

52

Catenative verbs followed by the bare infinitive

This is one of the least common patterns of catenative verbs, though it is familiar from the use of the bare infinitive after auxiliaries:

I don't think (bare infin.) *so.*
I will talk (bare infin.) *to him.*

Three common multi-word verbs take the bare infinitive: *had better*, *have (got) to*, *would rather/sooner*.

I think I **had better talk** *to this Colonel Wei.*

he **had to turn up** *the trouser legs . . .*

These verbs, having no non-finite forms, are not full lexical verbs. Yet they are not auxiliary verbs, since we do not use them as operators. They are classed as modal idioms. The only common verbs in this pattern (and even they are in restricted use) are *make*, *let* and *help*:

You must **make do** *with him.*
Don't **let go***.*
Hyde **helped save** *him.*

GUIDELINE

Since these three verbs are more common in transitive use, the corresponding pattern, v. + o. + bare infinitive, is much more productive.

see

48	Auxiliary verbs	139	Lexical verbs
117	Bare infinitive	157	Non-finites
51–60	Catenative verbs	184	Operator

Explain: **He didn't aim to kill/He aimed not to kill**

53

Catenative verbs followed by the *to*-infinitive

We use many verbs in this pattern to talk about aims, purposes and intentions which are expressed in the infinitive of the second verb:

I intend **to sue** *for libel.*
. . . they had chosen deliberately **to ignore** *him.*

The forward-looking verbs in this group include:

agree	*deserve*	*pretend*
aim	*fail*	*promise*
arrange	*hesitate*	*refuse*
claim	*hope*	*struggle*
consent	*long*	*swear*
decide	*manage*	*threaten*
decline	*offer*	*volunteer*
demand	*prepare*	

These verbs are followed by the *to*- infinitive only and never appear in other catenative patterns.
Notice that these verbs may take progressive, passive and perfect infinitives:

He did not seem **to be apologising**.
Zimmermann will have **to be exposed**.
Zimmermann appeared **to have lost** *interest.*

A small group of verbs which take the *to*- infinitive also appear in a related pattern with introductory *it*. This category includes *appear*, *happen*, *seem* and *turn out*:

The stars seemed **to drip** *light.*
It seemed that the stars dripped light.

Zimmermann appeared **to have lost** *interest.*
It appeared that Zimmermann had lost interest.

GUIDELINES

We express interestingly subtle differences in meaning with the negative forms of this pattern. Making the main verb negative is not the same as making the non-finite negative. See how changing the scope of negation alters the sentence meaning:

She hasn't decided to leave him. (She may or may not stay.)
She has decided not to leave him. (She will stay.)
He didn't deserve to die. (But he died.)
He deserved not to die. (He may or may not have died.)

see
51–60 Catenative verbs
116 Infinitives

54

Catenative verbs followed by *-ing*

The *-ing* form often carries the meaning of ongoing activity (as it does in the progressive tenses):

Lin took her arm and they began ***walking****.*

In this case the action, *walking*, continues after the action of the main verb, *began*. In other cases, the action of the *-ing* form take place before that of the main verb:

He stopped ***moving****.*

The two examples above are examples of those starting and stopping verbs which we use with a following *-ing* form (among others):

begin	*carry on*	*resume*
cease	*continue*	*start*
commence	*quit*	*stop*

A much larger group which takes the *-ing* form consists of emotive verbs like *love* and *hate*:

Zimmermann disliked ***being*** *followed.*

Verbs in this group include:

can't bear	*enjoy*	*loathe*	*resent*
detest	*not fancy*	*love*	*can't stand*
dislike	*hate*	*not mind*	
dread	*like*	*regret*	

GUIDELINE

The verbs *can't bear*, *can't stand*, *not fancy*, and *not mind* obviously have negative bias. We do not use them in affirmative sentences: they are non-assertive:

She couldn't bear ***travelling*** *by bus.*
Could she bear ***going*** *by taxi?* but * *She can bear* ***flying****.*

Verbs taking *-ing* include:

admit	*escape*	*need*	*require*
avoid	*forget*	*permit*	*save*
confess to	*can't help*	*recommend*	*try*
deny	*imagine*	*remember*	*want*
deserve			

Lin could not help ***smiling****.*

A number of multi-word verbs also belong to this category, e.g.:

He was ***engaged in computing*** *the risks . . .* [prepositional verb]
The face ***went on looking*** *down at him.* [phrasal verb]

Other prepositional verbs include:

bank on	*decide on*	*play at*
count on	*delight in*	*see about*

Phrasal verbs include:

break off *keep on* *put off*
carry on *leave off* *take up*
give up

The few phrasal-prepositional verbs include:

get around to *go in for* *put up with*
get out of *look forward to*

Notice that, unlike members of other groups of verbs followed by *-ing* these multi-word verbs, in catenative use, are always followed by *-ing* and never the *to-* infinitive.

GUIDELINES

Several *-ing* forms like *swimming*, *dancing*, *walking* and *shopping* are rather like non-count nouns – they can follow the definite article and take an adjectival modifier: *The **living** is easy*. Such forms commonly follow *come* and *go*:

Come dancing. *Let's go skating.* *She's gone shopping.*

Notice that the large majority of catenative verbs which select *-ing* have the same subject for both verbs in the pattern. That is, in the sentence *They began walking*, *they* did the walking as well as the beginning.

A small number of verbs in this pattern assume a different (although sometimes unidentified) subject. Consider:

You need training/feeding etc.
He deserves punishing/rewarding etc. } ~ someone else will do it.
It requires painting/mending etc.

see

46	Assertion/non-assertion	194, 195	Phrasal verbs
51–60	Catenative verbs	196	Phrasal prepositional verbs
123	*-ing* form	221, 222	Prepositional verbs

55

Catenative verbs followed by *-en*

In this limited pattern, the verb *to get* is followed by the *-en* form:

*'Don't get **lost**,' Schiller added.*

We commonly (and informally) speak of *getting* ***caught/dressed/drunk/ found out***, etc.

GUIDELINE

Although this pattern appears almost identical with the pattern for linking verbs, the above are not examples of linking use. *Don't get lost* has a close transitive parallel, *Don't get him lost*. *Get* in catenative use does not always have the same subject for the main verb and the *-en* form; linking verbs always have subjects and complements which refer to the same person/ thing.

see
51–60 Catenative verbs
94 *-en* form
141 Linking verbs

56

Catenative verbs followed by object + bare infinitive

A common application of this pattern is with verbs of perception. For example:

He saw (v.) *Meng's mouth* (o.) *fall* (*bare inf.*) *open.*

He dimly heard (v.) *the door* (o.) *open* (*bare inf.*).

He felt (v.) *his stomach* (o.) *revolt* (*bare inf.*).

Schiller watched (v.) *Hyde* (o.) *move* (*bare inf.*) *to the Land Rover.*

In every case, the sentence describes a single, complete action. In contrast, we use verbs of perception with the *-ing* form to mean ongoing, incomplete action. Compare:

He felt the heat ***assail*** *him.* (single brief event – bare infinitive)

Aubrey felt his clothes ***beginning*** *to stick to him.* (extended ongoing action – *-ing* form.)

Verbs of perception include:

feel	*notice*	*perceive*	*smell*
hear	*observe*	*see*	*watch*

Notice that we use passive forms with *feel*, *hear*, *observe* and *see*, but only with the *to-* infinitive:

The door was heard ***to open.***

GUIDELINES

The above use is true for verbs of perception with their literal meaning. When, however, we use them metaphorically, we must use a *that-* clause:

Buckholz felt (that) he had at last learned the truth.

However, because *that* may be deleted, in a few situations, we could use the same form for both the literal and metaphorical uses. Consider:

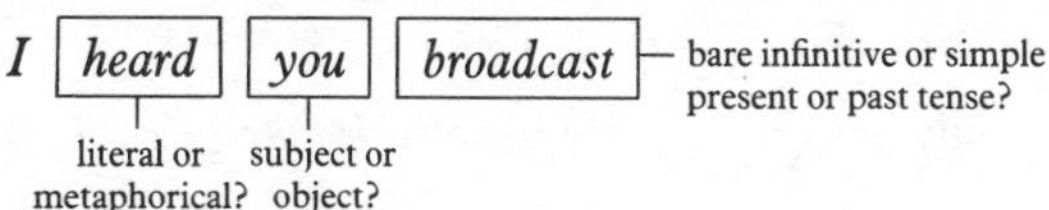

Either *I listened when you broadcast*, or *Someone said that you broadcast*. (Of course any potential ambiguity would be resolved by context in both speech and writing, and largely by selection of stress and intonation patterns in speech. Indeed this rather ambiguous sentence is the result of grammatical juggling, rather than of any genuine situation. If a genuine common source of ambiguity existed, the English language would have resolved it long ago.)

> *'Poggio's, where people go to watch each other watch each other.'*
>
> Lawrence Durrell, *Tunc*

Other verbs which catenate with object + bare infinitive include: *have*, *help*, *know*, *let* and *make*.

Don't let it bring me down.

His grin was awkward and boyish, making him appear absurdly young.

We use the passive forms of *help*, *know* and *make*, but only with the *to-* infinitive:

He is known to be KGB.

GUIDELINE

Have in this pattern carries the meaning of *cause*, *bring about*:

*I'll **have** them **meet** you in the lobby.*

see
117 Bare infinitive
51–60 Catenative verbs

57

Catenative verbs followed by object + *to-* infinitive

One fairly large group of verbs which follow this pattern is concerned with letting or making people do things – suasion. The objects, therefore, are usually animate:

Lin forced (v.) himself (o.) to keep (to- infin.) the gun steady.

Hoardings exhorted (v.) the population (o.) to continue (to- infin.) the . . . work.

Verbs in this group include:

advise	*depend on*	*get*	*permit*
allow	*direct*	*impel*	*persuade*
ask	*drive*	*implore*	*rely on*
assist	*empower*	*instruct*	*remind*
bribe	*enable*	*invite*	*request*
cause	*encourage*	*lead*	*teach*
challenge	*forbid*	*leave*	*tell*
command	*force*	*order*	*warn*
compel			

Most verbs in this pattern can also be used in the passive, still with the suasive meaning:

But people can be ***persuaded*** *to say things . . .*

As in other patterns, the *to-* infinitive carries a general meaning of forward-looking action.

Another group of verbs following this pattern are mental-state verbs:

The man had not ***expected*** *him to turn back.*

He ***knew*** *himself to be acting irrationally.*

He ***understood*** *himself to be closer to people like Davenport.*

Verbs in this group, centring round thoughts and opinions, include:

assume	*fancy*	*know*	*show*
believe	*feel*	*observe*	*suppose*
consider	*find*	*prove*	*think*
discover	*imagine*	*report*	*understand*
expect	*judge*	*reveal*	

All of these verbs also pattern with *that*-clauses.

He evidently ***assumed that*** *only the truth would keep the man quiet.*

Notice how a number of emotive verbs like *love* and *hate*, which can be followed by *-ing*, also pattern with the *to-* infinitive, both with and without an object.

I ***wanted*** *to negotiate.*
I ***want*** *you to do something.*

These verbs, carrying meanings about likes and wishes, when followed by the *to-* infinitive refer to the wishes of the subject about its own future:

I ***wish*** *to go to the United States of America.*

Followed by an object, the wishes are about the action of someone else:

He ***wished*** *the truth to reach Louvain.*

The emotive verbs which pattern in both ways include:

ask	*express*	*like*	*need*
beg	*hate*	*love*	*require*
choose	*help*	*mean*	*want*
dare	*intend*	*prefer*	*wish*

GUIDELINE

Occasional ambiguity is possible when the infinitive of purpose may be confused with a catenative verb + *to-* infinitive. Which is the following?

She reported him [*to be*] [*safe .*] — refers to she or him?

infinitive after mental-state verb or infinitive of purpose?

Fortunately the language affords us a number of ways of avoiding such ambiguity:

He was reported to be safe. (catenative passive)
She reported that he was safe. (that-clause after mental-state verb)
To be safe, she reported him. (fronting of infinitive of purpose)

Notice that when two or more *to*-infinitives are coordinated, the second and other infinitives often drop the *to*:

It enables Vogel to sit back in his chair, △ fold his arms across his chest, △ appear at ease.

> *'Missionaries teach them not only to serve the Lord but run a Ford car . . . then the American agent sells them one . . .'*
>
> Will Rogers, *Saturday Review*

see
51–60 Catenative verbs
116 Infinitives
118 *to*-infinitive

58

Catenative verbs followed by object + *-ing*

Verbs of perception take this pattern as well as the object + bare infinitive:

. . . he **heard** *the car engine starting.*
. . . he **saw** *the city retreating into the heat.*

Perception verbs include:

feel	*notice*	*perceive*	*smell*
hear	*observe*	*see*	*watch*

Certain mental-state verbs of assumption and opinion may also select object + *-ing*:

Aubrey **found** *the impression unnerving.*

Mental-state verbs include:

consider	*excuse*	*forgive*	*picture*
discover	*find*	*pardon*	*show*

A small group of verbs use the pattern in fixed idiomatic phrases:

to catch someone napping	*to get someone going*
to keep someone waiting	*to leave someone standing*
to send something flying	*to send someone packing*

see
117 Bare infinitive
51–60 Catenative verbs

59

Catenative verbs followed by object + *-en*

Unlike the *to*-infinitive patterns, this has a passive implication. Consider:

. . . *they want silence kept (-en).*
(or, they want silence to be kept.)
but *they want us to keep (to-infin.) silence.*

Some verbs of perception follow this pattern, particularly *feel*, *hear* and *see*:

They walked on, Lin ***feeling*** *himself drawn into Mary's chilly, ice-capped dreams.*

Mental-state verbs are used with object + *-en*:

The Americans ***want*** *the Treaty stopped.*

Mental-state verbs in this use include:

discover	*imagine*	*leave*	*report*
fancy	*keep*	*make*	*show*
find			

He ***kept*** *his eyes closed.*

He ***discovered*** *himself hurled into an adult, irrecoverable world.*

Notice in this last example, the use of the reflexive. In catenative patterns with objects we need to use reflexive pronouns when the subject of both verbs is the same, in order to avoid ambiguity. Compare:

He ***understood himself*** *to be closer to people like Davenhill.*

Lin ***forced himself*** *to keep the gun steady.*

He ***knew himself*** *to be acting irrationally.*

▶ GUIDELINE

An interestingly subtle distinction often occurs when we use *have/get* + O. + *-en*. We interpret the main verb (*have* or *get*) as having active meaning if the outcome is desirable, but as having passive meaning if the outcome is undesirable. Compare:

She ***had*** *the house* ***painted****.*	*He* ***got*** *the car* ***mended****.*
She ***had*** *both arms* ***broken****.*	*He* ***got*** *the car* ***smashed****.*

In the active sentences, the subject initiates the action, but suffers it in the passive.

▶ **see**
51–60 Catenative verbs
246 Reflexive pronouns

60

Verbs taking more than one catenative pattern

Davenhill said, 'The Americans want the Treaty stopped. We may – may – want it to proceed.'

Here, almost in the same breath, he uses *want* + object + *-en* and *want* + object + *to*-infinitive. Certain verbs of liking and disliking can also be followed by:

the *to*-infinitive	*I told him you'd still* ***like to go*** *in.*
the *-ing* form	*She won't* ***like being*** *interrupted.*
object + *-ing*	*He doesn't* ***like Zimmermann dropping*** *behind.*

We usually choose the infinitive pattern when referring to a single action or a positive choice, with a future meaning:

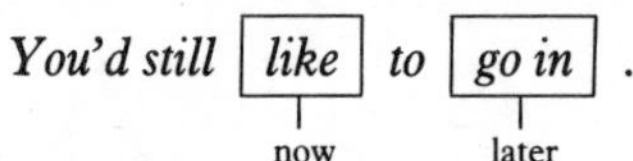

We select the *-ing* pattern to refer to an ongoing action or a general activity; the *-ing* form has a contrasting backward-looking sense:

He [*doesn't*] *like Zimmermann* [*dropping behind*].
now — earlier

GUIDELINE

Want is one of a small group of verbs we use with *-ing* when we wish to give a passive meaning to the second verb:

The house **wants/needs/requires/deserves** *cleaning.* ~
The house wants/needs/requires/deserves to be cleaned.

We also use *want*, *need* and *require* as mental-state verbs followed by object and both *-ing* and *-en* forms, with equally passive meaning:

We **want/need/require** *the house cleaned.* ~ *We* **want/need/require** *the house cleaning.*

> *'I like people and I like them to like me, but I wear my heart where God put it – on the inside.'*
>
> F. Scott Fitzgerald, *The Last Tycoon*

Verbs of perception (*feel*, *hear*, *notice*, *observe*, *perceive*, *see*, *smell*, *watch*, etc.) can be used with both object + bare infinitive and object + *-ing*. Compare:

The doctor **saw** *Lin . . . approach him.*
Lin **watched** *him pass.*
Aubrey **saw** *the city retreating.*
Lin **watched** *him moving away.*

We select the bare infinitive to refer to a single complete action or event. Craig Thomas makes this choice when he describes Aubrey left alone at noon in the burning Australian desert:

Aubrey felt the heat [*assail*] *him.*

a single event, like a blow

By contrast, we use the *-ing* form to refer to an action in progress. Thomas chooses *-ing* after the same verb to describe Aubrey's slow, continuing perspiration:

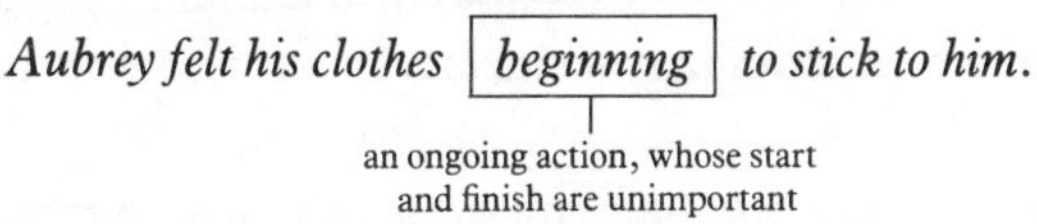

GUIDELINE

We do not always have a free choice after verbs of perception. Dynamic verbs may describe a single event – *to blink*; an ongoing one – *to breathe*; or a repetitive one – *to hammer*. We are more likely to choose the bare infinitive for event verbs and *-ing* for those with repetitive meaning. Consider the verb *to trip*, which can have both senses:

I ***heard*** *her* ***trip*** *over the doormat.* ~ fall, a single event.
I ***heard*** *her* ***tripping*** *down the corridor.* ~ dancing, a repetitive action.

Begin/start verbs, or aspectual verbs, which also include *cease*, *commence* and *continue*, are followed by both the *to*-infinitive and *-ing*:

They ***began walking****.*
They ***began to stroll****.*

In such cases there is little difference in meaning and the choice between the two patterns is open. However, when the second verb is in stative use – and stative verbs are not normally used in the progressive tenses – the *to*-infinitive is preferred to *-ing* after *begin/start* verbs:

Zimmermann . . . ***continued to gaze*** *at the Russian.* = *continued gazing.*

but, *He* ***continued*** *to* [*recognise*] *the Russian.*

stative verb

NOT * *continued recognising*

For stylistic reasons we do not use the *-ing* form after *begin/start* verbs in the progressive tenses:

You are beginning ***to learn*** *the game.*
NOT * *beginning learning.*

Notice that *to stop* is not a member of this group, although *to cease* is:

We ***ceased having*** *breakfast.*
= *We* ***ceased to have*** *breakfast.*
= *We* ***stopped having*** *breakfast.*
} *We gave up the habit.*

But, *We* **stopped to have** *breakfast = We stopped in order to have breakfast.* When we use the *to-* infinitive after verbs like *to stop*, it is to express purpose.

GUIDELINE

Sometimes we make a subtle distinction between *begin* + *-ing* and *begin* + *to-* infinitive. For deliberate actions we tend to prefer the *-ing* pattern. When your doctor asks: *When did you start losing weight?* he is asking about your deliberate slimming. *When did you start to lose weight?* implies that the weight loss was unintentional and therefore a symptom of possible illness. If you continue losing weight you both may be happy. If you continue to lose it, the reverse.

Remember and *forget* can precede both *-ing* and the *to*-infinitive, but the choice reflects differences in meaning. With both verbs, when we are thinking of a past action, we use the *-ing* form:

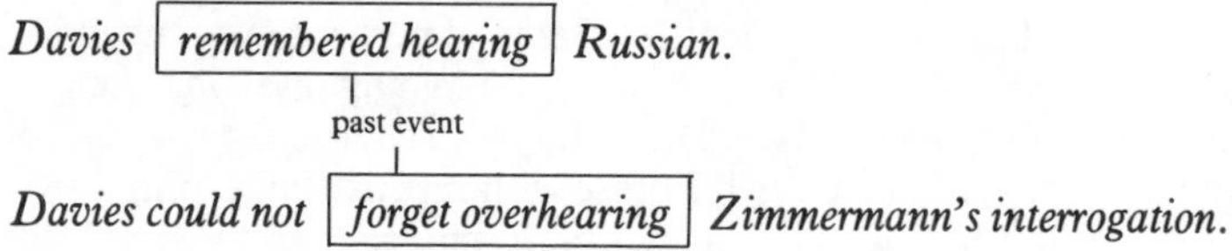

Here, as elsewhere, *-ing* has the sense of an ongoing activity. When we are thinking ahead to a future action, we use the *to-* infinitive:

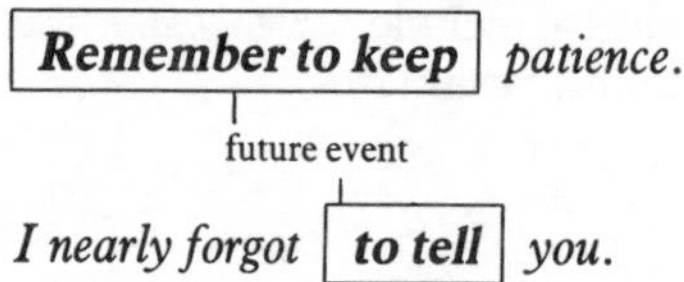

We use *to regret* in the same way, though with the forward-looking sense with the *to-* infinitive we limit this verb's use to reporting verbs:

I **regret to** *say/report/announce . . .*

We also use *to try* with the same two catenative patterns. The *to*-infinitive after *try* has the infinitive's common meanings of purpose and futurity:

They're **trying to tear** *it all down.*

The *-ing* pattern has the meaning of more general activity when *try* is used with its secondary meaning of experimentation:

Try talking *to him.*

Certain verbs of suasion like *advise*, *allow*, *encourage*, *forbid*, *permit*, *recommend*, and *urge* take object + *to-* infinitive when an object intervenes:

I cannot . . . **permit Zimmermann to be judged** *guilty.*

(Once more, we use the infinitive to indicate future action.) Without an object, the same verbs take the *-ing* pattern, and denote a general activity:

. . . wide enough **to permit overtaking**

▶ GUIDELINES

Catenative verbs are very common in English. For details of non-finite and other forms following individual ordinary verbs consult a good modern dictionary.

The association of verbs in catenative patterns with certain non-finite forms is closely related to the complementation of cognate nouns and adjectives. Consider:

*I **hesitate to agree**.* *I'm **hesitant to agree**.*
*My **hesitancy to agree***
*He **insists on going**.* *He's so **insistent on going**.*
*His **insistence on going***

▶ **see**
51–60 Catenative verbs
87 Dynamic/stative

61

Clauses

In traditional grammar, a clause contains a subject and a finite verb.

They (s.) *were* (v.) *executed.*

Modern grammar finds it convenient to extend the meaning of clause to include not only main and subordinate finite clauses, but non-finite clauses and verbless clauses:

[main: *He noticed*] [subordinate: *that both Aaronson and Rutherford had broken noses.*]

It was not wise [non-finite: *to be seen in the neighbourhood of such people.*]

All three had written long, abject articles in The Times, [non-finite: *analysing the reasons for their defection.*]

[verbless clause: *When in Siberia*] *. . . they had betrayed important military secrets.*

So nominal clauses, acting as nouns, regularly stand as subjects, objects and complements of verbs:

[s.: *To keep them in control*] *was not difficult.*

The Party claimed [o.: *that 40 per cent of adult proles were literate.*]

It was [c.: *like a single equation with two unknowns.*]

Adjectival clauses operate as adjectives in premodifying and postmodifying positions:

One never-to-be forgotten day.
He thought of a man ***whom he had passed in the street.***

Adverbial clauses function as adverbs in a wide range of meanings:

time
The instant he had flattened it out, he saw its significance.

reason
The date had stuck in Winston's memory, because it had been midsummer day.

GUIDELINE

Remember that non-finite and verbless clauses are always subordinate.

see

24 Adverbial clauses
96 Finite/non-finite
156 Nominal clauses
200 Postmodifiers
204 Premodifiers
261 Subordination

62

Cleft sentences

In *A Passage to India* by E. M. Forster,

A servant . . . handed Aziz a note. 'Old Callender wants to see me at his bungalow.'

Each of these two sentences consists of one clause. But they can also be expressed as two clauses, each with its own verb:

It was a servant who handed Aziz a note. 'It's old Callender who wants to see me at his bungalow.'

These are both cleft sentences, which are alternative forms constructed to give focus to a particular part of a sentence. There are two main kinds of cleft sentences: the first type starts with introductory *it* and can give focus to most parts of the sentence:

It was **a 'servant** *who handed Aziz a note.*
(subject is focus)

It's **'me** *old Callender wants to see at his bungalow.*
(object is focus)

It was **'Aziz** *the servant handed a note to.*
(indirect object is focus)

It's **at his 'bungalow** *old Callender wants to see me.*
(adverbial is focus)

The second type of cleft sentence is the *wh-* type:

What the servant handed to ˇAziz was a **'note.**
(object is focus)

*What ˇCallender wanted was to see ˋ**Aziz** at his ˋbungalow.*
(object is focus)
What he ˇdid was ***to send Aziz a ˋnote.***
(predication is focus)

An alternative *wh-* type puts the *wh-* clause second:
To see ˋAziz was ***what Callender wanted.***
(object is focus)

This second type of cleft sentence is sometimes called pseudo-cleft and the focus is final.

GUIDELINE

Cleft sentences are found in written English more commonly than in spoken English, where the same information is likely to be given in short answers to focusing questions:

Q. *Who handed Aziz the note?* A. *A servant.*

However, cleft constructions are a flexible device, since the *it*-type gives focus on the topic and the *wh*-type provides end-focus.

see
61 Clauses
97 Focus
134 Introductory *it*
273 *wh-* clauses

63

Comment clauses

Comment clauses, like sentence adverbials, are parts of a sentence to which we add, in parenthesis, a comment or an expression of our attitude. They may consist of finite and non-finite clauses. In writing, we separate them off by commas. In speech, we tend to say them without stress and more quickly and softly than the rest of the sentence. Without them, daily conversation would sound jerky and artificial. Comment clauses can take front- mid- or end-position.

There's some	*I don't mind telling you*	*, I'd like to change place with.*

Finite comment clauses include the commonest kinds: those designed to keep the hearer's attention in a friendly way – *you know, mind you, as you say* – or to express the speaker's attitude – *I suspect, I feel sure, I'm afraid, I've no doubt.*

You see, *most boys are so selfish.*
Not too good, ***I hope.***
I mean, *when shall I start to earn my living?*

Non-finite comment clauses tend to be a little more formal, using the *to*-infinitive, an *-ing* clause or an *-en* clause:

To put it mildly, *Eustace was rather nervous.*
He was, ***roughly speaking,*** *an accountant.*
*'**All things considered,** I think . . .'*

Many comment clauses are fixed phrases, some being little more than verbal tics:

you see	*I guess*	*as it happens*
you know	*I must say*	*don't you know*
if you follow	*as I said*	*to tell you the truth*

GUIDELINE

Non-finite comment clauses are adverbial in nature. Compare: *frankly speaking, to put it frankly, frankly* . . . But finite clauses are more like main clauses followed by *that*- clauses:

It's difficult, ***I think****.* ~ *I think (that) it's difficult.*

We do not regard non-finite comment clauses as unattached participles.

> *'What a queer thing Life is! So different from anything else, don't you know, if you see that I mean.'*
>
> P. G. Wodehouse, *My Man Jeeves*

see
96, 157 Finite/non-finite
185 Participles
257 Sentence adverbials

64

Comparisons with adjectives

Adjectives help us to say that things are alike:

Nottingham is ***as big as*** *Leicester.*

Gradable adjectives more often help us to say that things are different:

Manchester is not ***as large as*** *Birmingham.*
Liverpool is ***larger*** *than Sheffield.*
Glasgow is the ***largest*** *city in Scotland.*
Cardiff is the ***largest*** *of Welsh cities.*

Equal and unequal comparisons

We make equal comparisons with the pattern *as* + *adj.* + *as* . . .

> *'We are married now: but just as happy as we were before.'*
>
> Bertrand Russell

Many colourful fixed similes have become almost proverbial. Someone who is totally blind is *as blind as a bat*. A very fit person is said to be *as fit as a fiddle*. An unintelligent person is *as thick as two short planks* (slang).

GUIDELINE

After the second *as* of this pattern use the object form of the personal pronoun: *as old as* ***me/him/her/us/them***.

not as + adj. + as or *not + so + adj. + as* make unequal comparisons. If someone is better than people say they are, we say they are ***not as black as*** *they are painted*. Notice that *so . . . as* is used only to make a negative comparison: *not so . . . as*. Another difference between *not as . . . as* and *not so . . . as* is that we can shorten sentences using *not so*, when we cannot shorten with *not as*:

Cyclists are not so common on London streets today as they were.
Cyclists are not so common (today)△.
Cyclists are not as common on London streets today as they were.
**Cyclists are not as common.*

GUIDELINE

You will never be wrong if you use *as . . . as* with positive clauses and *so . . . as* with negatives.

Comparative and superlative forms

All gradable adjectives have a comparative and a superlative form. These are formed in one of two ways:

add the suffixes *-er* and *-est* to the adjective.

put *more* and *most* in front of the adjective.

All regular one-syllable adjectives take *-er* and *-est*:

low/lower/lowest *rich/richer/richest*

two-syllable adjectives ending in unstressed

-y -ly -ow -le and *-er* also take *-er* and *-est*:

greedy/greedier/greediest *lovely/lovelier/loveliest*
narrow/narrower/narrowest *gentle/gentler/gentlest*
clever/cleverer/cleverest

Notice the following irregular forms:

good/better/best *bad/worse/worst*
less/lesser/least

Some two-syllable adjectives in *-le* and *-er* do not take *-er/-est*:

sterile/more sterile/most sterile
eager/more eager/most eager

GUIDELINE

It you are not sure when to use *-er/-est* or *more/most*, use *-er/-est* with one-syllable adjectives and *more/most* with two and more syllables (with the exceptions listed above).

Notice that two adjectives have both regular forms in *-er* and *-est* and irregular forms:

far/farther/farthest are used for distance.

> *Manchester is* ***farther*** *from London than Sheffield or Birmingham.*
> *Manchester is the* ***farthest*** *of the three from London.*

far/further/furthest are also used for distance, but can mean *extra*, *advanced*.

> *A College of* ***Further*** *Education*

old/older/oldest are the commonest forms to talk about age.

> ***Older*** *cupboards were less deep than more modern ones because clothes hangers were not introduced until the 1920s.*

elder and *eldest* are becoming old-fashioned, but are still used with names to show relationships:

> *William Pitt the* ***Elder*** *and William Pitt the Younger were important British statesmen.*

All other gradable adjectives and three common one-syllable adjectives – *right*, *wrong* and *real* – when used as gradables form their comparatives and superlatives using *more* and *most*: *important/more important/most important*, and form their opposites by using *less* and *least*: *important/less important/least important*.

Comparative and superlative adjectives – use

We use the comparative form of the adjective to compare one object or group with another, separate, object or group:

> *The pen is* ***mightier*** *than the sword.*

We use the superlative form of the adjective to refer to one object or group that is part of a larger group:

> *The* ***Worst*** *Journey in the World.*

Traditional grammars say that we use the comparative to compare two things, and the superlative for more than two. But this is neither helpful nor true. Consider the four Brontë children:
Charlotte (b.1816) Branwell (b.1817) Emily (b.1818) and Anne (b.1820).

Charlotte was ***older*** *than Branwell.*	[compares 1 to 1]
Charlotte was ***older*** *than the others.*	[compares 1 to 3]
The others were all ***older*** *than Anne.*	[compares 3 to 1]
Anne was the ***youngest*** *child.*	[refers to 1 of 4]
Emily and Anne were the ***youngest*** *girls.*	[refers to 2 of 4]

Comparative adjectives *not as ... as ...*

These two sentences mean the same thing:

> *Westminster Abbey is* ***older than*** *Westminster Cathedral.*
>
> *Westminster Cathedral is* ***not as old as*** *Westminster Abbey.*

So when do we choose to use the *-er* form and when the *not as . . . as* pattern? In general statements the *-er* form is more common. It is also more direct.

GUIDELINE

Use *not as . . . as* to make less direct statements, particularly to avoid the harshness of a direct one. To say someone is *not as young as he was* is a kind way of saying he is getting old. To say *he's not as kind as he might be* is an understatement of his unkindness.

Also use *not as . . . as* to stress surprise or a change of opinion:

It was ***not as far as*** *he thought.*
He was ***not as ugly as*** *they had imagined.*

Parallel increase
We use comparative adjectives to show that two increases are related. The pattern is:

the adj. -er . . . the adj. -er . . .
the more adj. . . . the more adj. . . .

This pattern is also used with adverbs or can include both adjectives and adverbs together. It is a very neat way of expressing a relationship between different things: *The* ***higher*** *you go, the* ***further*** *you fall.* Some phrases have become almost proverbial: *The* ***sooner,*** *the* ***better.*** *The* ***more,*** *the* ***merrier.***

> *'An archaeologist is the best husband any woman can have: the older she gets, the more interested he is in her.'*
>
> Agatha Christie, Attrib.

Gradual increase
We repeat a comparative adjective to show that a change is not continuing. The pattern is: *adj. -er and adj. -er* or *more and more adj.*

Alice's Adventures in Wonderland included growing *smaller and smaller, then bigger and bigger.* She often became *more and more puzzled* and once she cried (ungrammatically), 'Curiouser and curiouser.'

GUIDELINE

Repeat the entire *-er* form for gradual increase: *colder and colder, better and better.*

But with longer adjectives only repeat *more/less*:

more △ and more beautiful,
less △ and less interested.

The pattern is also used with adverbs.

> *'An expert is one who knows more and more about less and less.'*
>
> N. M. Butler, Address at Columbia University

see
4 Adjectives
13 Adverbs: comparison
105 Gradable/non-gradable

Which four prepositions can complement **pleased**?

65

Complementation of adjectives: prepositional phrases

Many adjectives are regularly followed by one particular preposition: *to be* ***fond of*** *someone*. Others are regularly followed by two or three prepositions, sometimes with slight changes of meaning: *to be angry* ***about*** *something/angry* ***at*** *something* and *angry* ***with*** *someone*.

When adjectives are always followed by one particular preposition, the two words make up a single unit of meaning; without the preposition, the adjective has a different meaning. Compare:

King Charles was ***proud of*** *his horse. King Charles was* ***proud.***

Common examples of adjectives which are always followed by one particular preposition:

accustomed to	*fond of*	*opposed to*
allied to	*inclined to*	*proud of*
averse to	*incompatible with*	*reliant on/upon*
based on	*intent on*	*set on*
conscious of	*liable to*	*short of*
due to	*likely to*	*taken by*

> *'I may be very fond of her, but I am not quite so fond of her company.'*
>
> Marcel Proust, *Cities of the Plain*

Other adjectives are followed by two, three or four prepositions, with small changes of meaning. Common examples are:

amused about/at/by/with	*impatient about/for/with*
angry about/at/with	*lucky in/with*
annoyed about/at/with	*mistaken about/by/for/in*
anxious about/for	*pleased about/at/for/with*
careful about/with	*sad about/at/for*
certain about/of	*satisfied about/by/with*
confident about/with	*sorry about/for*
delighted about/by/with	*successful at/in/with*
different from/to	*sure about/of*
disappointed about/with	*surprised about/at/by*
embarrassed about/at/with	*terrible at/with*
excited about/at/by/with	*terrified about/at/by/with*
frightened about/by/of	*tired by/from/of/with*
furious about/at/with	*useful at/for/with*
glad about/of	*useless at/for/with*
happy about/for/with	*worried about/at/by.*

GUIDELINES

Think of the adjective and preposition as a single unit:

to be fond of ~ *to like* *to be short of* ~ *to lack*

Often the adjective is linked with a preposition which is similarly linked with cognate nouns and adjectives:

Adjective	**Verb**	**Noun**
careful about	*to care about*	*care about*
free from	*to free from*	*freedom from*
hesitant about	*to hesitate about*	*hesitation about*
reliant on	*to rely on*	*reliance on*

But there are exceptions:

full of but *to fill with* *fond of* but *fondness for* *proud of* but *pride in*

'People are always rather bored with their parents. That's human nature.'

Somerset Maugham, *The Bread-Winner*

---

see

4 Adjectives
218–20 Prepositional phrases

66

Complementation of adjectives: *that*-clauses

In predicative position, several adjectives with a personal subject are followed by a *that*- clause:

Hamlet was **suspicious that** *his father had been murdered.*

Sometimes, more formally, to express a possibility, we include *should* in the *that*- clause:

He was **horrified that** *he* **should** *have been murdered.*

And the *should* is unavoidable when the reference is to the future:

He was **determined that** *the ghost* **should** *speak to him.*

Many adjectives complemented with *that*- clauses can have introductory *it* as subject:

He was **certain** } **that** *the ghost was his father.*
It was certain }

So we have four patterns of complementation:

Paired *-ing* and *-en* adjectivals in both patterns

He *was shock***ed** *that his mother had remarried.*
It *was shock***ing** *that his mother had remarried.*

When we omit initial **that** from a clause are we being more or less formal?

Other adjectives used in this way include:

alarmed	*disappointed*	*shocked*
amazed	*frightened*	*surprised*
annoyed	*horrified*	*worried*
astonished	*pleased*	*upset*

Adjectives used unchanged in both patterns:

He was ***unfortunate*** *that he could not take decisions.*
It was ***unfortunate*** *that he could not take decisions.*

Other adjectives used in this way include:

certain	*hopeful*	*sad*	*unfortunate*
fortunate	*lucky*	*sure*	*unlucky*

Adjectives used only with the personal subject pattern:

He was ***angry*** *that his mother had married his uncle.* NOT **It was angry that . . .*

Other adjectives used in this way include:

appreciative	*grateful*	*proud*
content	*happy*	*sorry*
glad	*pleased*	*thankful*

Adjectives used only with introductory *it*:

It was ***fatal*** *that Hamlet should be so hesitant.* NOT **He was fatal that . . .*

Other adjectives used in this way include:

clear	*evident*	*obvious*	*strange*
curious	*extraordinary*	*odd*	*tragic*
disappointing	*likely*	*plain*	*true*
disastrous	*logical*	*possible*	*well-known*

GUIDELINE

We use the personal subject when we want to be direct and informal. We use introductory *it* when we are being impersonal and more formal. In informal styles we can usually drop the *that*.

> *'It is paradoxical that every dictator has climbed to power on the ladder of free speech. Immediately on attaining power each dictator has suppressed all free speech except his own.'*
>
> Herbert Hoover, *Speeches*

see

5 Adjectives: position
134 Introductory *it*
156 Nominal clauses
150 *Should*

67

Complementation of adjectives: *to*-infinitive

The *to*-infinitive complements adjectives in a range of meanings, the infinitive acting as a reduced clause. We often use introductory *it* to introduce the adj. + infinitive pattern:

It's ***nice to play*** *games occasionally.*
It's ***good to see*** *you.*

Here the grammatical subject of the sentence is the non-finite clause, which we place in end-position to avoid the clumsiness of a long subject:

To play games occasionally is nice.(?)

Two related patterns with adjectives + *to*-infinitives can carry similar meanings:

Her hair was ***long enough to reach*** *her shoulders.*

Her hair was ***not too short to reach*** *her shoulders.*

The structure with *adj.* + *to*- infinitive is intriguingly complex in its range of meanings, which we can only appreciate by paraphrasing. Consider the following six sentences:

The Government was ***wrong to do*** *it.*

Here the subject of the sentence is also the subject of the infinitive. We can paraphrase the pattern with introductory *it*:

It was wrong for the Government to do it.

Other adjectives in this pattern include:

brave *cruel* *mad* *right*
careful *foolish* *mean* *silly*
careless *greedy* *nice* *wise*
clever *kind*

Gabrielle was ***quick to reply****.*

Again the two subjects are common, but the paraphrase calls for a related adverb ~ *She replied quickly.*
Other adjectives in this small group are: *prompt*, *slow*.

I'm ***glad to hear*** *it.*

The subjects are common, but here the paraphrase requires an adverbial clause ~ *I'm glad because I've heard it.* Adjectives in this pattern include emotive words like:

afraid *angry* *furious* *happy* *proud* *sad* *sorry*

and many *-en* participles like:

annoyed *disappointed* *surprised*
delighted *interested* *worried*

He wasn't ***prepared to argue.***

Explain the ambiguity in: **Is she fit to leave?**

The subjects are once more common. Adjectives in this pattern have volitional meaning or a modal meaning of ability or possibility. The infinitive refers to activity in the future. Other adjectives are:

able *hesitant* *ready*
anxious *impatient* *reluctant*
certain *keen* *willing*
eager

and *-en* participles like *determined* and *prepared*.

I was always ***difficult to please***.

Here the subject (I) is the object of the infinitive. ~ *To please me was difficult.*

Common adjectives in this pattern include:

awkward easy hard impossible pleasant tricky unpleasant

Her hair was ***soft to touch***.

Again the sentence subject is identified with the object of the infinitive. But we cannot paraphrase this pattern as **To touch her hair was soft.*

Usually we can omit the *to*-infinitive without loss of meaning: *Her hair was soft.*

Adjectives in this pattern are very numerous.

GUIDELINE

Some adjectives can be used in more than one pattern, as can most infinitives. Not surprisingly, therefore, ambiguous sentences may occur. So: *The bull is ready to eat* may describe feeding time at a stud farm or the climax of a medieval ox-roast. Fortunately only grammarians allow themselves to be tantalised by such problems.

see
97 Focus
134 Introductory *it*
156 Nominal clauses

68

Complementation of adjectives: *wh*-clauses

Adjectives with *wh*-clauses often have introductory *it* as subject:

It was ***unclear what*** *Hamlet should do.*
It became ***obvious who*** *the ghost was.*

Some other adjectives:

clear doubtful puzzling uncertain unknown

Notice that no prepositions appear with adjectives after *It*. It does not make sense to say **It became clear about who the murderer was.*

After a personal subject, several adjectives are complemented by a *wh*-clause. These adjectives usually have a negative meaning, and have a following preposition: *Hamlet was* ***uncertain about what*** *to do.*

He was ***hesitant about who*** *he could trust.*

Some other adjectives:

careful about	*uncertain about*
doubtful about/as/to	*unclear about*
puzzled about	*undecided about/as to*
sure about/of	*unsure about/of*

Occasionally the preposition can be left out:

*He was **careful (about) who** he spoke to.*
*He was **uncertain (about) what** to do.*

GUIDELINE

With personal subjects, you are always correct if you do not drop the preposition. Then you can think of these as adjectives complemented by a prepositional phrase, as in 65.

see
65 Complementation with prepositional phrases
134 Introductory *it*
156 Nominal clauses

69

Compound adjectives

There are several compound patterns for adjectives. The main groups are:

Noun + adjective/participle	→	*horror-stricken, traffic-free*
Adverb + adjective/participle	→	*over-confident, forthcoming*
Participle + adverbial	→	*laid-back, broken-down*
Adjective + adjective	→	*Indo-European, red-hot*
Preposition + noun	→	*underhand, down-market*
Phrasal	→	*up-to-date, off-the-peg*

The first three patterns above are most productive, with new compounds regularly appearing.

Dylan Thomas was particularly fond of *N. + Adj.* compounds meaning *as Adj. as N.* Examples from *Under Milk Wood*:

*his nicotine **egg-yellow** weeping walrus moustache*
*the **bible-black** sea*

And a TV football commentator recklessly claimed

*The marking has been **shirt-close**.*

A recent claim by a dairy company that its milk is always *doorstep-fresh* presumably wants us to paraphrase the compound *as fresh as when it arrived on the doorstep*. A correspondent to *The Times*, however, asked *How fresh is a doorstep?* In recent years N. + *-ing* has spawned ***heat-seeking*** (missiles), ***mind-blowing*** (experiences) and ***stress-inducing*** (occupations).

New N. + *-en* compounds include ***brain-damaged*** (children), ***computer-assisted*** (design) and ***self-motivated*** (employees).

Participle and adverbial coinings include ***hung-up***, ***laid-back*** and ***switched on/off***. Perhaps the most available pattern for the inventive writer is the phrasal compound.

Here is Kingsley Amis running wild in *That Uncertain Feeling*:

> *After a brief left-right-left of platitude ('Good evening' 'Lovely drop of weather, what?' 'Marvellous isn't it?') I at once went on to rehearse the nice-room-this gambit, the it-must-be-a-tie-running-a-pub gambit, the but-I-suppose-it's-an-interesting-job gambit, the tax-on-beer gambit, and finally silence. The landlord offered the what-do-you-do gambit, the of-course-television's-ruining-this-business gambit, the still-I-always-say-with-customers-you-can't-have-quantity-and-quality gambit, the how-do-you-like-these-titchy-bottles-I-only-got-them-just-for-silly gambit, and finally silence.*

There appears to be little logic about the use of hyphens in compound adjectives. The best guide is a reliable dictionary, which should also be consulted for compound stress patterns.

GUIDELINE

Comparison of compound adjectives is a shady area. Some inflect the first element:

better looking, *better off*, *better known*
lesser known, *harder wearing*, *worse off*, etc.

The majority, however, use *more/most*: *more bad-tempered*, *more good-humoured*, *more well-thought-of* etc.

see
64 Comparison of adjectives
185 Participles
204 Premodifiers

70

Compound nouns

Compound nouns are common and new ones are appearing all the time. Almost all compound nouns have the stress on the first element: *'book-case*, *'vacuum cleaner*, etc. This helps us to tell the difference between compound nouns and phrases made up of adjective + noun.

Compound noun	**Phrase**
a'blackbird (a species)	*a'black'bird* (any bird that is black)
a'gold-fish (a species)	*a'gold'fish* (a fish made of gold!)
a'model-shop (it sells models)	*a'model'shop* (the shop is a model)

Think of compound nouns as sentences which have been telescoped together. *Lightswitch* is a telescoped form of *The* ***light*** *has a* ***switch***. There are several compound patterns for nouns. The main groups are:

Subject + verb → *headache, workman, sailing boat*
Verb + object → *haircut, paperclip, chewing gum*
Verb + prep. phrase → *sun-bathing, sleepwalker, swimming-pool*
Subject + object → *cornfield, toothbrush, policeman*
Subject + complement → *bluebird, fir tree, whiteboard.*

There are two subject + verb groups of compound nouns:

Subject + verb → *headache* – **the head aches**
rainfall – **the rain falls**

So: *landslide* *nightfall* *sunrise* *tape-measure*

Verb + subject → *sliderule* – **the rule slides**
wrapping-paper – **the paper wraps**

So: *tow-rope* *turn-table* *washing machine* *working party*

GUIDELINE

In all the above examples, the first word is stressed. Occasionally you will find compounds of this kind, like *working class*, which have the main stress on the second word.

There are two verb + object groups of compound nouns:

Verb + object *killjoy* – **someone kills joy**
hold-all – **it holds everything**

So: *chewing gum* *mincemeat* *postcard* *stopwatch*

Object + verb *shoelace* – **something laces the shoe**
self winding – **it winds itself**

So: *spot remover* *stocktaking* *word processor* *windscreen wiper*

New compounds of this type continue to appear, especially those ending in *ing* and *-er*: **mind-blowing, asset-stripper**

There are several verb/noun + prepositional phrase groups of compound nouns. The prepositional phrase has an adverbial role, indicating place, time, purpose and other relationships.

place *bathroom* – **bath in a room**
space travel – **travel in space**

time *afternoon tea* – **tea in the afternoon**
birthday party – **party on a birthday**

purpose *bookcase* – **case for books**
keyring – **ring for keys**

other *dry cleaning* – **clean when dry**
science fiction – **fiction about science**
fire-escape – **escape from fire**
telephone message – **message via the telephone**

There are many subject + object forms of compound nouns, since the verb of the underlying sentence is not represented. Common examples are:

Subject belongs to object – ***the leg belongs to a chair*** ~ *chairleg*
So: *bottleneck, doorknob, lampshade, shoelace, window-pane*

Subject produces object: ***the bee produces honey*** ~ *honeybee*
So: *boat-builder, credit card, oilwell, raincloud, shotgun*

Subject is produced by object: ***juice is produced by fruit*** ~ *fruit-juice*
So: *camelhair* *milk powder* *oatmeal* *photocopy*

Subject makes object work: ***the foot makes the brake work*** ~ *footbrake*
So: *airbrakes* *atom bomb* *motor mower* *wind instrument*

Subject works with object: ***the man works with the post*** ~ *postman*
So: *cameraman* *locksmith* *policewoman* *wine waiter*

There are three main subject + complement groups of compound nouns:

Subject + noun complement: *fir-tree* ~ ***the tree is a fir***
So: *ice-cube* *paperwork* *pipeline* *raindrop* *tape-measure*

Subject + adjective complement: *wetsuit* ~ ***the suit is wet***
So: *blueprint* *flatfish* *long jump* *madman* *safe deposit* *software*

Subject + noun complement: *soap-stone* ~ ***the stone is like soap***
So: *cat-burglar* *egghead* *frogman* *stick-insect*

The spelling of compound nouns is not regular.

Even dictionaries do not always agree when a compound is one word, or two, or hyphenated. We write very common, well-established compounds as one word: *daylight*, *shorthand*, *boyfriend*, etc. If you are unsure about other compounds, write them as two words.

> *'Lord Byron was born with a club-foot which (it is generally supposed) had a profound effect on his future temperament.'*
>
> Margaret Drabble, *Oxford Companion to English Literature*

▶ **see**

23 Adverbials
218–20 Prepositional phrases

71

Concord

This traditional term means the 'agreement' between singular and plural subjects and their following verbs. Since English verbs are not commonly inflected, concord is not as important as in some other languages. Perhaps for this reason, we sometimes appear to break the rules.

English non-plural verb inflections are limited to the third person singular of the present simple tense of lexical verbs: *walk**s***, *buy**s***, *use**s***, etc. and third person singular forms of to be (*is*, *was*), to do (*doe**s***) and to have (*ha**s***).

Non-count nouns and singular count nouns are naturally followed by a singular verb form. With noun phrase subjects, the verb usually agrees with the head:

*A **line** of grey ships **was** steaming across the Aegean.*

Notice however that when a singular head is not as important as a later plural noun, it is that second noun which decides the concord: *a **lot** of*

things, *a* ***group*** *of* ***children***, *a* **number** *of* ***reasons*** usually attract a plural verb. Sometimes we use a plural verb form with a singular collective noun, to show that we are thinking of the individuals that make up the group:

The staff (sing.) don't (plur.) speak English.

Similarly, adjectives in a generic sense – as in *the young and the aged, the living and the dead* usually use a plural verb – to show that we are thinking of the membership of the groups.

The dead (sing.) live (plur.) by love.

Coordinate subjects are often felt to be a single entity and therefore attract singular concord:

Gin and tonic was (sing.) served.

Noun phrases referring to money and times are also notionally single:

Six hundred pounds was (sing.) enough to live on.

... of a (sing.) very disagreeable twelve hours

Five seconds was (sing.) enough to set him dreaming of falling in love.

Clauses, both finite and non-finite, are felt to call for singular verbs:

What I am employing is (sing.) a very new psychiatric technique.

To be uninhibited ... is (sing.) not the same as being unshockable.

GUIDELINE

Given a choice of concord between a subject's grammatical number and its notional number, we usually choose the latter, as does *The Times* newspaper in:

[One] in three houses in Britain [are] more than 50 years old.

see

162 Collective nouns
80 Count/non-count
7 Generic adjectives
178 Noun phrases

72

Conditional sentences

A conditional sentence usually has two clauses, a main clause and a subordinate conditional clause. We use conditional sentences to imply that the events of the main clause depend upon those of the conditional clause. So:

conditional clause | main clause

If I can produce the letter ... the matter will be forgotten.

The speaker means that his employers will forget that he has lost a certain letter if (and only if) he can show them it. But if he is unable to produce it, his carelessness will not be forgotten. Most conditional clauses start with *if*, the other common subordinator being *unless*. *Unless* is the negative form of *if*:

If I can't produce it ~ **Unless I can produce it**

Open conditions most often refer to past, present or future time – which?

Other subordinators include: *provided/providing that*, *on condition that* and, to introduce questions, *Suppose/supposing (that)*.

***Suppose he** himself gave her the injections . . .*

Conditional sentences are of two kinds: open and hypothetical. In both, the conditional clauses can be initial or final, though imperatives tend to come first.

> *'Never speak loudly to one another, unless the house is on fire.'*
>
> H. W. Thompson, *Body, Boots and Britches*

▶ **see**

29 Adverb clauses of condition
74 Hypothetical conditions
73 Open conditions

73

Conditional sentences: open conditions

These are open or real in the sense that they are a real possibility, now or at some later time. All modal verbs may appear not only in the main clause, but also in the *if*-clause. We use open conditions most often to talk about the future:

***If you interrupt again,** you will have to go outside.* [threat]
***If I give you the letter,** will you come back again?* [plea]
***If this is mentioned in court,** deny it.* [instruction]
*You can go away **if you like.*** [offer]
*She'll die **if she doesn't take it.*** [prediction]
You threaten me and I'll wake up the house. ~ ***If you threaten me** . . .* [threat]

We also use open conditions to talk about habits, past or present, using appropriate tenses:

***If Isobel stays in London,** I go to her.*
*I go into churches and pray, **if the doors are open.***
*He worried about his old mother **if he went away for a weekend.***
***If he should keep Patrick too long in the waiting room,** Patrick would say, 'When are you coming to another seance?'*

Sometimes we use an open condition to show logical reasoning – past or present – if A, then B – where we assume that the **if-** clause is likely:

***If he's your friend,** I can only say –*
***If he's so sure he's going to get off,** why does he bother to tell you?*
*Why didn't you keep it confidential, **if it's confidential?***

▶ GUIDELINES

Sometimes we say things like: ***If he's an army officer,*** *I'm a Dutchman.* ***If that's gold,*** *I'll eat my hat.* We are claiming that the *if-* clause is as unlikely as the main clause. In fact these are rhetorical conditions and function as strong statements: *He isn't an army officer, That isn't gold.* Similarly Muriel Spark's Elsie said, *'I'm damned* ***if I'll part with the letter.'*** ~ I certainly will not give you the letter. We use rhetorical conditions referring to minimal amounts to give strong assertion to the main clause:

She's fifty ***if she's a day.***

If there's one thing a bachelor does not like *it is another bachelor who has lost his job.*

Freda will not proceed with the case, ***if I know anything of Freda.***

But the judge in Freda's court case used an indirect condition when he said –

The evidence . . . ***if I might say so,*** *is less than useless.*

We insert such idiomatic phrases to be more polite: others include:

if I may be frank	*if you'll allow me to say so*
if you don't mind	*if you'll forgive me for being serious*

Other fixed phrases of indirect condition show uncertainty:

if you know what I mean	*if I remember correctly*
if I'm not mistaken	*if I'm right*

Notice how we can use the imperative in the main clause of an open condition and also to replace the *if-* clause. When the main clause refers to the future, the *if-* clause may be in any present tense. Occasionally we can use inversion of subject and operator without *if* to form open conditions, mostly with tentative *should*, but it gives a formal tone. Compare:

If Tim should be there, *give him my regards.*
Should Tim be there, *give him my regards.*

▶ **see**

72	Conditional sentences	136	Inversion
109	Imperatives	150	Tentative *should*

74

Conditional sentences: hypothetical conditions

These are unreal conditions, rejected in the speaker's mind and therefore the main clause is felt to be unlikely. Both clauses may refer to past, present or future, using appropriate tenses:

The police wouldn't (pres.) *allow him his freedom* ***if they thought*** (pres.) ***he was guilty.***

If Alice were (fut.) ***to take too much insulin*** *. . . she might* (fut.) *die.*

I'd adopt (fut.) *the child* ***if I married*** (fut.) ***Alice.***

I'd like (fut.) *Alice for a wife* ***if I was*** (fut.) ***to marry.***

She would (past) *have stopped* **if your mother hadn't** (past) **made her life a misery.**

> ***If you'd seen*** (past) ***as much as I have,*** *you would* (pres.) *know the gift can descend on anyone.*
>
> *A silly question because* ***if he hadn't*** (past) ***been born*** *he could* (past) *not have asked it.*

Verb forms in hypothetical conditions are back-shifted as in indirect speech. So when we refer to present or future time, the *if*-clause takes the simple past tense and the main clause the past tense form of the modal. When we refer to past events, the *if*-clause takes a verb in the past perfect tense and the main clause modal usually takes the past perfect form. We can use subjunctive *were* for all persons in hypothetical conditions, to suggest unlikeliness: ***If she were to take too much insulin*** . . . though *was* is commonly heard in such sentences. Similarly the idiomatic *If I were you* is often heard with *was*.
More often than open conditions, certain hypothetical structures can delete *if* and invert the subject and operator to give a more formal tone:

> ***Were Alice*** *to take too much insulin . . .*
>
> ***Had your mother not*** *made her life a misery . . .*

Had is the most commonly used operator of this inversion.

▶ **see**
49 Back-shift
72 Conditional sentences
73 Open conditions
136 Inversion

75

Conditional sentences: ellipsis and substitution

As in other subordinate clauses, we use the devices of omission and substitution to avoid needless repetition and sentence length. Occasionally in hypothetical conditions we omit subject and operator in the conditional clause but only after *if* and *unless*.

> *You would make an excellent medium,* ***if△ properly trained.***
>
> *Alice would certainly die,* ***if△ deprived of her insulin.***

Similarly we often omit subject and operator after *if* before *necessary* and *possible*, and occasionally before *anything*:

> *Dr Lyte suggested the baby could be adopted,* ***if△ necessary.***
>
> *Patrick asked for an appointment.* ***'If△ at all possible,'*** *he said.*
>
> *. . . it would go against him,* ***if△ anything*** *(∼ if it did anything)*

Subject and operator may in certain cases also be omitted in conjunction with the pro-forms *so* and *not*.

> *Patrick might be found guilty, and* ***if so,*** *would go to prison.*
>
> *Tim . . . hoping someone married would take him home to supper, but prepared* ***if△ not*** *to dine alone at eight o'clock.*

The omitted words are less exactly retrievable in the idiomatic phrase, *What if . . .?*

> ***What if*** *Patrick did her harm?*

but their sense is clear.

Several expressions of volition, possibility and deduction may involve concealed conditionals. Consider:

I wouldn't do that (if I were you).
You might have passed (if you had worked harder).

'And here is the lesson I learned in the army. If you want to do a thing badly you have to work at it as though you want to do it well.'

Peter Ustinov, *Dear Me*

▶ **see**

72 Conditional sentences
73 Open conditions
74 Hypothetical conditions
88 Ellipsis
143 Modal verbs
263 Substitution

76

Conjunctions

This is a closed class of words which join together clauses and other sentence elements. When we join two equal elements, we use coordinating conjunctions.

We entered the great gate **and** *found ourselves immediately in a warren of cobbled streets.*

When we join a main clause to a less important and dependent clause, we start that dependent clause with a subordinating conjunction.

I was wrong, **as** *it turned out.*

The simple conjunctions *and*, *but* and *or* regularly coordinate clauses. Subordinating conjunctions may be simple or compound:

although	*because*	*once*	*while*
as	*even though*	*since*	etc.
as long as	*if*	*unless*	

Many conjunctions are closely related to adverbial meaning:

after, before, since, until, when, while [time]
everywhere, where, wherever [place]
as long as, assuming that, if, in case
provided that, supposing, unless [condition]

But, see the list of subordinators of adverbial clauses as a demonstration that many carry more than one adverbial meaning. Unlike coordinators, subordinators frequently start new sentences, when the subordinate clause has been fronted to give special emphasis:

As we emerged on the balcony overlooking the courtyard*, we heard the sound of voices.*

Comment on: **He cooks and sings beautifully**

GUIDELINE

Notice, however, that we do not usually front clauses subordinated by *as far as* (= distance) and *as long as* (= time, duration).

The superb view stretched **as far as the eye could see.**

see

24–34 Adverbial clauses
77 Coordination
78 Coordinators
98 Fronting
261 Subordination
262 Subordinators
276 Word classes

77

Coordination

This is the linking by coordinators of clauses and other sentence parts of equal meaning and grammatical value.

The darkness was restful **and** *I felt inclined to doze.*

(He was) conscious of the elegance of his beard **and** *beautiful hands.*

When we coordinate two clauses into a compound sentence we do not usually repeat the same subject and auxiliary in the second clause:

He seemed extremely troubled, and△ looked up nervously.

Coordination can link:

nouns	*(He made) a few friends* **and** *many enemies.*
verbs	*. . . circling slowly* **and** *running the whole length of the horizon*
adjectives	*She was lean* **and** *half-starved.*
adverbials	*Autumn is lengthening into winter, slowly* **but** *surely.*
conjunctions	*. . . if* or *when*

Common coordinators include:

and, both . . . and . . ., but, either . . . or, not only . . . but also . . ., or

GUIDELINE

Where two coordinated verbs are close in meaning, we usually omit a common adverbial from the first clause:

He eats△ and drinks too much.

If this is always true, then here is a car component advertiser who does not mean what he says:

Children's seats supplied and fitted FREE

see

253 Compound sentences
76 Conjunctions
78 Coordinators
79 Correlatives
261 Subordination

78

Coordinators

These are the coordinating conjunctions, related adverbs like *once* and *so* and correlatives which link (coordinate) clauses and other sentence elements of equal meaning and grammatical value.

They look ragged and thin **but** *not actually starving.*

The moon was all but gone, **yet** *the light brimmed the whole amphitheatre.*

Coordinating conjunctions stand at the beginning of a clause or between the words or elements they join:

People will buy the newspapers all right,
but *he can't guarantee readers.*

They need (paper) for wrapping fish in,
or *eggs.*

Many modern writers, reflecting the pauses of speech, often start a new sentence with *and*, *but* or *or*. In effect this coordinates the new sentence with the last one:

'Come,' he cried. 'Come with us.' **And** *led us by the hand into the darkness.*

GUIDELINE

Occasionally, for reasons of style, writers place coordinate clauses together without coordinators – zero coordinator.

We followed them up stairs, down alleys, △ *round corners.*

He was in build short, in character voluble, △ *in colouring blond as a kingcup.*

'I came, I saw, I conquered.'

Julius Caesar, *Divus Julius*

---

see

76	Conjunctions	79	Correlatives
77	Coordination	277	Zero forms

79

Correlatives

These are pairs of conjunctions used mainly in coordination and also in subordination. Correlatives join two equal forms, the most important being:

both . . . and . . ./either . . . or . . ./neither . . . nor . . ./not only . . . but also . . .

With noun phrases, adjectives, adverbs, prepositional phrases and non-finites they are used for emphasis:

This does not imply ***either*** *lack of spontaneity* ***or*** *of goodwill.* [N.P.]

Both *geographically* ***and*** *temperamentally, Rhodes lay outside . . . trouble.* [adv.]

. . . its effect, ***not only*** *on the rotation of crops,* ***but also*** *on the forest.* [P.P.]

We also use all these to coordinate parallel finite clauses:

It seemed hopeless, ***both*** *because the noise was so great* ***and*** *the invective so continuous.*

But with negative correlatives, inversion is necessary:

No sooner ***does he*** *see a cicada . . . than he must buy it.*

Not only ***does one*** *turn to the icon in adversity, but also in trouble.*

As subordinators of two equal noun phrases, reduced clauses or finite clauses, we use *whether . . . or (whether) . . .*

Tomorrow I should see ***whether*** *it was still a reality* ***or whether*** *we had invented it.*

Other correlatives are:

just as . . . so . . . , rather . . . than . . . , not so much . . . as . . .

''Tis neither here nor there.'

William Shakespeare, *Othello*

---

see

76 Conjunctions 136, 137 Inversion

77 Coordination 261 Subordination

80

Count/non-count nouns

This is the major division of common nouns. Those which have plural forms, can be counted and usually follow a form of the article are called count nouns (also countable, and sometimes unit nouns). Examples:

desk girl pen roundabout

Common nouns which have no plural form are usually followed by a simple verb and are not counted are non-count nouns (sometimes called mass or uncountable nouns). Examples:

blood dynamite happiness malaria swimming

Many languages have the count/non-count distinction. But a non-count noun in one language is not necessarily a non-count noun in another language. For example *anger*, *baggage*, *dancing*, *furniture*, *information*, *parking* and *poetry* are non-count in English but count nouns in other languages. Several English nouns can be both count and non-count, some items of food for example. When we buy *potatoes* (count) there may be twenty *potatoes* (count) in a kilo bag. But Van Gogh's painting 'The Potato Eaters' shows people who live on the food we call *potato* (non-count). Similarly:

> ***Cheese*** (non-count) *is heavy in calories.*
>
> *Cheshire, Cheddar and Stilton are well-known English* **cheeses** (count).

Other common nouns which we use as both count and non-count nouns are:

brick	*plastic*	*wood*	*fish*	*tea*	*time*
cotton	*rock*	*wool*	*fruit*	*tobacco*	*youth*
hair	*silk*	*cake*	*liquor*	*water*	*war*
material	*stone*	*coffee*	*meat*	*age*	*work*
metal	*tile*				

GUIDELINE

If in doubt about whether a noun is count or non-count consult a good dictionary. Otherwise look for plurals, *a/an* and numbers which are signs of count nouns. A safe test is with *much/many*. *Much* patterns with nouns used as non-count, *many* with nouns in count use: *much time*, *many times*.

> *'Life is doubt, and faith without doubt is nothing but death.'*
>
> Miguel de Unamuno, *Poesias*

see
160 Common nouns

81

Declaratives

Declaratives are one of the four types of simple sentence. Formally they have subject and verb as their basic word order and typically end with a falling intonation in speech.

Traditional grammar taught that the function of declaratives was to make statements. In many cases this is true, but we also use the declarative form in other functions, as discussed in sentence form and function.

see
254 Sentences: form and function
255 Sentences: four kinds

82

Defining/non-defining

This concept is most familiar when used to distinguish two kinds of relative clause. A defining clause postmodifies and restricts a preceding noun and is an essential part of the noun phrase. It is not separated off from the noun head by commas in print or, in speech, by pauses:

She despised men ***who were weak.*** ~ *She despised those men who were weak.*

A non-defining relative clause can have the same form, but it is not essential to the meaning of the sentence and can be deleted without loss of communication. In writing we mark it off with commas and in speech by pauses and intonation:

She despised men, ***who were weak.*** ~ *She despised all men; they were weak.*

The concept of defining/non-defining applies equally however to adjectives and appositive clauses. Whilst most adjectives are defining by nature, we do sometimes use them in a non-defining way:

How's your ***beautiful*** *mother?*

Here, *beautiful* is not identifying one mother of several, and is non-defining. Similarly, ***Happy*** *Hampstead*, ***Little*** *Dorrit*, ***Simple*** *Simon*, ***Dear*** *John*.

GUIDELINES

Poets often place adjectives in non-defining use when loading their verse with descriptive detail. Consider:

He holds him with his ***glittering*** *eye.*
(Ponder the defining meaning!)

The ***fair*** *breeze blew, the* ***white*** *foam flew.*

Intensifying adjectives are usually non-defining. Consider:

a ***true*** *friend* *a* ***real*** *idiot* *a* ***sure*** *winner*

In apposition an appositive clause may be an essential part of the meaning of its sentence (defining) or a disposable embellishment (non-defining). Consider:

defining

The belief ***that the earth was flat*** *did not encourage distant exploration.*

non-defining

The Copernican theory, ***that the planets orbit the sun,*** *withdrew sailors' fear of the end of the world.*

> *'Happy the people whose annals are blank in history books.'*
>
> Thomas Carlyle, *Frederick the Great*

see

4 Adjectives 130 Intensifying adjectives
37 Apposition 248 Relative clauses

83

Demonstratives

The words *this*, *that*, *these* and *those* are demonstratives. *This* and *that* are singular, *these* and *those* are plural, *this* and *these* mean *here* and *now*, and *that* and *those* mean *distant* in time and/or space. Compare:

She was born in **this** *place, within* **these** *four walls.*

In **that** *ancient cornfield many a man had made love-promises to a woman.*

We use demonstratives as pronouns and as determiners. Compare:

On a morning like **this** (pron.)
This (det.) *ancient track ran east and west.*

Demonstrative pronouns usually refer to things, rather than people.

This *seems all right.* ~ *this beer . . .*

Jude did not think of **that** *then.*

Occasionally we use *these/those* to refer to people, as in ***those*** *in charge* but only when we know who we are thinking about. Such cases are really examples of ellipsis – *those men*. We can use *this* and *that* to refer to an event or something that has happened:

Arabella introduced Jude to her parents and neighbours. They all spoke in a congratulatory manner and took him seriously as Arabella's intended partner . . . He had not meant **this***: a mere afternoon of pleasant walking:* **that** *was all he had meant.*

Demonstrative pronouns can stand for earlier clauses (as above) which are anaphoric reference, pointing backwards. We also use *this/those* (but not *that/those*) to point forwards (cataphoric reference) as in:

All his reading had only come to this: that he would have to sell his books to buy saucepans.

That and *those* are used in formal written English as relative antecedents.

Their lives were ruined . . . by the fundamental error of their matrimonial union: **that** *of having based a permanent contract on a temporary feeling.*
Here, *that* ~ *the fundamental error*

turning on the ladder, Jude knelt on the third rung, where, resting against **those** *above it, he prayed that the mist might rise.* Here, *those* ~ *the rungs*

As relative antecedents *that* and *those* are pronouns of definite meaning substituting for preceding nouns or noun phrases, and meaning *the one/ones*. The only time when we use demonstrative pronouns to refer to people is in identifying sentences:

This *is Arabella.* ***Those*** *are my friends. Who was* **that?**

▶ GUIDELINES

We often use *this/that* to identify or introduce more than one person if we feel they are a unit. ***This*** *is my mother and father.* ***That's*** *the Fawley family.*

On the telephone we identify ourselves and others with pronouns:

__This__ is Joy McKellen. Is __that__ Peter?
Who is __that?__ (Americans prefer *Who is __this?__*)

Demonstrative determiners: When *this/that*, *these/those* are followed by a noun we are using them as determiners. *This* and *that* refer to singular count and non-count nouns. *These* and *those* refer to plural count nouns only.

__That__ night he went out alone.
Throw aside __those__ stupid books.

Like other determiners, the four demonstratives are placed before adjectives in a noun-clause:

__that__ old woman's shop window

They also stand before the pronouns *one/ones*.

We can use *one* to refer to both things and people:

The place I mean is __that__ one yonder.
__this__ person or __that__ one

GUIDELINES

The determiners *this/these* usually refer to something known in the context or already mentioned (anaphoric reference), but notice this contemporary forward (cataphoric) reference:

I saw __these__ beautiful green leather shoes this morning. ~ the ones I am going to tell you about

Notice that *here* and *there* are demonstrative adverbs of place.

> *'We are here today and gone tomorrow.'*
>
> Mrs Aphra Behn, *The Lucky Chance*

see
84 Determiners
88 Ellipsis
228 Pronouns

84

Determiners

These are a closed list of words like *the*, *his* and *this*, whose function is to determine or limit a following noun. They usually come at the beginning of a noun phrase, and always stand before any adjectives in the phrase:

__all the__ way *__next__ day*
__three__ whole years

There are limitations on how we use determiners:

according to the following noun (we only use *a*, *every* and *neither* for example with singular count nouns, but we never use *few*, *many* and *several* with singular count nouns).

some are mutually exclusive (we cannot use *the* and *my* together for example).

determiners have different positions relative to one another. (we always place *all* before *the*, for example, and *my* before *several*).

Determiners and nouns

Three classes of common nouns affect our choice of determiners: count nouns singular (like *man*), count nouns plural (like *men*) and noncount nouns (like *sympathy*). The classification of determiners into articles, demonstratives, numerals, possessives, quantifiers and *wh*-words is quite separate from the restrictions on usage with count and noncount nouns.

Of the articles, for example, *a/an* is marked for singular and appears with singular count nouns only, whereas we use *the* with count nouns, singular and plural, and with non-count nouns. The table below lists the most common determiners, indicating which noun classes we use them with, and giving examples:

Determiners	count singular	count plural	non-count	Examples
the	√	√	√	**the** *words*, **the** *sunlight*
all possessives	√	√	√	**my** *mother*, **her** *jewels*, **their** *people*
what, *which*, *whose*	√	√	√	**what** *kind*, **whose** *feet*
stressed *some* and *any*	√	√	√	**some** *enemy*, **any** *stone*
no, *such*	√	√	√	**such** *men*, **no** *harm*
all multipliers, *all*, *half*	√	√	√	*a* **half** *year*, *with it* **all**
ordinals, *past*, *other*	√	√	√	**second** *nature*, **other** *matters*
unstressed *some* and *any*		√	√	**some** *guests*, **any** *hurt*
zero		√	√	*I felt*△ *anger*, *It is*△ *time*
enough		√	√	**enough** *ships*, *trouble* **enough**
more, *most*, *plenty of*		√	√	**more** *cunning*, **most** *dancers*
a lot of, *lots of*		√	√	**lots of** *the myths*, **a lot of** *blood*
another, *next*, *last*	√	√		**next** *day*, **last** *noises*
this, *that*	√			**this** *last year*, **that** *blood*
one, *a/an*	√			**a** *light step*, **an** *ox*
each/every, *either/neither*	√			**each** *other*, **every** *day*, *on* **either** *side*
these/those, *both*, cardinals		√		*in* **those** *days*, *a* **hundred** *oxen*
many (a), *few/fewer/fewest*		√		**many** *times*, **a few** *steps*
several, *a good many*		√		**several** *youths*, **a good many** *people*
(a) little, *less*, *least* }			√	**less** *time*, **too much** *pride*
much, *a good deal of* }				**a good deal** *of pain*

Order of determiners
Determiners usually precede the noun they determine, but we do not use them in random order. It is useful here to identify three groups of determiners:
central determiners, the most important group;
predeterminers, which, when present, come before central determiners; and
postdeterminers which follow them.

Predeterminers	**Central determiners**	**Postdeterminers**
some quantifiers *all, both, half*	articles *a, an, the*	cardinals *one, two* etc.
multipliers *once, twice, double* etc.	demonstratives *this, these* etc.	ordinals *first, second* etc.
intensifiers *such, what*	possessives *my, your* etc.	general ordinals *last, other, next*
	some quantifiers *some, any, no* etc. *wh-* determiners *what, which, whose*	some quantifiers *few, less, little* *many, more* etc.

Notice that not all predeterminers can be used with all central determiners – for semantic reasons. But where we use two or more determiners together, the order follows the table above. For example:

Predet. + central	**Central + postdet.**
all their *jewels*	***the other*** *side*
such a *thing*	***the third*** *time*
all this *way*	***her two*** *hands*

The combination of two determiners, as in these examples, is common. We less frequently combine three:

> ***All these six*** *boys . . . were threats to my honour.*
> predet. + central + postdet.

GUIDELINE

Think of determiners as part of the premodification system in the noun phrase. Here we frequently combine determiners with adjectives and other premodifiers:

> ***all that great height of*** *rock*

see

38	Articles	181	Ordinals
180	Cardinals	198	Possessives
80	Count/non-count	204	Premodifiers
83	Demonstratives	229	Quantifiers
130	Intensifiers	274	*wh-* words
179	Numbers	276	Word classes

85

Direct and indirect speech

To report someone else's words we have two alternatives. One is to repeat the actual words used, writing them in quotation marks. This is direct speech. The alternative is to report the words indirectly, making certain changes. This is indirect speech.

He said, 'You're silly.' [direct speech]
He told me I was silly. [indirect speech]

(Some grammars use the term reported speech to mean the same thing as indirect speech, others give the terms slightly different meanings. To avoid confusion, we will use indirect speech only.)

Occasionally we use a mixture of the direct and indirect reporting:

indirect: *They invited me to dinner* — direct: *and would I bring a friend.*

They invited me to dinner and would I bring a friend.

The very large number of reporting verbs gives us many forms of reporting, with varying degrees of recoverability of the original. Consider:

'I wonder if you'd like to play.'
- *She wondered if we'd like to play.*
- *She invited us to play.*
- *She suggested a game.*

One special kind of indirect speech is used by fiction writers to report the stream of thoughts in a person's mind. This is free indirect speech, which usually drops the reporting clause and retains direct questions, exclamations and interjections. These features give it more immediacy, despite its back-shifted verbs and shifts in pronouns, time/place adverbials and demonstratives.

Here are Miriam's tumbling thoughts when Paul Morel breaks with her in *Sons and Lovers*. This is free indirect speech.

> *She had known. Only why, as he sat there, had he still this strange dominance over her? . . . Why, even now, if he looked at her and commanded her, would she have to obey? . . . But once he was obeyed, then she had him in her power, she knew, to lead him where she would. She was sure of herself . . . Ah, he was not a man!*
>
> D. H. Lawrence

▶ **see**

49 Backshift
110, 111 Indirect speech
252 Reporting verbs

86

to do

As well as its function as an operator, *to do* is used as a lexical verb with a range of meanings:

I'll see what I can **do**. (perform)
I don't know how you **do** *it*. (succeed in)
But it wouldn't **do** *at all*. (be acceptable)
That **does** *it*. (completes)

Like regular lexical verbs, it uses auxiliary *do* as operator in negative and interrogative forms:

Why **did** (op.) *you* **do** (lex.) *it? But I* **didn't** (op.) **do** (lex.) *it*.

▶ **see**
48 Auxiliary verbs
139 Lexical verbs
184 Operator

87

Dynamic and stative use

We usually think of verbs as referring to actions or events. These may be an extended action in progress, a single happening or one that recurs:

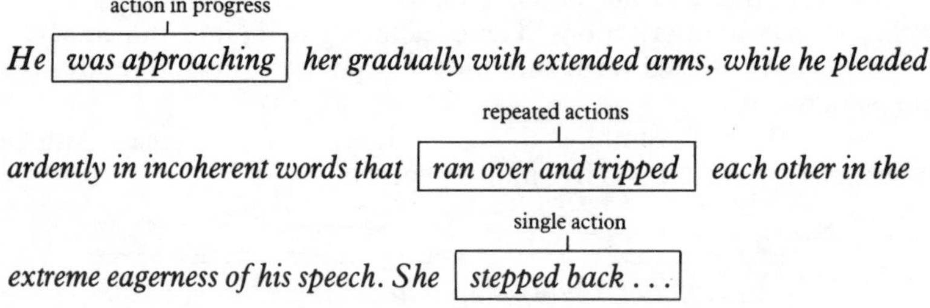

All the above verbs are dynamic: verbs which we use in simple tenses for single or repeated actions, and progressive tenses for actions in progress. But certain verbs usually refer, not to events and actions, but to states – hence the name stative verbs. Some, like *be* and *have* refer to qualities and states:

That white man **is** *not content*.

Others refer to emotional and intellectual states:

I **wish** *you would do something*.
What did she **mean** *by it?*

Also verbs of perception:

He **watched** *the canoe dart away*.

Verbs with stative meaning refer to states which continue for a long time and are not temporary. It would often be inappropriate to use them in progressive aspect, which stresses an action's temporary nature. We do not usually find statives in progressive tenses. Similarly stative verbs rarely occur in the passive voice. Consider, **You to do something is wished (by me)*, **The canoe was watched dart away (by him)*. With verbs in stative use there is no idea of verbal action transferring from grammatical subject to object.

GUIDELINE

It is more accurate to speak of verbs in dynamic/stative use than dynamic/stative verbs, since several verbs may be used in both ways with quite different meanings. Consider:

Are you ***following*** *me? (Am I being* ***followed****?)*	dynamic
Do you ***follow*** *(understand) me? (*Am I being* ***followed****?)*	stative
They all ***had*** *a good time. (A good time was* ***had*** *by all.)*	dynamic
She ***had*** *fair hair. (*Fair hair was* ***had*** *by her.)*	stative
We ***recognised*** *the new government. (The new government was* ***recognised****.)*	dynamic
We ***recognised*** *Peter's back. (*Peter's back was* ***recognised****.)*	stative

Notice that most verbs have corresponding nouns and adjectives: *know/knowledge/knowledgeable*; *possess/possession/possessive*.

The terms dynamic and stative can be applied equally to verbs, nouns and adjectives but the distinction is most significant with verbs.

see
45 Aspect
271 Verbs: general

88

Ellipsis

Ellipsis, sometimes called omission, takes place when we leave out parts of sentences to avoid needless repetition. Ellipsis, together with substitution, are the two processes of the principle of reduction. We omit words which carry information which we know from the situation or from our shared cultural knowledge or from our knowledge of linguistic structure. These are all weak forms of ellipsis. Sometimes we omit words which are already present in the sentence(s) used. This last, when the omitted words are fully recoverable from the text (textual ellipsis) is technically the only true kind of ellipsis, the strong form.

Situational ellipsis

A Margaret Drabble character tells his friend:

And you've had a bad time. Being ill △. And then, Alison △ . . .

The elliptical reference to Alison omits information which the two characters know, and which the reader shares from earlier chapters. The speaker really means *And then, you must be worried about your mistress, Alison, who is still in an unfriendly country, where her feckless daughter has been arrested* – or words to that effect. Situational ellipsis of this kind is a common feature of intimate and informal conversation – probably the most economical form of communication.

Cultural ellipsis

Margaret Drabble describes two lovers meeting in a roadside café:

Karel ordered two teas, one with△ and one without△.

She is able to omit *sugar* because she assumes her readers to be familiar with the kind of café involved, even to the lengths of mentally conjuring up the likely underlying (informal) dialogue: *Two teas, please. Sugar? One with, one without.*

Structural ellipsis

When a Drabble character writes in a friendly letter,

You will be pleased to hear△ they say△ I will be able to get around quite well . . .

she uses an informal conversational style in which *that* is omitted twice. An optional *that* has been omitted from two *that*-clauses in direct object position.

Textual ellipsis

In the following examples, ellipsis avoids needless repetition, but the omitted words are completely recoverable from the text.

Alison was very good at looking after him, when she chose to be△.

I want you to tell me what I ought to do,△ who I should talk to.

The above examples show anaphoric ellipsis, in which the omitted words have already been used. Cataphoric ellipsis, in which the omitted word(s) occur later in the text, is less common:

Malice and justice united, to persecute the once so prosperous△, once so arrogant△, once so powerful of nations, the nation on whose empire the sun never set.

His sourness took a common△, but to Babs and Anthony (unworldly innocents) a rather surprising course . . .

GUIDELINE

Anaphoric ellipsis is by far the more common and typical of conversation and informal writing. Cataphoric ellipsis is a conscious, stylistic device: it tightens up the structure of a sentence, but at the same time makes the sentence less easy to read.

Ellipsis – what do we omit, and where?

There are two functional situations where we omit items and two formal situations. Although these overlap, each is sufficiently frequent and useful to be separately identified.

The omission of words which carry obvious or known information is very common in casual, intimate speech, where we often drop the early, unstressed words – initial ellipsis.

In shorter spoken exchanges, the second speaker usually takes up an already stated topic, by way of agreement, disagreement, comment or other response. In such cases we use various kinds of ellipsis to avoid needless repetition – ellipsis in response structures. Phrases and sentences using *and*, *but* and *or* usually repeat information and are structures in which we frequently omit words – ellipsis in coordination. In a similar way, subordinate clauses often share information with their main clauses, giving rise to ellipsis in subordination.

GUIDELINE

Ellipsis is a very useful and natural device in English. There is nothing sloppy or inferior about omitting items in the appropriate places. Consider the result of replacing the omissions from the dialogue quoted in 90.

'Don't you disapprove of capitalism?'
'No, I don't disapprove of capitalism. Why should I disapprove of capitalism? Do you disapprove of capitalism?'
'Of course I don't disapprove of capitalism.'
'Well then, why should I disapprove of capitalism?'

Ridiculous and totally unnatural. Ellipsis and substitution both serve the same purposes of shortening messages and making the relationships of meaning clearer. Sometimes we use ellipsis, sometimes substitution, and occasionally both.

see
91 Ellipsis in coordination
90 Ellipsis in response structures
92 Ellipsis in subordination
89 Initial ellipsis
245 Reduction
263 Substitution

89

Initial ellipsis

In casual speech we often drop initial unstressed syllables and words – *' k you* ~ *Thank you, 's OK* ~ *it's OK, 'fraid not* ~ *I'm afraid not, Sorry* ~ *I am sorry*.

One explanation is that the omitted items have been so unstressed that we don't hear them. Many common elliptical phrases have become almost fixed expressions appearing more often than not in elliptical forms: *Very good. Wonderful. Crazy. Out! Fire! Bad luck. No chance. No problem.* And most people will agree on what unstressed words have been left out. From infancy we constantly use similar elliptical sentences – *Again. Nice. Can't. Got it.* As children we learn to reduce sentences to the minimum when calling over some distance – *Finished. Ready. Coming.*

As adults we similarly drop from the beginning of casual speech and thoughts words which carry little or no new information. The commonest items omitted in initial ellipsis are:

it is/was *'△Not my mistake,' said Anthony.*

there is/are *Still, △ no point in moaning.*

Pronoun subject

'△Can't adapt, poor old fellow.'
△Belongs to the local Archaeological Society.

Pronoun subject + auxiliary verb (in both statements and questions)

'△Sorry,' she said.

'△Depressed?' he said gently.

'△A man after my own heart,' said Francis.

'How's Maureen? △Keeping all right . . .?'

Auxiliary verb in questions

'△You there, Mrs Ellerenshaw?' he said.

'△She still here?'

▶ GUIDELINES

When we are making statements we leave out personal pronouns before ordinary verbs – *Thought so*. Also before a negative auxiliary verb – *Don't think so* – and modal auxiliaries – *△Must go. △Couldn't say. △Have to wait*. But we do not usually drop the pronoun subject before auxiliary *have*, *be* and *will*. (This does not apply to telegrams, which have separate rules: Drabble's telegrams saying WILL BE WITH YOU BOTH SOONEST and AM CATCHING NEXT PLANE TO ADRA would not be acceptable in speech.)

With questions, we can drop the pronoun subject, auxiliary verb, or both: *Are you happy? You happy? Happy?* But we do not omit the auxiliary verb before *I* or *It*. The only elliptical forms of *Am I too late? Is it working?* are *Too late? Working?*

▶ see

88 Ellipsis

90 Ellipsis in response structures

91 Ellipsis in coordination

92 Ellipsis in subordination

90

Ellipsis in response structures

We use a response structure as a spoken reaction to someone else when we answer a question, agree or disagree with a statement, or comment on what someone has said. In most of these cases a full response would repeat information from the earlier sentence. We avoid this repetition by using ellipsis.

'Don't you disapprove of capitalism?'
'No. △ Why should I? △ Do you? △'
'Of course I don't. △'
'Well then, why should I? △'

The commonest omissions in response structures are:

subject and operator

'What will you do with them?' '△Put them back.'

subject and verb

'What's he called, your baby?' '△Hugh.'

predicate

'Who says you can't drink?' 'My doctor. △*'*
'And where were you?' '△*Me?'*

main clause

'Are you going now?' 'Yes. △*'*
'He's never shown any signs of getting married, has he?' '△*Not that I know of.'*

wh- question

'They're false teeth.' 'Good heavens. Whose? △*'*

after *wh-* word

'She let him have them both. Why not? △*'*

full clause

'Give my regards to Karel.' 'I will. △*'*

after operator

'My family come from there.' 'So do mine △*.'*

after *to*

'Don't wait for the train to go.' 'I want to △*,' he said.*

after verbs of saying and thinking

'What are you going to do about Karel?' 'I don't quite know △*.'*

GUIDELINES

Notice that when a short answer reduces a clause with two auxiliaries, the second one is omitted:

'You'll have to wait a bit.' 'Yes, I will △*.'*

Notice also that in short answers with *so*, *nor* and *neither*, there is inversion of subject and auxiliary verb:

'I think this is paradise,' she said. And so ***did he****.*

'I do not know.' 'No,' said Evelyn, 'neither ***do I****.'*

see
136 Inversion
241 Response questions
238 Tag questions
263 Substitution

91

Ellipsis in coordination

When we use conjunctions like *and*, *but* and *or* to join two words, phrases or clauses, we give them equal value. Coordinate phrases and sentences of this kind usually have at least one grammatical item in common, and this item is frequently omitted, especially when it is used for the second time. Indeed, in coordinate phrases joined by *and* we drop a common determiner more often than we repeat it: *a boy and* △ *girl, some bread and* △ *butter, your uncle and* △ *aunt.*

What has been omitted from **He turned left and right**?

Other common items omitted in coordinative ellipsis are:

it was

It wasn't an arm she'd lost, but△ a baby.

subject

The curtains were heavy and△ shut out the light.

subject and operator

In a hotel room, one could look oneself at least in the eyes,△ throw oneself on the bed . . .

subject and verb

The great-uncle who had hanged the cat and then△ himself.

subject and object

'I can't divide myself in two,' Alison said and from time to time,△ repeated.△

predicate

Where the others had got to, God alone knew, or possibly God and Alison△ . . .

(after *than*)

People got much worse than Peter.△

main clause

A man on a tractor shouted at them that they were walking on private property and△ to keep off.

non-finite verb

'It's very near,' Galletti assured her, firmly grabbing her arm and△ her briefcase.

main verb

He had given away nothing, the others△ all.

auxiliaries

a large area . . . had been devastated by bombs, and△ not yet rebuilt.

complement

I thought I was a revolutionary, but I'm not.△

prepositional phrase

She is both self-conscious△ and curious about it.

nouns

Stan's hair was silver, short back and sides, but Len's△ was black and curly . . .

adjectives

a man of indeterminate age and△ background.

prepositions

licence to use bad language at committee meetings and△ editorial conferences

conjunctions

Kate leaned over, helped herself to one,△ ate it.

▶ GUIDELINE

The Drabble quotations suggest that ellipsis in coordination may be a stylistic feature of written prose, which in her case is true. But it is widely common in everyday conversation to omit subjects – *I'll go and△ see;*

objects – *buying*△ *and selling clothes*; complements – *he's rich but I'm not*△; main verbs – *Bring your toothbrush and*△ *pyjamas*, etc.

The general rule is: omit whenever you can without losing or confusing the meaning.

▶ **see**

77	Coordination	88	Ellipsis
78	Coordinators	263	Substitution

92

Ellipsis in subordination

Subordinate clauses do not always have information or grammatical items in common with main clauses. That is why ellipsis is less common in subordinate clauses than in coordinate. The commonest items omitted are:

subject and operator
(She) proceeded to give illustrations, until△ *checked by Evelyn.*

subject and verb phrase in *if not* clauses
Don't men know how to cook vegetables? If △ *not*△, *why don't they learn?*

predicate
Frances arrived in England several months before her postcard△.
He was better than the television△.

main clause (in response structure)
'Why couldn't you take a note of it?' △*'Because I was busy.'*
I don't see why△ *not.*

wh- clause after *know, ask, tell* (response structure)
'What are you going to do?' 'I don't know△.'

verb from verbless clauses
There it floated, its fine winter plumage△ *still iridescent.*

(with verbs of uncertainty)
I don't suppose I ever will△.

whole clause after *to*
Are you sure you really want to△?

whole infinitive clause after *ask* and *want*
You can kill yourself if you want△.

complement
We have to be firm because we can't afford not to be△.

relative pronoun
This was something △ *she by no means understood.*

relative and operator making non-finite clauses
It was . . . one of those obstacles△ *intended to prevent children from rushing straight across the road.*

that when *that-* clause is object or complement (informal)
I thought△ *they all made sense.*
She said△ *she never understood people who said*△ *they felt submerged by hotel rooms.*

GUIDELINES

We usually omit a repeated coordinated subject, but we cannot do so in a similar subordinate clause. Compare:

He felt angry, and △ *shouted.* coordination
**He felt angry, because* △ *shouted.* subordination

Also, notice, we can omit the rest of a *wh*-clause after *what*, *who*, *when*, *why*, *where*, *which* and *how*, but not after *whether*, *if* etc. Compare:

I don't know how. △ **I don't know whether.* △

see
88 Ellipsis
261 Subordination
262 Subordinators

93

Empty *it*

Empty *it*, also known as dummy *it* and prop *it*, is used in a variety of structures where there is no obvious subject or object. It is the English pronoun with least inbuilt meaning and is best suited to the role of empty subject or object. We use *it* as an empty subject when talking about time, distance, weather and certain other common topics:

*What time is **it**?*	***It**'s four o'clock.*
*When was **it**?*	***It** was Sunday the ninth.*
*How far is **it**?*	***It**'s only ten minutes' walk.*
*How long was **it**?*	***It** was about six inches long.*
*What's **it** like?*	***It**'s raining.*
*Who is **it**?*	***It**'s only me.*

We use *it* to mean *whatever is happening* (*stop* ***it***) or *whatever has happened* (*I couldn't help* ***it***) or *life in general* (*take* ***it*** *easy*). Indeed, a number of parallel idiomatic expressions suggest that *it* and *things* may be equally without meaning:

*Take **it** easy/Take **things** easy*
*Think **it** over/Think **things** over*
*How's **it** going?/How are **things** going?*

GUIDELINE

Do not confuse empty *it* with introductory *it*. In the latter case, *it* is also in the subject slot of the sentence, but stands for a later clause.

> *'Football, it seemed to me . . . is a species of fighting.'*
> George Orwell, *Such, Such were the Joys*

see
134 Introductory *it*

94

The *-en* participle

This is the past participle of verbs. Although most past participles end in *-ed* (*hurried*, *placed*, *tried*, etc.), so do the corresponding past simple forms (*I hurried/placed/tried*, etc.). Also, the term past participle is confusing since it does not always refer to past time. For these reasons, modern grammar prefers the term *-en* participle. Compared with the *-ing* participle, its meaning is relatively passive. We use it for several purposes:

in the formation of the present and past perfect tenses

Someone has/had ***seen*** *it.*

in the formation of all passive tenses

He has been ***seen****.*

in catenative use after certain verbs

Get yourself ***settled*** *in.*

as complement after linking verbs

Garcia looked ***hunted****.*

in postmodification

. . . shirt sleeves ***rolled*** *up to the elbow*

The *-en* participle can stand alone as a member of other word classes. We use it as a noun: *the wounded*.

as a participial adjective

He was ***tired****.*
a highly ***respected*** *figure*

and even occasionally as a modifier of an adjective

Damned *cold out tonight.*
Dead *simple!*

GUIDELINE

Interestingly, we use a number of *-en* forms of intransitive verbs with active meaning:

a ***distinguished*** *actor*	***slanted*** *eyes*
varied *interests*	*he looked* ***relaxed***

see

51	Catenative verbs	188	Past perfect tense
141	Linking verbs	200	Postmodification
3	Passive voice	223	Present perfect tense
186	Participles as other word classes	187	Pseudo-participles

95

Exclamations

These are a small class which are the least common sentence type. The form of exclamatory sentences starts: *What* + (adj.) + *noun* . . . *How* + adj. adv. . . .

How good and kind you are!

They are usually written with a final exclamation mark, though they should not be confused with interjections, which also have exclamation marks, but are single words. Exclamatory sentences often appear in shortened forms, with omission of what follows the *What/How* introduction patterns:

What a ghastly accident△*!* *What a shame*△*!*
Austin! How lovely△*!*
How eagerly he was looking forward△*!*

GUIDELINES

A less common exclamatory form deletes the adj/adv after *how*:

Oh, how (well/cleverly/frequently) he lied!
How (tall, big) she's grown!

We only use this pattern with verbs in dynamic use. So:

How foolish (he is) but never **How*△ *he is!*
How well I understand△*!* but never **How*△ *I understand!*

see
131 Interjections
253 Sentences

96

Finite verbs

All lexical verbs have finite and non-finite forms. Finite verb forms usually have a subject and can stand as the only verb in a sentence. The finite verb may be marked for time and aspect through its tense forms. In some cases (particularly with *be*) the finite verb has concord, or agreement, between itself and its subject:

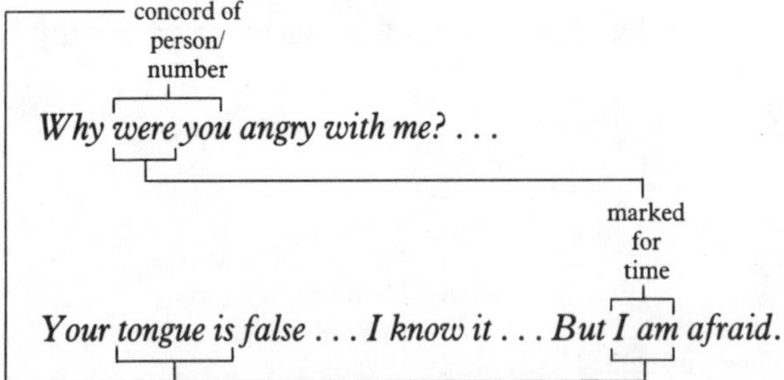

Non-finite verb forms (the infinitive, the *-ing* form and the *-en* form) cannot stand as the only verb in complete sentences. But we do use them in combination to make finite complex tenses and to combine with finite verbs in catenative use.

see
45 Aspect
51 Catenative verbs
71 Concord
157 Non-finites
264 Tenses
271 Verbs

97

Focus

We can divide sentences up into pieces of information – in simple terms we can say that in writing these are usually separated out by punctuation; in speech each piece of information has a separate tone unit and each tone unit has a nucleus. The nucleus is the heart of our message and we give it greater prominence together with the appropriate intonation contour. Consider:

The boy liked to 'watch (nucleus) *them.*

I want you to tell me about the 'bear (nucleus) *again.*

The nucleus identifies the focus of information. It usually comes at the end of a tone-unit and usually falls on the last noun/verb/adjective/adverb of the central idea. (It is the idea itself which carries the focus, not just the stressed syllable or even the head word of the phrase.)

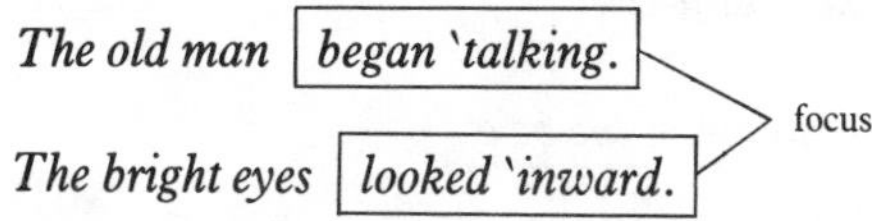

The placing of the nucleus/focus at the end of a tone unit is the normal, unmarked position, matching the main sentence types of English. It is called end-focus. The principle of end-focus is clearly at work in complex sentences. See from these examples how the second of two clauses, whether main or subordinate, carries greater focus:

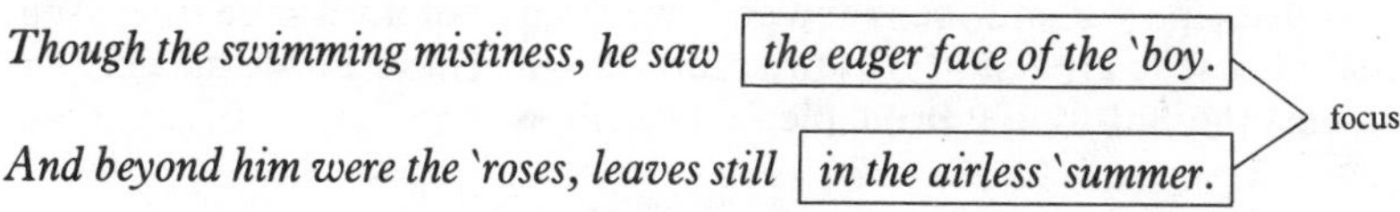

A number of grammatical devices help us to place end-focus on part of a clause which normal word order would not allow: introductory *it* is a device we use to place end-focus on a different part of a clause:

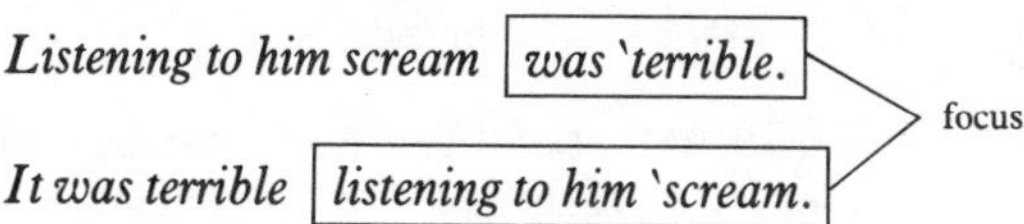

Inversion has the same effect:

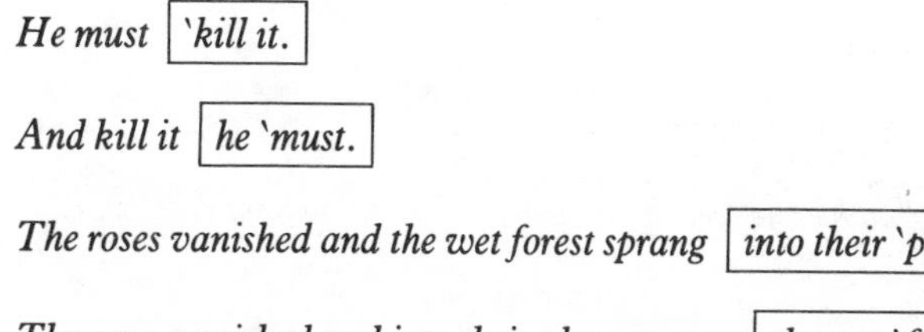

The passive can be used to give end-focus on the subject or verb of a corresponding active sentence:

A rash of delicate wrinkles marked | *the 'skin.* |

The skin was marked by | *a rash of delicate 'wrinkles.* |

He had started | *the 'battle.* |

The battle | *had been 'started.* |

Pseudo-cleft sentences are used to give end-focus to a chosen part of a sentence:

The chain | *brought the bear down.* |

What the chain did was | *bring the bear down.* |

What was brought down by the chain was | *the bear.* |

This principle of end-focus usually works together with another tendency in English: that is our preference for end-weight. We tend to put longer, heavier parts of a clause or sentence at the end. This avoids unbalanced sentences:

He lay ***feeling the warm wetness spread across the broken shin.***

The principles of end-focus and end-weight are not invariable rules. We may choose to give end-focus to a sentence element in a way that goes against the end-weight principle:

end focus and end weight

When it was in use was the only time it was not with him.

weight | focus

The only time it was not with him was when it was in use.

When we need to give special emphasis to part of the clause/sentence other than the end, we can shift the nucleus to an earlier part of the tone unit. This is contrastive focus. It is clearly marked by intonation in speech, though in print we can use italics and underlining in script. Consider:

Did | *'you* | *cry, Mali?*

What things | *'can* | *a man cry for?*

A man can only cry when he feels his | *'heart* | *is going to break.*

> *'The wild places are where we began.*
> *When they end, so do we.'*
>
> David Brower, Attrib.

▶ **see**

98	Fronting	142	Marked/unmarked
134	Introductory *it*	3	Passive
136	Inversion	62	Pseudo-cleft sentences

98

Fronting

Fronting is one way of making part of a sentence more important, by changing its normal word order: it takes place when we move something to the front of the sentence:

__Elephants__ he had a great feeling for.

By writing the above sentence, in which the object *elephants* is fronted, Graham Greene gives the word greater emphasis. He makes it into the topic of the sentence. With the normal, unmarked word-order, the grammatical subject, *He* is the topic. We often place nuclear stress on a fronted topic and therefore give it even greater emphasis. When we front *never*, *nor*, *not*, *nowhere* and other negatives which normally take mid-position we use inversion of subject and operator:

Nor __had Louise__

As with inversion for questions, we use *Do* if there is no other operator:

I didn't ask, nor __did I__ give him your address.

Semi-negatives are often fronted in this way to give a rather formal tone. They include:

barely little hardly only rarely scarcely seldom

In only one other country __had he__ felt more happy.

So meaning *too* is often fronted in an elliptical second utterance. The effect here is to give emphasis to the subject, which is now final and has end-focus.

'And my – hic – father?'

'A bit of a hound, but __so are most men__(s.).'

So and *such* introducing amount or degree-clauses may be fronted but must have subject/operator inversion:

'I hadn't really thought about it, so occupied __had I__ been with all the arrangements for the funeral, the interviews with the solicitor . . .'

With the fronting of complement, object or adverbial of place, inversion of subject and verb takes place, but we do not use *Do*.

At the very moment __in walked__ the whole grand party, Mr and Mrs Bernard Shaw, Mr H. G. Wells, Miss E. Nesbit . . .

I realised . . . how deep __was the disturbance__ my aunt had caused.

__Here's Rose.__

Explain: **Here is John/* Here is he**

GUIDELINES

Although we commonly say *Here'***s the bus**, *There* **are the boys**, we do not use subject/verb inversion when the subject is a pronoun. Compare:

Here ***are your keys****. Here* ***they are****.*
*There'****s Henry****. There* ***he is****.*

Sometimes we front a piece of direct speech, when it is the object of a reporting verb (*announce*, *answer*, *call*, *reply*, *say*) and use inversion of subject and verb:

'There,' ***said the Governor's cousin,*** *'I can spare you that.'*

But in such cases the inversion is not obligatory:

'There,' ***the Governor's cousin said,*** *'take it or leave it.'*

The inversion is much less common with a pronoun subject. Compare:

'A priest?' ***said the woman*** *at last.*
'A priest?'* ***said she* *at last.*

Various sentence elements may be fronted without inversion:

And ***cheered up*** *she certainly was by the waxworks.* [fronted subject complement]

The weekends *he spent with his wife and family . . .* [fronted direct object]

It was understood that I had to wait for the ashes, and ***wait,*** *I did.* [fronted main verb]

Then it was *that in the fifty-first room he had his second stroke.* [fronted adverbial]

GUIDELINE

Most of these sentence elements are fronted for reasons of style. For purposes of everyday communication the only common kind of fronting is that starting with *here/there*.

see
97 End-focus
136 Inversion
252 Reporting verbs
266 Topic

99

Future time

Although English has no future tenses we use a variety of tense forms and other devices to talk about future states and events. We use the present simple tense to identify future events already planned now – *We* **leave** *at dawn*. An everyday use of this form is in timetables and their announcements:

This train **stops** *at Grantham, Doncaster and York.*

This use, however, is formal and not very common. More frequently we use the present simple with future meaning in subordinate clauses, notably *if*, *when* and other time clauses:

If we ***get*** *away, I'm not going to let him run everything.*

We use the present progressive tense to refer to future events arising from present human decisions or arrangements. When no time adverbial is included, we are thinking of an imminent event:

Are *you* ***coming*** *along?* *(Now is the time we'd agreed.)*

*I'****m*** *certainly* ***going.*** *(I'm ready now.)*

Notice that we do not use progressive tenses with verbs of stative meaning, so we cannot say things like, **It's* ***being*** *cold tomorrow.** *They are* ***costing*** *more next year.*

Shall/will + bare infinitive

This is a common way in which we talk about the future, using *shall* for first persons only and *will* with all persons. We use this for the pure future of prediction (*shall/will*) and for volition:

We ***shan't be*** *too badly off.*	[prediction]
*I'****ll show*** *you what we've got.*	[volition – offer]
*We'****ll come*** *again some time.*	[volition – promise]
*'Go,' said Hazel, 'or we'****ll kill*** *you.'*	[volition – threat]

We also use *shall/will* with future meaning with *if*- and other subordinate clauses:

They ***won't*** *be able to go on, if we don't rest.*

When I get to the bend, ***I'll*** *signal.*

Shall/will + progressive infinitive

In this way we stress the activity. Typically we use this form as a background tense for future events:

*They'****ll be waiting*** *for you when you get there.*

Be going to + bare infinitive

Very commonly in informal speech we use *going to* to mean a present intention, or certainty resulting from present causes:

They're ***going to leave*** *tonight.* *(they've decided)*

I got him into this and I'm ***going to get*** *him out.* *(I'm determined)*

There's ***going to be*** *rain tonight.* *(look at the sky)*

Be to/be about to + bare infinitive

These semi-modals have future meaning, *be to* referring to planned actions, including strict instructions:

You ***are*** *both* ***to*** *come with me.*

If we come upon any strange rabbits, you ***are to*** *attack them at once.*

We use *be about to* when talking about imminent action:

He ***was about to*** *speak.*

Hazel ***was*** *just* ***about to*** *run.*

▶ GUIDELINE

As the last two examples remind us, all of these ways of talking about the future are available to us in back-shifted forms as future-in-the-past. The key to the English tense system is to remember that we see events from the speaker's/writer's/thinker's point in time of speaking/writing/thinking. In this way we can see the logic of future-in-the-past and other back-shifted forms. Consider:

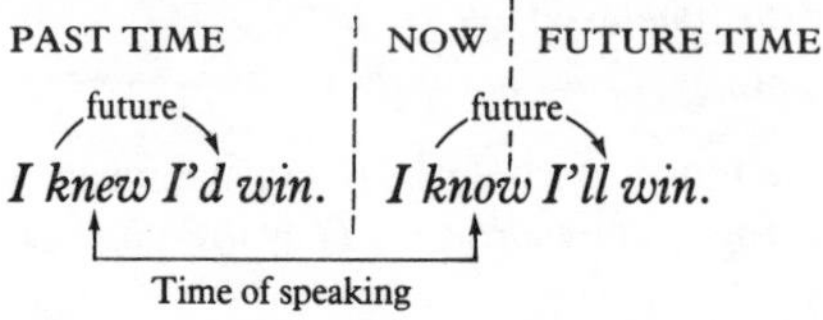

Motorists are to use dipped headlights at night when crossing the runway

Gibraltar road sign

▶ **see**

49	Back-shift	148, 149	*Shall/will*
87	Dynamic/stative use	264	Tenses
225	Present progressive tense	148	*Will/would*
226	Present simple tense		

100

The genitive: general

The genitive form is also called the possessive. The traditional term, genitive, is perhaps more useful because it parallels concepts in some other languages, and because it has a suitably wider meaning than possessive. The genitive form in English has several common meanings other than possession. Both count and non-count nouns can be inflected for the genitive.

an hour's time   *time's winged chariot*

▶ **see**

80	Count/Non-count nouns	103	Genitive and the *of* construction
104	Double genitive	102	Meanings of the genitive
101	Formation of the genitive		

101

The genitive: formation

In writing we add *'s* to the noun. If the noun is a plural that already ends in *-s* we simply add the apostrophe. So:

John – John's
the child – the child's
the boy – the boy's
the children – the children's
the man – the man's
the waitress – the waitress's
the waitresses – the waitresses'

Some first names and family names end in *-s*:
Agnes Brass. We used to have a choice between 's or apostrophe only in forming the genitive. Compare:

St Thoma(*s'*) *Mount* near Madras, and *St Thoma* (*s's*) *Hospital* in London.

St Agne(*s'*) *Eve*, Tennyson's poem and *St Agne* (*s's*) *Day*, 21 January.

The *'s* form is more often heard and used today.
The rules of pronunciation are the same as for plural nouns in *-s* and for the *-s* of the third person singular present tense. So the genitive form for singular nouns is pronounced:

/ɪz/ after the sibilants /s/ /z/ /ʃ/ /ʒ/ /tʃ/ /ʤ/
Sikes's *Jaggers's* *Pinch's* *Defarge's* *Magwitch's* *Rudge's*

/z/ after all other voiced consonants and vowel sounds
Trabb's *Copperfield's* *Wegg's* *Fagin's* *Wickham's* *Grove's* *Emily's* *Trotter's*

/s/ after voiceless consonants other than sibilants
Quilp's *Twist's* *Wemmick's* *Steerforth's* *Pecksniff's*

Regular plural nouns in -s do not change their pronunciation when an apostrophe is added (*boys* and *boys'*-/bɔɪz/). Therefore the above rules apply to the genitive forms of regular plurals. So:

the Rudges' (/ɪz/) *house* *the Wickfields'* (/z/) *home*
the Wemmicks' (/s/) *cottage*

The only genitive plural forms which can be identified in pronunciation are for those irregular plurals made by a vowel change: *child's/children's*, *man's/men's*, *woman's/women's*. This is why some grammars say that the genitive of regular nouns is only pronounced in the singular.

> *'Cowards' hearts beat faster than heroes',*
> *But last longer.'*
>
> Zarko Petan, *The Times*

102

The genitive: meaning

The genitive is used most commonly with people, groups of people, countries and the higher animals to show their relation with something or someone. Some of these relationships are the *have* relationship, the subject/verb relationship, the verb/object relationship, the subject/complement relationship, the originator relationship, the descriptive relationship, the time relationship and the place relationship.

The *have* relationship (the possessive genitive)

Mrs Morel's sons – Mrs Morel has sons (William, Paul and Arthur).

Here the genitive means the same as *to have*.

Mrs Morel had great affection for her second son,
Paul; she had blue eyes, and later a malignant tumour.

So the *have* relationship can identify both her personal qualities and parts: *Mrs Morel's affection for Paul*, *Paul's mother's blue eyes*, *Paul's mother's tumour* (Sometimes called the partitive genitive).

The subject/verb relationship (the subjective genitive)

William's departure ~ *William*(s.) *departed* (v.).

Here the genitive form identifies the subject and the second noun represents the underlying verb. William hated his father. He applied for a better job. He later died of an illness. So:

William's hatred *William's application* *William's death*

Notice that the subject/verb relationship may include not only a derived noun but the *-ing* form: *William's dying.*

The verb/object relationship (the objective genitive)

Paul's appointment ~ *someone appointed* (v.) *Paul* (o.)

Here the genitive identifies the object of a verb and the second noun represents that verb. Paul was appointed to a clerk's job in a factory. The girls embarrassed him. Someone introduced him to Miriam. So: *Paul's appointment to a clerk's job*, *Paul's embarrassment*, *Paul's introduction to Miriam.*

▶ GUIDELINE

Sometimes ambiguity can arise. *William's memory* may show the subject/verb relationship: *William remembered (something)* or the verb/object relationship: *(Paul) remembered William* – after his death, for example. Conversely a photograph of the princess taken by Snowdon may be both *Snowdon's photograph* and the *princess's photograph.* If you are not sure about an ambiguous phrase, use the subject/verb interpretation. We tend to regard genitives as subjective. We also tend to lean towards a human subject rather than a non-human. So:

The fox's capture ~ *Someone captured the fox*, rather than *The fox captured something.*

The subject/complement relationship

Miriam's timidity – *Miriam* (s.) *was timid* (c.).

Here the adjectival complement is represented by a corresponding abstract noun. Paul found Miriam fascinating. But his mother was jealous. Paul felt guilty. So:

Paul's fascination   *His mother's jealousy*   *Paul's guilt*

The originator relationship (the genitive of origin)

Clara's birthday present ~ *Clara* (originator) *sent Paul a birthday present.*

Here the genitive names the originator of the second part of the phrase. Paul made a drawing of Clara's hands. Paul told his mother about Clara. D. H. Lawrence created Paul Morel in *Sons and Lovers*. So:

Paul's drawing, Paul's narrative to his mother, Lawrence's Paul Morel and Lawrence's 'Sons and Lovers'.

The descriptive relationship (the descriptive genitive)

a women's college ~ a college for women

Paul's sister, Annie, went to a college for teachers. She finally got a certificate qualifying her to teach. Paul's lover, Clara, supported the rights of women. So:

a teachers' college,   *a teacher's certificate,*   *women's rights.*

The genitive in its descriptive relationship is a classifier of the second noun.

The time relationship (the temporal genitive)

a day's work – work lasting one day

Paul took his mother to Lincoln for a day. He took Clara for a walk along the Trent one evening. He spent a week on holiday with her. So:

a day's visit to Lincoln   *an evening's walk*   *a week's holiday*

The place relationship (the local genitive)

at the butcher's – at the butcher's shop

Here the genitive often stands alone, referring to a person's home, a shop, restaurant, business, college, etc.

Paul last saw Miriam when she stayed with her cousin. Clara rejoined her husband at Paul's lodgings. Paul worked at Jordan's factory. So:

at Miriam's cousin's   *the meeting at Paul's*   *working at Jordan's*

At the barber's, George S. Kaufman was asked how he liked his hair cut. He replied, 'In silence.'

103

The genitive and the *of-* construction

Sometimes the genitive and the *of-* construction can be used as alternatives in the same situation.

What's your MP's name? What's the name of your MP?

Both are correct, but even here there is a slight difference in meaning, because the last important word of a phrase usually carries the important information. So the genitive form of the question above gives more attention to *name*, and the *of*- construction gives more attention to *MP*. Usually, however, the two constructions have different meanings and are not alternatives. We prefer the genitive for people, groups of people and higher animals. For inanimate nouns and non-count nouns we prefer the *of*- construction. So:

the government's seats, but *the seats of government*
the Ministers' faces, but *the four faces of Big Ben* (the clock)

Notice, however, the fixed formal phrases:

The House of Commons, *the Chancellor of the Exchequer*, *the Minister of Sport*, etc.

Other examples:

John's head, *Mary's age*. Never **the head of John*, etc.
The Head of the school, *the age of the furniture*. Never **the school's Head*, etc.

We can use both the genitive and the *of*- construction with collective nouns which have a human connection:

the party's policy ~ *the policy of the party*

Other examples:

the union's support ~ *the support of the union*
the crowd's anger ~ *the anger of the crowd*

We use the genitive for the *have*- relationship, since the subject is usually animate:

The Prime Minister's residence is Number Ten Downing Street.

Other examples:

Father's car, *mother's favourite*, *the cat's litter*, Never **the car of father*, etc.

We prefer the genitive for the subject/verb relationship; we prefer the *of*-construction for the verb/object relationship:

The Queen's arrival (s./v.) *for the Opening of Parliament* (v./o.).
The government's success (s./v.) *means the defeat of the opposition* (v./o.).
Big Ben's famous chime (s./v.) *stops during the cleaning of the clock* (v./o.).

Notice that in phrases like *Jack's agreeing to go* . . . the genitive is essential. Notice also that with generic adjectives we must use the *of*- construction.

the needs of the poor, *the education of the young*, Never **the young's education*, etc.

Similarly when the object is a generic adjective in the verb/object relationship, we use the *of*-construction:

the care of the sick, *the protection of the innocent*

Both the genitive and the *of*-construction may be used for subject/complement relationship with animate subjects:

the Chancellor's (animate) *ingenuity* ~ *the ingenuity of the Chancellor* (animate) but: *the passing of the bill* (inanimate), *the Opening of Parliament* (inanimate).

Notice the difference between:

the country's peace ~ *the country is peaceful (not at war)*
the peace of the countryside ~ *the countryside is peaceful (not noisy)*

We prefer the genitive for the originator relationship:

The Queen's speech ~ *the speech she made*
the speech of the Queen ~ *her way of speaking*

Other examples: *Jane Austen's novels, Stephenson's Rocket, Bach's Air on a G-string.*

We only use the genitive for the descriptive relationship: *the Members' bar, the Commons' library, the Lord Mayor's Show.*

We prefer the genitive for the time relationship: *a month's recess, yesterday's order paper, two minutes' silence.*

We prefer the genitive for the place relationship when followed by a superlative: *London's most famous square, the world's highest mountain, England's best known composer.*

With a longer noun-phrase we do not use the genitive, but the *of*-construction. Compare:

the law's demands, the new law's demands;
but *the demands of the laws concerning terrorism.*

GUIDELINES

As a general rule, use the genitive with people, groups of people and the higher animals, but the *of*-construction with inanimate nouns. Of course, such rules are broken, especially by poets.

> *'And the wheel's kick and the wind's song and the white sails shaking,*
> *And a grey mist on the sea's face and a grey dawn breaking.'*
>
> John Masefield, 'The Seafarer'

Do not think of the genitive and the *of*-construction as alternatives. They are two, related, forms of noun phrases, also related to the construction with a noun as a premodifier. Compare:

a'bird call	noun as premodifier
a'bird's'call	genitive
the'call of a'bird	*of*-construction.

Notice the different stress patterns.

see

97 Focus
7 Generic adjectives
178 Noun phrases
204 Premodifiers

104

The Double genitive

This is the combination of the inflected genitive and the *of*-construction:

a novel (*of*) *V.S. Naipaul* (*'s*).

The *of* is followed by either a definite, personal noun phrase, or a possessive pronoun:

an idea of John Ruskin's ~ *one of Ruskin's ideas*
a neighbour of ours ~ *one of our neighbours*

The above examples of the double genitive show its non-unique meaning, when the indefinite article is used – Naipaul wrote several novels/ Ruskin had more than one idea/ we have numerous neighbours.

But the double genitive with unique reference is a useful construction when we want to front a certain part of our sentence for emphasis:

The particular novel of V. S. Naipaul's *that I like is . . .*
This idea of John Ruskin's *– can we come back to it?*

GUIDELINE

Notice the difference between

a student of Karl Popper ~ *one who studied Popper's works*
a student of Karl Popper's ~ *one who studied under Popper personally*

see
98 Fronting
103 The genitive and *of*

105

Gradable and non-gradable words

Some adjectives, adverbs, nouns and a few verbs are gradable; they describe qualities or things which have varying degrees or strength. A tall person can *be fairly tall* (adj.), *quite tall*, *rather tall* and *very tall*. We can live *comfortably* (adv.), *more comfortably*, *less comfortably* or *least comfortably* in various homes. Accidents can result in *major* or *minor damage* (N.), *superficial damage*, *great damage*. And an optimist can *rather hope* (v.) or *hope very much*.

Other words are non-gradable. Non-gradable adjectives include *married* and *single*; non-gradable adverbs include *firstly* and *lastly*; non-gradable nouns include *birth* and *death*.

Most verbs are non-gradable.

The difference between gradable and non-gradable words is their meaning. It is largely a matter of common sense. If you understand *parallel*, *finally* and *infinity*, you are unlikely to say **rather parallel* **very finally* or **a small amount of infinity*.

GUIDELINES

But notice how the grading is not always in the same direction. This interesting feature of gradable words is particularly apparent with polar adjectives and adverbs. Consider:

→

least fast, less fast, fast, faster, fastest (speed rises)

←

least slow, less slow, slow, slower, slowest (speed slows)

No oddity of language, this, but a reminder that the mechanics of grammar must follow the directions of meaning.

see
4 Adjectives: characteristics
13 Adverbs
130 Intensifiers

106

to have/to have got

As well as its use as operator *have* is used as a lexical verb. When we use it with stative meanings of possession, permanent qualities, states or relationships, it forms questions by inversion and forms negatives with *not*. In British English we often use *have (got)* in this sense when American English favours *to have*.

__I've got__ a dead woman on my hands. (possession)
Priscilla __had (got)__ privileged eyes. (quality)
He __has (got)__ three children. (relationship)
Morgan __hadn't (got)__ a clue. (negative)
__Have__ you __got__ a needle and thread? (question)

Notice that *got* forms are commonest in spoken English. Even then we use it less frequently in past forms partly because of the perfective feel to *have got* which is often inappropriate for past reference:

Did you __have__ a happy childhood? He __didn't have__ a car at that time.

When we use *have* as a lexical verb in a dynamic sense, we form negatives and questions with *do* as an operator. Dynamic *have* can be used with progressive and perfect tenses and the imperative:

We __don't have__ a great deal of time. (negative)
__Did you have__ a good trip? (question)
It was all some frightful dream he __was having__. (present progressive)
Priscilla's __had__ a bit of a sticky time, lately. (present perfect)
__Have__ a good game. (imperative)

What's the difference between **I've got to** and **I have to**?

▶ GUIDELINE

Have as a dynamic lexical verb (questions and negatives with *do*) shows a wealth of meanings in the many common fixed phrases we use it in:

to have . . .

a baby	*a fright*	*a peep*	*an understanding*
a bath	*a good time*	*a quarrel*	*a word* etc.
breakfast	*a holiday*	*a relationship*	
a chat	*a look*	*a shower*	
a dream	*a moment*	*a swim*	

American lady: *Do you have children?*
English lady: *Not very often.*

▶ **see**
87 Dynamic/stative use
136 Inversion
139 Lexical verbs
184 Operator

107

to have got to/have to

Both these forms, followed by a *to*-infinitive carry the meaning of obligation/necessity:

You ***have (got) to*** *help me.*

In general, British English uses the *got* form, and American English the *have* form, especially in present tenses:

I've ***got to****/I* ***had to*** *do it.* (British English)
I ***have to****/I* ***had to*** *do it.* (American English)

But British English sometimes makes a distinction. We tend to use *have got to* for a single present or future activity. But we use *have to* for habitual action or a series of actions, present or future:

'I'm sorry,' he said, 'but I've ***got to*** *do it.'* [future obligation to do one thing]

We'll just ***have to*** *take our chances on that.* [future obligation of habitual action]

This is by no means a hard-and-fast rule. When William Boyd's character, Fanshawe, feels immediate action is called for, he uses both forms to make his point:

*'That does it,' he said vehemently. 'She'****s got to*** *go. She* ***has to****.'*

As with *to have/to have got*, the *got* form is less common in past reference, when we are concerned about a completed action – which calls for the past simple tense:

I ***had to*** *make preparations.*
She ***had to*** *go and lie down.*

This is also the case when we are reporting *have got to*: it becomes *had to* in indirect speech:

I knew I ***had to*** *do it.*

Notice that we can use *shall/will* with *have to*, but not with *have got to*:

You'll ***have to*** *see if you can make any more sense of it.*

But both forms can be followed by the present passive infinitive:

It's clear what ***has (got) to*** *be done.*

GUIDELINES

What is the difference between *have (got) to* and *must*? Usually *must* refers to an obligation felt by the speaker: *have (got) to* usually refers to an externally imposed obligation or necessity. Talking to a friend we would say:

There's something I ***must*** *tell you* (a secret, a joke, gossip).

There's something I've ***got to*** *tell you* (a message, information from elsewhere).

Negative forms of *have (got) to* mean the same as *needn't* – absence of obligation:

Morgan realised he ***needn't/didn't have to/hadn't got to*** *resign.*

> *'I always find I have to write something on a steamed mirror.'*
>
> Elaine Dundy, *The Dud Avocado*

see
106 *to have/have got*
110 Indirect speech
146 *must*

108

Had better

This is a fixed phrase, meaning *it is advisable*, followed by the bare infinitive. The *had* never changes, even though the phrase refers to present or future action:

I'd better *get you home.*
We'd better *go, I suppose.*
He thought ***they'd better*** *have a closer look.*

When does a pronoun subject take mid-position in imperatives?

GUIDELINES

We also use the phrase with *not* to threaten or warn, often with a final rising intonation:

You'd ***better not*** *let`me catch you' stealing.*
They'd `* ***better not*** *come`back.

In its question form, with subject/operator inversion, we use the phrase to make polite suggestions:

Had I better *give you a hand?*
Hadn't you better *stop seeing him?*

see
117 Bare infinitive
136 Inversion

109

Imperatives

Imperatives are one of the four types of simple sentence, the others being declaratives, interrogatives and exclamations. The form of imperatives is the verb base, usually without subject, though with any appropriate complementation. Here are two examples of imperatives in their traditional role of giving commands:

'Sit down,' *the old man said.*
*'****Put*** *your kukri away . . . and then* ***make*** *a fire between two stones.* ***Stand*** *them on edge about four feet apart.'*

Occasionally, to avoid ambiguity, or to give emphasis, we include the subject (always the addressee); this can take both front- and end-position:

You *sit down there.*
Let me see, ***Mali.***

We negate imperatives by using *do* as the operator with *not/n't*, unless a negative pronoun or adverb is present:

Don't *let me down, leg.*
Nobody *move.*

But notice the position of subject *you* when added to a negative imperative:

Don't ***you*** *shout at me!*

We also use do for an emphatic imperative:

Do *let me try.*

In reported form, the imperative takes the *to-* infinitive pattern:

*'****Have*** *one of my sandwiches, Mali,' the boy offered.*
He invited the gardener ***to have*** *a sandwich.*

GUIDELINE

The imperative illustrates with colourful profusion how grammatical form is not necessarily identified with one particular communicative function.

Consider some of the informal uses to which we put the form, besides commands:
Think nothing of it [acknowledging apology/thanks]
Do it my way [advice]
Do have another [invitation]
(Do) forgive me [apologising]
Please do! [giving permission]
Look here! [attention-getting]
Tell me another! [disbelief]
Let me see [prevarication]
Stone the crows! [exclamation]
Get lost [rebuffing]
Take care! [saying farewell]
Help me, would you? [request]
Watch out! [warning]

Duck or Grouse!

Warning over low door in pub

▶ **see**
110 Indirect commands
184 Operator
254 Simple sentences

110

Indirect speech

Indirect speech is the reported form of other people's, and sometimes our own, words and thoughts. All sentence types can be reported into indirect speech: declaratives, interrogatives, imperatives and exclamations.
Indirect declaratives are formed with nominal *that*- clauses:

She said, 'It's a nice stone.'
~ *She said* ***(that) it was a nice stone.***

In both cases, the words following *said* may be analysed as its grammatical object.

Indirect interrogatives are formed with nominal *wh*- or *if*- clauses:

He asked, 'Why should I lie?' [*wh*- question]
~ *He asked* ***why he should lie.***

(Notice the inversion after *wh*-)

She asked, 'Were there any flowers?' [*yes/no* question]
~ She asked (***if/whether***) ***there were any flowers***.
She asked herself, 'Is it suicide or not?' [alternate question]
~ *She asked herself* ***whether or not it was suicide***.

Indirect imperatives are formed with a *that*- clause or a *to*-infinitive clause:

'Don't be late,' she said.
~ *She said* ***that I shouldn't be late***.
~ *She ordered me* ***not to be late***.

(Notice that with the *to*-infinitive, the reporting clause needs a direct object or a prepositional object:

**He ordered not to be late.*)

Indirect exclamations are formed with a nominal *wh-* clause:

'What a wonderful day it is,' I said.
~ *I said* ***what a wonderful day it was.***

(Notice that only complete sentence exclamations can be reported. In verbless exclamations, we need to provide the omitted verb in indirect speech).

'What weather! △' I exclaimed.
~ *I exclaimed* ***what weather it was.***

GUIDELINE

In indirect declaratives, *that* may be omitted after the commonest reporting verbs, but not others:

He said △ it was good. He thought △ it was good.
He told me △ it was good. but not **He replied △ it was good. *He muttered △ it was good.*

see

85	Direct/indirect speech	156	Nominal clauses
111–15	Indirect speech	252	Reporting verbs

111

Indirect speech: tense changes (back-shift)

In indirect speech we often need to make changes to the original direct forms. These are mainly different verb tenses, pronouns and adverbs. The reason for this is simple. When we change from direct to indirect speech there is often a time shift in the viewpoint. Consider:

Sir Ronald ***said,*** *'Mark* ***is*** *dead.'*

The novelist is narrating NOW (i.e. in present time) a past event and uses the simple past tense: *Sir Ronald* ***said*** . . . Sir Ronald's actual words were said during that past event, THEN (i.e. in past time) so in reporting them directly, the writer must reflect Sir Ronald's viewpoint at the time of speaking – *My son* ***is*** *dead.* In reporting the words indirectly, our viewpoint is NOW, the time of speaking/writing, so we use the simple past both for *to say* and for *to be dead*. From the NOW viewpoint the boy ***was*** dead. *Sir Ronald* ***said*** *that Mark* ***was*** *dead.* Cordelia, the detective, asked questions. She asked: *Did he leave a note?* The novelist's viewpoint is NOW, therefore in narrating a past event before-NOW, she uses ***asked***. Cordelia's question, asked THEN, refers to an earlier event before-THEN, and so needs a past tense, *Did he leave . . .?*

before-THEN   THEN   NOW

note?   Cordelia's question   novelist writing

So the direct speech sentence has two viewpoints, the novelist's NOW and the character's THEN. But when we report the question indirectly, our only viewpoint is NOW, demanding a past tense of THEN and a past perfect tense for before-THEN: *She asked if he had left a note.*

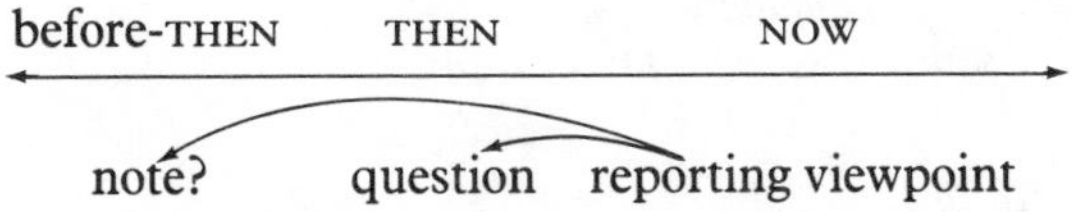

before-THEN THEN NOW

note? question reporting viewpoint

This tense change in indirect speech, shared with other structures, is called back-shift. Sometimes back-shift is unavoidable in indirect reporting, sometimes it is optional and at other times it is not necessary. The key is in the viewpoints.

see

49 Back-shift
110, 112–15 Indirect speech
252 Reporting verbs

112

Indirect speech: when tense changes are necessary

When the direct words are reported indirectly, back-shift is unavoidable, with a reporting verb in a past tense marking a change of viewpoint. This happens to reported verbs in all present tenses and to modals *shall*/*will*/*can* and *may*.

Direct	**Indirect**
'I'm sorry.' [present simple]	*She told him that she* **was** *sorry.*
'No one is working late.' [present progressive]	*She thought no one* **was** *working late.*
'He's been shot.' [present perfect]	*She suggested he* **had** *been shot.*
'I've been wondering . . .' [present perfect progressive]	*She said she'***d** *been wondering.*
'I shall try.' [*shall*]	*She claimed she* **would** *try.*
'There will *be expenses.'* [*will*]	*She suspected there* **would** *be expenses.*
'Can you do that.' [*can*]	*He asked whether she* **could** *do that.*
'They may ask questions.' [*may*]	*She feared they* **might** *ask questions.*

GUIDELINES

When we are reporting suggestion or offers we use *should* in indirect speech with third person subjects:

Shall we go? *He suggested they* **should** *go.*
Shall I help? *He asked if he* **should** *help.*

Notice that when back-shift already exists in the direct words, they are reported unchanged. Here *might/should* have been chosen for polite distancing:

I might need/should like a photograph.
I said I ***might need/should like*** *a photograph.*
BUT *I want a photograph. I said I* ***wanted*** *a photograph.*

▶ **see**

49	Back-shift	150	*should*
49	Distancing	252	Reporting verbs
144–9	Modals		

113

Indirect speech: when tense changes are optional

When the reporting verb is in a past tense, and the reported verb is in the past, we have a choice of using back-shift or not:

'He saw you at the inquest,' she said. [direct]
She said **he saw/had seen** *you at the inquest.* [indirect]

In reported statements like this, we often feel that the message is unimpaired by not changing the verb one tense back. Likewise with the reported verb in any other past tense:

'I was coming to see Mark,' she said.
She said she **was/had been** *coming to see Mark.*

We only need to use the optional back-shift where it is necessary to separate THEN and before-THEN. In thinking about the mystery of Mark's death, Cordelia has a sudden thought:

'Someone else found the body first!'
She realised that someone else **had found** *the body first.*

We also have a choice of using back-shift or not when there is no change of time reference. When, for example, a reported verb in the simple present tense has timeless or habitual meaning, the time viewpoint remains the same.

'What are your fees?'
He enquired what my fees **are/were**.

When a reported verb in the present talks about eternal truths, we are unlikely to select the option of back-shift.

He always said, 'Dead men can talk.'
He always told me dead men can talk.

▶ GUIDELINE

The choice between repeating or back-shifting a present-tense reported verb can provide a delicate balance of meaning. Compare these two scenarios:

Walker (fiercely): *I won't do it.*	Walker (fiercely): *I won't do it.*
Helm (threatening): *What's that?*	Helm (threatening): *What's that?*

Walker (undeterred):	Walker (weakening):
I said I [*won't*] *do it.*	*I said I* [*wouldn't*] *do it.*
(same time reference = same decision)	(change of time reference = change of mind)

▶ **see**
49 Back-shift
252 Reporting verbs

114

Indirect speech with no tense changes

When the reporting verb refers to present or future time, we make no tense changes in the reported verbs. Clearly the time reference has changed little from the first speaker to the second.

Direct	**Indirect**
*'I **think** you'll find it interesting.'*	*She **thinks** I'll find it interesting.*
*They'll **say** 'Did you know?'*	*They'll **ask** if you know.*
'It's nothing.'	*I've told you it's nothing.*

We cannot back-shift in reporting what has already been back-shifted for another reason. Therefore there is no tense change made in reported forms of hypothetical clauses:

*'It **would** be helpful.'*	*I said it **would** be helpful.*
*'I **might** have guessed.'*	*He knew he **might** have guessed.*

This applies to the past forms of modal verbs:

could might should would (rather) had better

Also *ought to*. In the same way, back-shifted verbs after *wish/if only* remain unchanged:

*'I **would** rather have left him.'*	*She said she **would** rather have left him.*
*'I wish he **were** reliable.'*	*Cordelia wished that he **were** reliable.*

Must usually remains unchanged:

*'We **mustn't** waste any more time.'*	*Cordelia said they **mustn't** waste any more time.*

No changes are made after *It's time*:

*'It's time you **were** getting home.'*	*He said it was time she **was** getting home.*

Back-shifted forms used for distancing and tentative offers, requests, etc. remain unchanged:

*'I **shouldn't** think so.'*	*I said I **shouldn't** think so.*
*'I'm sure I **could** help.'*	*Cordelia was sure she **could** help.*
*'I wonder if I **might** have a look.'*	*She wondered if she **might** have a look.*

Which word classes, besides verbs, often need changes in indirect speech?

Obviously we do not change past perfect and past perfect progressive tenses, if only because there are no remoter tenses available:

*'I **had lived** in just such a cottage.'*
*She recalled she **had lived** . . . in just such a cottage.*
*'I **had been living** in the cottage . . .'*
*She told them that she **had been living** in the cottage . . .*

GUIDELINE

Where the first person with *shall/should* is used in direct speech, we may need to use *would* in the reported form to match the change of person.

*I **should** like a photograph.*
*She said she **would** like a photograph.*

see

49 Back-shift
74 Hypothetical clauses
252 Reporting verbs
275 Wishing

115

Indirect speech: changes other than tenses

We change tenses between direct and indirect speech to acknowledge the shift of viewpoint from that of the original speaker to that of the reporter. For exactly the same reason, we need to change certain pronouns, adverbs and determiners. Pronouns need to change only with a shift in viewpoint:

Direct	Indirect
'I'm on my own.'	*I realised I was on my own.* *She realised that **she** was on **her** own.*
'Are you enjoying yourself?'	*He asked if **I** was enjoying **myself**.* *He asked if **she** was enjoying **herself**.*
'That wasn't our idea.'	*We knew it wasn't our idea.* *He knew it wasn't **their** idea.*

Adverbs of time and place frequently need adjustment to match a shift in viewpoint:

'He worked well here.'	*She said he worked well **there**.*
'Now I realised . . .'	*I admitted that **then** I realised . . .*
'Isabelle has a party tonight.'	*Sophie told me Isabelle had a party **that night**.*
'. . . about five weeks ago'	*. . . about five weeks **previously***

Other adverb changes include *today (that day)*, *tomorrow (the next day)*, *yesterday (the day before)*, *at this moment (at that moment)*.

A few verbs also reflect viewpoint and require a switch when the viewpoint changes:

'You can come too.'
*She said I could **go** too.*

'Come round to my house.'
*She invited me to **go** round to her house.*
'Bring a friend.'
*She suggested that I should **take** a friend.*

GUIDELINES

Traditional grammar taught that direct and indirect speech were related by a set of semi-mechanical rules whereby tenses, pronouns and adverbs are switched with unfailing accuracy. This is not so. There are areas where sometimes a shift is felt to be necessary and sometimes not. We make tense and other changes between direct and indirect speech to carry the message we intend, which may need to identify differences of viewpoint in time, space or person.

see
110, 111–14 Indirect speech

116

Infinitives

Infinitives are non-finite parts of the verb, and have no obvious subject or tense. The most familiar infinitive is the *to*- infinitive – *to go*, *to sell*, etc. We also use it without *to* when it is known as the bare infinitive – *go*, *have*, etc. These are simple infinitives. The complex forms are marked for progressive and perfect aspect and passive voice:

to be sold	simple passive infinitive
to be selling	progressive active infinitive
to be being sold	progressive passive infinitive
to have sold	perfect active infinitive
to have been sold	perfect passive infinitive
to have been selling	perfect progressive active infinitive

We use the infinitives most commonly to form complex verb groups with catenative verbs:

*Let's **get** down to business.*
*. . . waiting for him **to take off***
*You seem **to be giving** them a hard time.*

GUIDELINES

One rare use of the infinitives is as replacement for the main verb in a sentence. We use the bare-infinitive after *why (not)* as a reduced question form or for suggestions:

*Why **bother**? Why **worry**? Why **go** to all this trouble?*
*Why not **go** by train? Why not just **shoot** him?*

We use idiomatic *to think* as a reduced form of

It is amazing to think . . .
***To think** I never knew! **To think** that she's in Paris!*

'To be, or not to be: that is the question:
Whether 'tis nobler in the mind to suffer
The slings and arrows of outrageous fortune,
Or to take arms against a sea of troubles,
And by opposing end them? To die: To sleep;
No more; and by a sleep to say we end
The heart-ache and the thousand natural shocks
That flesh is heir to. 'Tis a consummation
Devoutly to be wished.'

William Shakespeare, *Hamlet*

▸ see

117	Bare infinitive	157	Non-finites
51	Catenative verbs	118	*to*-infinitive

117

Infinitives: the bare infinitive

This is the infinitive without *to*. We use it in three common ways:

after modal verbs

I can't **believe** *that.*
He won't **sell** *it.*

after *going to*, *be about to*, *be to*, to talk about the future

He's going to **keep** *me informed.*
. . . about to **make** *herself up*

and with catenative verbs

. . . heard the lift door **clang** *outside*
Let's **go**.

Three modal idioms use the bare infinitive to show preference:

rather/sooner than

Rather than **cross** *the slope diagonally, he went straight up.*

had better/best

They'd better **think** *again.*
I'd better **go**.

and *have (got) to*

Raul had to **catch** *a plane.*

Notice also the use of the bare infinitive after *why (not)*:

Why **go** *to the trouble?*

'Many people would sooner die than think, in fact they do.'

Bertrand Russell, Attrib. in *Flew, Thinking about Thinking*

▶ **see**

51	Catenative verbs	116	Infinitives
99	Future time	143	Modal verbs

118

Infinitives: *to*-infinitive

This is one of the four non-finite verb forms, for example *to go*. The *to*-infinitive has a wide range of functions. We use it to form complex finite verb groups after some auxiliaries and catenative verbs:

If we have ***to do*** *anything, it must be within a week.*

Tell him ***to get*** *the shuttle . . . I want* ***to see*** *him before noon.*

We use it to complement adjectives:

It's so good ***to see*** *you.*

and after nouns (and pronouns) as a post-modifier:

Give you something ***to think about****, won't it?*

It functions alone in its own clauses, as nominals:

God knows ***what I'll find to say*** *to his mother.*

and as adverbials:

She was saying this ***to work it out for herself****.*

and as sentence adverbials:

To put it frankly*, you'll be running out of pilots.*

As the above examples show, the *to*-infinitive often carries a general future meaning.

'To everything there is a season, and a time to every purpose under the heaven. A time to be born, and a time to die; a time to plant and a time to pluck up that which is planted.'

Ecclesiastes, The Holy Bible

▶ **see**

48	Auxiliary verbs	157	Non-finites
51, 53, 57	Catenative verbs	200	Post-modifiers
65	Complementation of adjectives	119–21	*to*-infinitive clauses
		257	Sentence adverbials

119

to-infinitive clauses as nominals

The *to*-infinitive has several uses as a nominal, either alone, after a *wh*-word or with introductory *it*.
As subject of a sentence the infinitive can stand alone:

__To leave things any longer__ would be fatal.

Usually, however, we prefer to preface a non-finite subject with introductory *it:*

It takes time __to get used to it__.

As object, *wh-* + infinitive is common, the clause being a reduced finite *wh*-clause:

She told him __what to do__.
She debated __whether to go to bed__.
__What__ does the Foreign Office have __to say__?

When the object infinitive has an associated adjective, we usually start the pattern with introductory *it*:

She found it hard __to lie__ to him.

As complement of *to be*, we use both plain infinitive and *wh-* + infinitive:

His ambition was __to marry Gabrielle__.
The problem was __where to get new supplies__.

A related function is in apposition to nouns:

His ambition __to marry Gabrielle__ dominated his life.
This question, __where to get new supplies__, sent him to the Embassy.

Notice how the non-finite clause can be defining or non-defining. We also use *wh-* + infinitive as complements of adjectives and prepositions:

She was undecided __how to refuse__.
It was a question of __how to refuse__.

The *to*-infinitive commonly stands in object position after catenative verbs.

> *'To travel hopefully is a better thing than to arrive, and the true success is to labour.'*
>
> R. L. Stevenson, *Virginibus Puerisque*

see

37	Apposition	134	Introductory *it*
53, 57	Catenatives and *to*-inf.	156	Nominal clauses
82	Defining/non-defining	274	*Wh*-words

120

to-infinitive clauses as reduced adverbials

These frequently appear in front- or in end-position. We most frequently use them to express purpose, but we occasionally use them for condition and result:

He turned ***to look up*** *at the window.* [purpose]
You're not going back ***to fly*** *again?* [purpose]
He reached ***to switch*** *it on.* [purpose]
To look at *Ferguson you would take him for a professor.* [condition]
He turned ***to find Jackson*** *there.* [result]

▶ GUIDELINE

Reduced adverbials should not be confused with catenative use. A large number of verbs in catenative use are followed by the *to*-infinitive, but can also stand alone and therefore may take an adverbial in end-position. Consider:

I refused to annoy *him.* (catenative)
I refused, to annoy *him.* (purpose adverbial)

The difference is clear in spoken English, because of the different intonation patterns and the slight pause we make before the adverbial – indicated in writing by the comma. But we can also place the adverbial in front-position – *To annoy him, I refused.* This option is of course not available in catenative verbs, with their strong bond between verb and infinitive.

> *'In this country we find it pays to shoot an admiral from time to time, to encourage the others.'*
>
> Voltaire, *Candide*

▶ **see**
53, 57 Catenative verbs and *to*-infinitive

121

to-infinitive after nouns

This is one form of post-modification. The relationship between the noun and infinitive takes a number of forms.

The noun can be the subject of the infinitive, as in

Donner was the ***only one to survive****.*

Here the infinitive clause is a kind of reduced relative clause. The noun can be the logical object of the infinitive:

I've got ***a plane to catch****.*
There's ***no time to lose****.*

In this pattern we sometimes include *for* + subject:

There's ***nowhere for her to go.***
There's only ***one thing (for us) to do.***

Sometimes the noun is the object of a preposition:

You have ***more important things to worry about.***
No ***space*** *left* ***to work in.***

We can use a formal version of the infinitive + preposition pattern: *No space left* ***in which to work*** – but this is not always possible, as in: **You have more important things about which to worry.*

Some nouns are related to verbs which we use as catenatives.

His ***decision to call*** *it a day* ~ *He* ***decided to call*** *it a day.*

An ***attempt to be*** *clever* ~ ***Attempting to be*** *clever . . .*

GUIDELINE

We sometimes use the passive infinitive with a sense of *must* as a postmodifier.

After *There is*, the two infinitives are often interchangeable, with little difference in meaning. Compare: *There's* ***no time to lose****/There's* ***no time to be lost.*** But notice – *There's* ***nothing to do*** ~ *it's boring*, *There's* ***nothing to be done*** ~ *it's hopeless.*

Otherwise we only use the passive infinitive if the subject of the sentence is the recipient of the action:

Every ***avenue is to be explored.*** Never **Every avenue is to explore.*

'I have nothing to declare except my genius.'
Oslash Wilde at the New York Customs House

---

see

53, 57	Catenative verbs	200	Post-modification
116	Passive infinitive	247	Reduced relative clauses

122

The split infinitive

A split infinitive is one where an adverb has been put between *to* and the base: *to* | *boldly* | *go.*

There is a strong traditional prejudice against this, although it is commonly heard in informal speech:

He promised ***to*** *really* ***try.***
She'd be the last ***to*** *even* ***want*** *to steal.*

In the first example there is no alternative. In the second, we could place *even* before the infinitive in front-position, less comfortably in end-position. The fact that adverbs often have three positions to choose from usually means we can avoid the split infinitive:

He wanted them **to** *quickly* **make up** *their minds.* – (no problem)

But sometimes we have no alternative to splitting the infinitive if we are not to change the meaning:

Perhaps you'd tell him to kindly stop it. (no alternative)

'When I split any infinitive God damn it, I split it so it will stay split.'

Raymond Chandler to his British editor, who tried to 'correct' his split infinitives.

123

-ing form

This is one of the non-finite verb participles, for example, *hoping*. It has a wide range of functions. Some of these we use in common with the *-en* participle and these are discussed under catenatives, participles, sentence adverbials and unattached participles.

We use some *-ing* forms as adjectives and nouns:

a ***working****-class family*
an ***appalling*** *prospect*
. . . returned to the ***packing***
. . . unable to bear the ***waiting***

and even as other word classes.

-ing can stand as nominals:

One thing only are you truly good at.
Killing people

and post-modify nouns:

massive cliffs ***rising steeply*** *from the sea*

We use *-ing* clauses with coordinating meaning:

They divorced, ***ending months of unhappiness****.*

in prepositional phrases:

one reason ***for taking an interest*** *in the business*

and in reduced adverbial clauses:

She folded her arms as ***if holding herself together****.*

Indeed *-ing* is possibly the most widely used of the non-finites.

GUIDELINE

Remember that the *-ing* form, whatever word class it is operating as, still carries a sense of ongoing activity.

> *'Amnesia is not knowing who one is and wanting desperately to find out. Euphoria is not knowing who one is and not caring. Ecstasy is knowing exactly who one is – and still not caring.'*
>
> Tom Robbins, *Another Roadside Attraction*

see

51	Catenative verbs	218	*-ing* in prep. phrases
128	*-ing* as coordinator	129	*-ing* in reduced clauses
125	*-ing* as nominals	157	Non-finites
126	*-ing* as other word classes	185–7	Participles
127	*-ing* as post-modifier	257	Sentence adverbials
124	*-ing* form, terminology	185	Unattached participles

124

The *-ing* form, terminology

The *-ing* form of a verb when used as a noun – *the shopping* – used to be called the gerund. When used as an adjective or verb – *shopping bag, going shopping* – it was called the present participle. But this is an over-simplification.

Some words ending in *-ing* are totally nominal.

Take *building* – we use it with all the qualities of a count noun – with articles, possessives, demonstratives and in a plural form:

the/our/his ***building(s)***

Other *-ing* forms, with no *a* or plural form, look more like non-count nouns:

the/my/that ***knitting***

Sometimes an *-ing* form is more verb-like:

Eating *mangoes cleanly is impossible.*

Here *eating* cannot take determiners or adjectives and it has a direct object and an adverb.

In adjectival use it is also more like a verb:

Eating *apples* ~ *apples for eating* ~ *apples for us to eat*

Modern grammar tends not to use the term gerund, but prefers to speak of the *-ing* form when it is used more like a noun, and participle when it is used in other ways.

GUIDELINE

A simple test of forms ending in *-ing* is to ask yourself if you can replace them with a pronoun. If so, they are noun-like and not participles, and hence are *-ing* forms. For example:

I love ***dancing****. (It)*
Dancing*'s a good pastime. (It's)*

▶ **see**
127–9 *-ing* clauses
185 Participles

125

The *-ing* form as nominal participle clauses

The nominal participle clause can act:
as subject of a sentence

__Flying planes__ is like that with me.

As direct object

I like __beating them__.

as subject complement

What you do best is __killing people__.

in apposition

I wonder how Tony took it, __being hauled out of action__.

as complement of a preposition

There are those who leave without __paying__.

and as complement of an adjective

It's been nice __seeing you__.

When the participle has a subject, there is a choice of pronoun or noun form before the *-ing*:

not long before {*Tony's* / *Tony*} *flying to Paris.*

within month a of {*his* / *him*} *taking up the appointment.*

In each case the first, possessive, alternative is formal; the second is conversational style. With the third person feminine pronouns, there is no choice, since they are identical:

. . . within a month of __her__ taking up the appointment.

Notice that we do not use the possessive after verbs of perception:

. . . she watched __him__ departing not **she watched his departing*

▶ GUIDELINE

With a few fixed phrases, introductory *it* is possible: *It's no use* **pretending**, *It's no good* **crying**, *It was great fun* **skiing**.

> *'Discovery consists of seeing what everybody has seen and thinking what nobody has thought.'*
> A. Szent-Gyorgyi, Attrib. in I. J. Good, *The Scientist Speculates*

Which **-ing** words are prepositions?

▶ **see**
134 Introductory *it*
156 Nominal clauses

126

-ing form as other word classes

A small number of *-ing* words, verb-related, are accepted as conjunctions and prepositions:

> ***Supposing*** *that he gets there first* . . . (conjunction)

Other conjunctions include: *considering (that)*, *providing (that)*, *seeing (that)*.

> *The news* ***concerning*** *her brother* (preposition) (~ *about*)

Other prepositions include: *excepting*, *including*, *regarding*.

There are also a few forms we use informally as pre-modifiers of adjectives:

blazing hot	*dripping wet*
freezing cold	*wringing wet*
starving hungry	*dazzling white*
hopping mad	*tingling fresh*

▶ **see**
12 Adverbs
76 Conjunctions
205 Prepositions

127

-ing participle clauses as post-modifiers

Like *-en* and *to*-infinitive clauses, *-ing* clauses can stand after nouns as post-modifiers. In this role they are reduced relative clauses. Like relative clauses they are either defining or non-defining:

. . . *the chandelier* ***hanging from the ceiling***	(defining)
. . . *the road* ***leading to Lancy***	(defining)
. . . *a dozen men* ***waiting***	(defining)
. . . *a suicide note*, ***regretting his involvement***	(non-defining)
. . . *on a yacht*, ***cruising the Greek islands***	(non-defining)

Possible paraphrases of *The road leading to Lancy* remind us that the *-ing* participle clause need not have the sense of progressive aspect:

> *The road which* ***leads/led*** *to Lancy*.

'. . . magic casements, opening on the foam
Of perilous seas, in faery lands forlorn.'

John Keats, 'Ode to a Nightingale'

▶ **see**
82 Defining/non-defining
94 *-en* participle
120 Infinitive clauses
185 Participles
200 Post-modifiers
247 Reduced relative clauses

128

-ing participle clauses as coordinates

In most cases, participle clauses are subordinate, the absence of a finite verb being enough reason:

He sat at a table in the corner, ***drinking coffee.***

Occasionally, however, a participle clause has coordinate meaning:

Stavron led his men into action, ***ending their days of hiding in the stable-block.***

Notice that no coordinator is necessary, but the relationship to the finite clause is more that of a sentence adverbial or a sentence relative clause.

▶ **see**
77 Coordination
257 Sentence adverbials
249 Sentence relatives
261 Subordination

129

-ing participle clauses as reduced adverbials

These are particularly favoured by narrative writers as economical ways of reduction. They express the regular meanings of full adverbials:

By joining him *on that plane, she could break her ties.* [means]

He had been more than attentive, ***taking her to concerts . . . encouraging her to talk about her work . . .*** [means]

Coming from a working-class background, *he lacked the aristocrat's social graces and easy manner.* [reason]

He slept well that night, ***the strain and fatigue of the past few weeks catching up on him.*** [reason]

Looking at you, *what else would he think?* [condition]

> *'Looking back at the age of eighty-eight I see clearly that I achieved practically nothing.'*
>
> Leonard Woolf, *The Journey Not the Arrival Matters*

▶ **see**
245 Reduction
257 Sentence adverbials

Of what kind is the intensifier in **It suits you to a 'T'**?

130

Intensifiers

These are adjectives and adverbials used with gradable adjectives, nouns, verbs and other adverbs. We use intensifiers to scale the meaning upwards (amplifiers) or to scale the meaning downwards (downtoners):

Amplifiers	**Downtoners**
more/most/very *successful*	***less/least/rather*** *successful*
he succeeded ***totally.***	*he succeeded* ***partially.***

Many related adjective/adverb pairs are available for intensifying:

Amplifiers

absolute(ly)	*high(ly)*	*pure(ly)*	*total(ly)*
complete(ly)	*immense(ly)*	*real(ly)*	*utter(ly)*
entire(ly)	*perfect(ly)*	*thorough(ly)*	*whole(wholly)*

Downtoners

bare(ly)	*partial(ly)*
mere(ly)	*slight(ly)*
near(ly)	*virtual(ly)*
part(ly)	

Adverbial intensifiers may take the form of noun phrases or prepositional phrases:

N.P. Amplifiers: *a lot, a good deal*
N.P. Downtoners: *a bit, a little*

Other intensifying noun phrases occur in idioms like *didn't sleep* ***a wink***, *don't care* ***a damn/a fig.***

P.P. Amplifiers: *to a large extent/degree, in all respects, in every respect*

P.P. Downtoners: *in some/a small extent, in some degree, in one way/some ways, in part, in one/some/certain respect(s)*

In informal conversation (and cheap advertising) we use certain amplifiers for their emotive force rather than their literal meaning. Examples are:

awful(ly)	*great*	*super*	*terrific(ally)*
fantastic	*marvellous*	*terrible/terribly*	*tremendous(ly)*

GUIDELINE

Non-gradable words like *dead*, *ultimate*, *equality* and *to halve* in their literal meaning cannot, by definition, be scaled up or down. Authors can, therefore, achieve humorous effects by intensifying them.

> *'All animals are equal, but some are more equal than others.'*
>
> George Orwell, *Animal Farm*

▶ **see**
105 Gradable/non-gradable
47 Intensifying adjectives
16, 17 Intensifying adverbs

131

Interjections

A minor, and least important, word class is that of interjections, usually shown in writing by exclamation marks – *Ah! Ouch!* Interjections have no linked grammatical relationship with other word classes and have only loose links with the sentences they appear in. In fact they are more usually found in isolation, and should not be confused with exclamations, which have sentence form. Unlike other minor word classes, this is not a closed one. New forms continue to appear in comic-strip language.

▶ **see**
95 Exclamations
276 Word classes

132

Interrogatives

We recognise a sentence as interrogative because it has at least one of the following features:
the operator stands before the subject: *Can* (op.) *you* (s.)?
the first word is a *wh-* question word: ***Where*** *are you?*
we speak it with a rising (questioning) intonation, and write it with a question mark at the end: *You are śure?*

Most interrogatives function as questions to seek information and expect an answer. Sometimes we show that we want a positive or a negative answer to our question. We can do this by giving it positive or negative bias, by using certain words and forms of question. Some interrogatives however do not expect a reply and fulfil a range of functions. Consider.

Will you please do as I say?	[command]
Won't you have a little more?	[invitation]
Would you mind giving me a hand?	[request]
Why don't you let me help?	[offer]
Don't you think you should ask him?	[advice]
Who would have thought it was you?	[disbelief]

As with other simple sentence types, we use the *-ive* word (interrogative) when referring to form alone. But the close relationship between form and function has led to the interchangeable use of the terms interrogative and question. We continue to use the latter for the various question types.

Why do people confuse **lie** and **lay**?

▶ **see**

239	Alternative questions	235	Questions, general
242	Declarative questions	244	Rhetorical questions
243	Echo questions	253–5	Simple sentences
240	Exclamatory questions	238	Tag questions
110	Indirect questions	237	*Yes/no* questions

133

Intransitive verbs

Although we use verbs intransitively, verbs which we use solely in intransitive use are uncommon.
Examples are:

appear	*fade*	*kneel*	*rise*
arrive	*fall*	*lie*	*sympathise*
come	*go*	*matter*	*tremble*
die	*happen*	*remain*	*wait*
digress			

Sometimes they appear in a simple subject + verb form:

I (s.) *sympathised* (v.).

More frequently, however, they take one or more adverbials:

I (s.) *remained* (v.) ***on the islet*** (adv.) ***for the Monday night* and all the *following day*** (adv.).

I (s.) *lay* (v.) ***there*** (adv.) ***for hours*** (adv.).

▶ GUIDELINES

The two irregular intransitive verbs *to lie* and *to rise* have similar transitive cognates, *to lay* and *to raise*. The existence of *lay/raise* ensures that *lie/rise* are never used transitively. Yet the similarity of the pairs often confuses native speakers, particularly into using *to lay* without an object:

irregular transitives			**regular transitives**	
lie	*lay*	*lain* (in bed)	*lay*	*laid* (eggs)
rise	*rose*	*risen* (early)	*raise*	*raised* (money)

Some verbs in common intransitive use are occasionally used transitively either with an obvious object, which is understood in the intransitive form, or with a very limited number of objects. In Geoffrey Household's sentence about a train journey, *We left again for Aldwych*, the verb has an understood object which every reader can supply –

We left [*the station*] *again for Aldwych.*
understood

When Household's hero is ambushed and shot at, the author's intransitive verb can be given only one object if made transitive: *Well he had missed* (me).

Other verbs used in this way are:

approach	*enter*	*play*
drink	*leave*	*win*
drive	*pass*	*write*

Notice that the subject/verb relationship is the same, whether those verbs are in transitive or intransitive use. Consider:

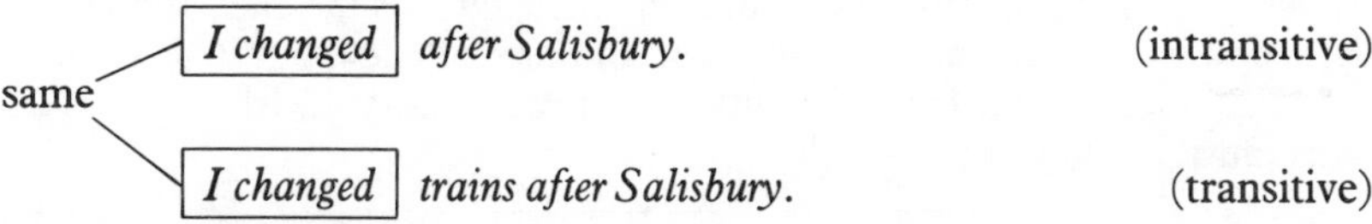

A small group of intransitive verbs are used transitively but with the former subject as object. At one point in *Rogue Male*, a character decides to stop a car for a lift. He makes a sign and – *the car stops.*

Other verbs we use in this pattern include:

begin	*cook*	*increase*	*stop*
boil	*drop*	*move*	*turn*
burn	*fly*	*open*	*unite*
change	*grow*	*sell*	*work*
close	*hurt*	*shut*	

> *'Most women set out to try to change a man, and when he has changed they don't like him.'*
>
> Marlene Dietrich, attrib. in A. Andrews, *Quotations for Speakers and Writers*

▶ **see**
270 Transitivity
271 Verbs: characteristics
272 Verb types

134

Introductory *it*

Also known as anticipatory *it* or preparatory *it*, this is the use of *it* to start a sentence when the *it* replaces a subject clause which is now placed at the end of the sentence:

. . . ***it*** *was plain* | *that her interest was in Strickland.* |

The usual word order in English sentences is subject + predicate: *Her interest was plain*. But when the subject is a clause, we often prefer to use introductory *it* + predicate + subject.

That her interest was in Strickland was plain. ~ *It was plain that her interest was in Strickland.*

Any kind of noun clause can take introductory *it*. There is a tendency in English for us to put longer parts of a sentence towards the end, giving them end-weight. Introductory *it* is part of this tendency, but it also gives the subject clause end-focus. We often use introductory *it* with a *that*-clause, to show our attitude:

***It** was quite clear* | *that she could not make head or tail of my announcement.* |

***It** was possible* | *that her reserve concealed a very deep feeling.* |

Sometimes the postponed subject is elliptical, having lost *that*.

***It** is true* | *I knew him more intimately than most.* |

The three examples above with introductory *it* are much more likely to be used and more acceptable than their corresponding normal word order (*That she could not make head or tail . . . was quite clear*, etc., could be stilted). For the *it* construction using *appear*, *follow*, *happen*, *seem*, *transpire* and other verbs, there is no possible normal equivalent:

It appeared that when everything was settled he would be four or five hundred pounds out of pocket.

Introductory *it* commonly refers to a clause starting with the *to*-infinitive, with and without *not*, also *for* + object + infinitive:

It was impossible **to keep up our social pretences any longer**.
It was impossible **not to laugh**. **Not to laugh was impossible.*

Other clauses which can follow *it* include:

wh- clauses
It was known **where Strickland was staying**.

as if/as though clauses
. . . it looked **as though he could not live more than a few hours**.

-ing clauses
It was a thankless task **taking care of Strickland**.

since clauses
It's a long time **since I was at the Louvre**.

Remember that introductory *it* always occurs first in a sentence, or immediately after an adverbial. Do not confuse introductory *it* with empty *it* as in:

It was about five years after this that I decided to live in Paris for a time.

In everyday speech we often use ellipsis to shorten sentences with introductory *it*, omitting the postponed clause, and relying on context to supply the meaning to *it*:

It won't take long. (to get there)
Will it hurt? (to have a tooth out)
It's OK. (to walk on the grass)
It can't be helped. (breaking things)

In such situations the shortened sentence is more likely to be used than the full one.

▶ GUIDELINE

In fact, with one exception, the end-position subject clause after introductory *it* is more common than the corresponding normal sequence of subject + predicate. Try, for example, putting the following sentence into normal sequence:

It is obvious that to lead such an existence and make so great a success of it, you must both have needed a strong will and a determined character!

The one exception, when introductory *it* is less commonly found, is with *-ing* clauses. Outside a few common informal sayings (*It's no good* ***talking***, *It's a waste of breath* ***explaining***), we prefer to put the *-ing* form in the topic position:

SMOKING IS FORBIDDEN

'It is better to be a fool than to be dead.'
R. L. Stevenson, *Crabbed Age and Youth*

▶ **see**

93	Empty *it*	119	*to*-infinitive clauses
97	Focus	266	Topic
125	*-ing* clauses	273	*wh-* clauses

135

Introductory *there*

Many English sentences start with an unstressed *there* usually followed by some form of *be*. This is introductory *there* (pronounced /ðəʳ/).

There *is something hostile in that soil.*

In such sentences *There* is an empty, grammatical subject, with the notional subject placed later (postponed) in the sentence, thereby giving it focus:

grammatical subject	v.	notional subject	c.	adv.	adv.
There	*are*	*six people*	*present*	*in my small room*	*already.*

Clearly there is a close relationship between this sentence and (the less likely):

Six people are present in my small room already.

But not all sentences starting with introductory *there* have equally obvious parallel sentences without *there*. Consider:

As the train jogged over the points, ***there*** *was* **time** *for agonised words.*

GUIDELINE

If you remember that introductory *there* is unstressed, you will not mistake it for initial demonstrative *there* (pronounced /ðeə/) when it is an adverb – and therefore stressed. When Ronny Heaslop was driving his mother and fiancée home, he was irritated by their demands to see India. Pulling up the mare, he said, ***'There's*** *your Ganges.'*

In this case *there* is an adverb, carrying nuclear stress and the focus of the sentence.

Sentences starting with introductory *there*, followed by *is*, *are*, *was*, *were*, etc., are often called existential sentences. Their interest is with the existence of their notional subjects:

Sitting in the courtyard of an Indian mosque, Dr Aziz listened to the night sounds: a distant European orchestra, Hindus drumming, mourners bewailing a corpse and – ***There*** *were owls, the Punjab mail (train) . . . His thoughts were on what existed around him.*

There is/are, however, introduce not only the idea of existence, but of happening. We can substitute the verbs *to exist* or *to occur* when looking for close paraphrases without *there*.

Between peoples of distant climes ***there is*** *always the possibility of romance ~ romance may possibly exist*

There has been *a terrible catastrophe about Aziz. ~ A terrible catastrophe has occurred about Aziz.*

Introductory *there* is followed by both singular and plural verbs:

There ***are*** *some exquisite echoes in India; there* ***is*** *the whisper round the dome at Bijapur . . .*

and like any normal subject, it has inversion with its verb for a *yes/no* question:

Is there *anything else I may tell you about my country?*

It also operates normally in the main sentence types:

Declaratives, both positive and negative

There was *the problem of Professor Godbole and his food.*

There was nothing *he would not do for her.*

Interrogatives

Are there *certain chambers that have no entrances?*

Exclamations

And how much illness ***there is*** *in the city!*

Introductory *there* is a most flexible structure.

It has passive forms

There *is nothing to be said.*

It can introduce main clauses

__There__ seemed a link between them at last.

It figures in subordinate *that*-clauses

Most of life is so dull that __there__ is nothing to be said about it.

in subordinate *if*-clauses

If __there__ was only a little food he would have it arranged nicely.

in subordinate relative clauses

... a beauty in which __there__ was nothing personal

Perhaps the commonest use of introductory *there* is the simple, existential sentence. Its structure is *there* + *be* + noun phrase:

There was *no quarrelling.*
There was *a moment's silence.*

One kind of introductory *there* sentence has a *to*-infinitive clause after the noun phrase:

There was *a tendency to see Fielding at the back of it.*
There was *always some little duty to be performed first.*

Occasionally we use introductory *there* before other verbs (with inversion of subject + verb) in formal literary style:

... __there went__ with them a desire for a good understanding ...

These (intransitive) verbs are usually either of existence: *There exist/lay/lived/remained/sat/stood* ... or of occurrence: *There appeared/arrived/came/emerged/entered/fell* ...

In literary style, when a sentence starts with a place adverbial, introductory *there* may be omitted before one of these existential verbs:

On this second rise △ is laid out the little Civil Station.
Immediately below △ was the scurf of life that an elephant always collects round its feet – villagers, naked babies.

GUIDELINE

Think of introductory *there* as a useful construction in its own right and not as an odd alternative way of saying things. It is a valuable – and often the only – way of giving focus to the notional subject; use it particularly to emphasise negatives: ***There's nothing***; *And soon* **there were none**; **There** *would have been* **nobody**.

The initial unstressed syllables have the same effect as a musical tune starting on the up-beat. In both cases, the emphasis is greater when it comes.

> *'There is probably nothing like living together for blinding people to each other.'*
>
> Ivy Compton-Burnett, *Mother and Son*

see
97 Focus
136 Inversion
254 Sentence types

136
Inversion

This means placing the verb before the subject.

There are two kinds of inversion; one in which we switch operator and subject (obligatory in many questions):

You (s.) *are* (op.) *going*. *(When) are* (op.) *you* (s.) *going?*

and the other in which the subject follows the whole verb phrase:

In his arms was lying (V.P.) *the infant* (S.).

In daily conversation and informal writing we use inversion in questions, question tags and certain exclamations:

*What'**s the answer**?*
*This is your work, **isn't it**?*
***Isn't it** stupid?*

We also use fronting with inversion in informal speech to give end-focus to the subject; and in contexts where substitution/ellipsis is appropriate:

Across the big yard **were the small houses for the masters.**
*Here'***s Robert.**
So **were François and Michel.**

More literary uses of fronting include obligatory inversion after fronted negative words and *such*:

Nor **did they** *mix with the rest of the company.*
Never before or since **have I** *endured hours of such misery.*
Such **was my introduction** *to glass.*

Other formal uses of inversion are with reporting verbs, in certain conditional clauses, after coordinating *as*, and after introductory *there*:

'Well,' **said Robert.**
Had my father *been alive he would have been proud.*
She made her way, **as was her custom,** *to the entrance.*
There **was only one thing** *I could do.*

'Never in the field of human conflict was so much owed by so many to so few.'

Winston Churchill, on the Battle of Britain

▸ **see**

72	Conditional sentences	138	Inversion with place adverbials
97	Focus	184	Operator
98	Fronting	235	Questions
135	Introductory *there*	238	Question tags
137	Inversion with negatives	252	Reporting verbs

137

Inversion with negative adverbials

Certain negative and semi-negative adverbials, usually taking mid-position, can be put at the beginning of their sentence (fronted) for emphasis. When we do this, inversion is obligatory; using *do/did* as necessary:

I little thought how near they would come. ~ *Little* ***did I*** *think how near they would come.*

The style is rather formal and literary. Consider:

Never ***had my aunt*** *seen the potash being prepared.*
Nowhere else ***did there*** *exist such closed communities.*

Other adverbials in this pattern include:

at no time	*rarely*	*scarcely*
on no occasion	*seldom*	*ever*
in no way	*not since*	*hardly ever*

Scarcely, *hardly* and *no sooner* can open sentences with inversion followed by a subordinate *when/than* clause:

Hardly ***had she*** *set eyes on him when she recognised him.*

No sooner ***did she*** *return than she started her narrative.*

Between *Not only . . . (but) also . . .* the first clause must have inversion:

Not only ***did he*** *live in a chateau . . . but our parents possessed it.*

In contrast, with *neither . . . nor* . . ., the inversion is on the second clause. But we use either of these correlatives to open a new sentence, followed by inversion:

Robert was neither a good husband, nor ***was he*** *an ideal father.*

Nor ***did we*** *visit Paris.*

Neither ***were they*** *betrayed to the authorities.*

▶ GUIDELINE

We use this last structure in everyday conversation to agree with an earlier statement. Here *so/nor* is followed by the inversion of subject and operator:

I love pasta. So ***do I****.*
We can't buy pitta bread. Nor ***can we****.*

On no account should visitors feed the animals

Zoo sign

▶ **see**
79 Correlatives
98 Fronting
136 Inversion
138 Inversion with place adverbials

138

Inversion with place adverbials

Place adverbs can be given front-position:

__Beside it__ stood the great furnace house.
__There__ stood my mother on the threshold.
__Here__ was a perplexity.
__Across the yard__ were the small houses.

Inversion is obligatory after the adverbial, unless the subject is a pronoun. Compare:

Here__'s mother__.	but	*Here she is.*
There __are the hills__.	but	*There they are.*

> *'Here lies one who meant well, tried a little, failed much.'*
>
> R. L. Stevenson, 'A Christmas Sermon'

see
20 Adverbs of place
136 Inversion
137 Inversion with negatives

139

Lexical verbs

Lexical verbs (sometimes called full verbs) have full dictionary meaning. We use them as main verbs to form with their subjects the basis of sentences. Examples of lexical verbs are: *hit*, *ride* and *seem*. Any word that has the following set of forms is a lexical verb:

the base form: *hit*, *ride*, *seem* (finite and non-finite)
the infinitive: *to hit*, *to ride*, *to seem* (non-finite)
the *-s* form (3rd person singular): *hits*, *rides*, *seems* (finite)
the *-ed* form (past simple): *hit*, *rode*, *seemed* (finite)
the *-en* form (past participle): *hit*, *ridden*, *seemed* (non-finite)
the *-ing* form (present participle): *hitting*, *riding*, *seeming* (non-finite)

Any word that can complete one or more of the following sentence patterns is a lexical verb:

They . . . intelligent. (are/proved/seem)
They . . . well. (act/worked/ride)
They . . . the wall. (built/painted/hit)

Lexical verbs are either regular or irregular in form.

GUIDELINE

Some grammars call both the past simple and the past participle the *-ed* form, because they both have an *-ed* ending with regular verbs. In order to distinguish between past simple and past participle, we follow a common convention in calling the past simple the *-ed* form and the past participle the *-en* form. Think of *swell, swelled, swollen.*

see

94 *-en* form
116 Infinitives
123 *-ing* form
185 Participles
191 Past simple tense

140

Linking adverbials

These are sometimes included with sentence adverbials, sometimes called conjuncts, connectors or discourse markers. They are the adverbs and adverbial phrases which bind ideas together in a text. We often place them at the beginning of sentences and mark their peripheral relationship with what follows by commas in writing and minor pauses in speech:

__Actually__, there were two other factors which added to my unease.

These adverbials serve a number of functions:

Initial *now* and *well* often signal the start of a new topic, or a return to an old one:

__Now__, where did we get to?

We can change the subject by starting with *incidentally*, *by the way*:

'__By the way__, McReadie, one thing I haven't been told . . .'

Summing up is indicated by adverbials like: *in a word*, *in short*, *in conclusion*, *altogether*, *thus*:

__In a nutshell__ . . . no.

Explaining can be signalled by:

that is (to say)
namely
for instance
for example
in other words
in point of fact
to put it another way

. . . an enormously high temperature – several million degrees, __in point of fact__.

Concession is expressed by:

however
nevertheless
only
still
in any case
at any rate
at all events
all the same

It was still curious, __all the same__ . . . about the corpse in the woolly jumper.

Result is signalled by:

therefore	*accordingly*
so	*as a result*
consequently	

I knew I would never forgive them for that.
***So** I just muttered . . .*

Other linking adverbials include:

Listing		**Adding**	
first(ly)	*last(ly)*	*furthermore*	*in addition*
second(ly)	*final(ly)*	*what is more*	*besides*
next	*to begin with*		

GUIDELINE

In formal writing we find the Latin abbreviations *e.g.*, *i.e.* and *viz.*, but we read them as *for example*, *that is* and *namely*.

see
23 Adverbials
257 Sentence adverbials
266 Topic

141

Linking verbs

These are sometimes called copular verbs. They link the subject of a sentence to its complement or adverbial. The subject complement is usually one or more adjectives or nouns, which refer to the same person or thing as the subject:

*He looked **trained and respectable**.* (adjectival complement)
*I became **a human being** again.* (noun complement)
*I was **out of any immediate danger**.* (adverbial)

The two types of linking verbs are current – where the complement describes a current attribute or thing – or resulting – where the complement names an attribute or thing which develops from the verb. Compare:

She looked a child. (current)
In love, one becomes a child again. (resulting)

Notice that the current type usually involves a stative verb, which we do not use in progressive tenses.

**He was seeming angry.*

The verb *to be* is by far the most commonly used linking verb. It links with only current attributes, but they may be nominal, adjectival or adverbial:

The road was a narrow track. (nominal)
This was depressing. (adjectival)
I was on the ridge. (adverbial)

Common linking verbs with their complementation include:

current		**resulting**	
appear	N./adj./adv.	*become*	N./adj.
be	N./adj./adv.	*come*	adj./adv.
feel	N./adj./adv.	*get*	adj./adv.
keep	adj./adv.	*go*	adj./adv.
lie	adj./adv.	*grow*	adj./adv.
look	N./adj./adv.	*turn*	N./adj./adv.
seem	N./adj./adv.	*turn out*	N./adj./adv.
smell	adj./adv.	*wind up*	N./adj./adv.
sound	N./adj./adv.		
stand	adj./adv.		
stay	N./adj./adv.		
taste	adj./adv.		

GUIDELINE

Verbs of perception – *appear*, *feel*, *look*, *seem*, *smell*, *sound*, *taste* – are followed by adverbials beginning *as if*, *as though*:

It looks as if it will rain.
You sound as though you are jealous.

Occasionally we hear *like* being used to introduce the complementation (**It looks like it will rain*, etc.), but this is not preferred English usage.

> *'She had a mannish manner of mind and face, able to feel hot and think cold.'*
>
> Joyce Cary, *Herself Surprised*

see
50 *to be*
87 Stative verbs
272 Verb types

142

Marked/unmarked

When two related words are contrasted by the presence or absence of an inflection, we call the former the marked form and the latter the unmarked form. So: *dog* – unmarked; *dog*(s) marked for plural.

As a rule the unmarked form is more general or neutral in meaning. The concept of marking is usefully applied to several word classes. Nouns may be marked not only for plural, but for case – *dog*(')*s*/*dogs*(') and gender *host*/*host*(ess). The same is true for pronouns *he*/*they*, *he*/*she*, *he*/*him*.

Verbs similarly have marked and unmarked forms. The unmarked form is the base form e.g. *eat*. By contrast verb forms can be marked for:

time	*(ate)*, marked for past time
aspect	*eat (ing)*, marked for progressive aspect
	eat (en), marked for perfective aspect
person	*eat (s)*, marked for third person singular

Marked and unmarked are terms we also apply to focus. When the focus of a structure is in its expected, normal, end-position it is unmarked. But we can mark the focus by a number of devices which move it to another position. One device is fronting, which in this case is achieved by using the passive form:

They will ask [*questions.*] ~ [*Questions*] *will be asked.*

unmarked focus — marked focus when fronted

GUIDELINES

Whilst in most cases of marked/unmarked noun pairs, it is the male which is the unmarked form (*host*, *waiter* etc.) in two cases it is the female form which is unmarked: *bride/bridegroom*, *widow/widower*.

Notice that the term unmarked is also used in the sense of neutral in meaning. So with measure adjectives after *how*, we ask:

How big/deep/heavy/long/old/tall/wide . . .?

Here the larger member of polar opposite adjectives has neutral meaning, compared with its opposite –

How big/ **small** (marked) *was Tom Thumb?*

> *'To be seventy years young is sometimes far more hopeful than to be forty years old.'*
>
> Oliver Wendell Holmes,
> On the seventieth birthday of Julia Ward Howe

see

45 Aspect 98 Fronting
97 Focus 3 Passive

143

Modal verbs: general

These are the largest group of auxiliary verbs, the commonest being *can*, *will* and *must*. Like other auxiliaries, they act as operators, form their negatives with *not* (*cannot*, *can't*, *will not*, *won't*, *mustn't*, etc.), make question forms by inversion with their subject (e.g. *Must* (v.) *you* (s.)*?*) and have an important role in the formation of tag questions, for example: *You must*, **mustn't you***?* Unlike the primary auxiliaries *be*, *do* and *have*, modal auxiliaries do not have infinitive forms, participles or third person inflections.

Modality is a range of attitudes we express towards the main situation or event of a sentence – possibility, permission, ability, likelihood, obligation and hypothesis among others. All modal verbs have more than one meaning; some can express near synonyms, like *ought to* and *should*; others can stand as antonyms, like *must* and *needn't*. The field of modality, therefore, is both complex and rich in ways of expressing a range of communicative functions. See how C. P. Snow in *The Conscience of the Rich* allots the contemplative Charles March no fewer than five categories of modality in as many sentences:

> *It* [*may*] *be a nuisance sometimes not to have a private income . . . there are*
> likehood
>
> *times when it's valuable for a doctor to be independent of his job. He*
>
> [*can*] *do things and say things that otherwise he* [*wouldn't*] *dare. Some of*
> freedom to act — hypothetical possibility
>
> *us* [*ought*] *to be able to say things without being frightened for our*
> obligation
>
> *livelihood, don't you agree? Well, I* [*shan't*] *be able to.*
> prediction

Such categories of modality may appear unrelated, but we can place them on a scale ranging from possibility to necessity.

At the same time we can identify two kinds of modal meaning: intrinsic, in which some kind of human control is present, and extrinsic in which the events are beyond human control, though not human judgement. Consider:

I ***won't*** *do it again.* [volition-intrinsic]
I'm sure ***it won't*** *last.* [prediction-extrinsic]

Similarly, all other modals have both intrinsic and extrinsic uses, which express one or more broad categories of modality in fulfilling a variety of communication functions.

▶ **see**

48 Auxiliary verbs
116 Infinitives
136 Inversion
144–52 Modal verbs, detail
184 Operators
185 Participles
238 Tag questions

144

Modal verbs: *can/could*

Can and *could* most often carry one of the four broad modal categories of ability and permission, opportunity and theoretical possibility.

Ability

With most verbs we use *can/could* to express general ability:

What do you think it **can** *mean?* [seeking information]
I wish to God I **could** *help.* [offering]

Referring to the present or past time we use *can* or *could* with verbs of sensation (*see*, *hear*, *smell*, *feel*, etc.).

I **could** *see the clear profile of his clever face.* [ability]

Here the plain verb without *can/could* would have much the same meaning. In the same way, certain other mental-state verbs (like *believe*, *imagine*, *remember*, *understand*) followe *can/could* with the intrinsic meaning of personal ability:

I'm afraid I **can't** *believe that.* [disbelief]

Both *can* and *could* often open requests, *could* being more tentative (and therefore polite):

I want to see you . . . **Can** *you manage to stay in?* [request]
Could *you possibly bear to have tea with me?* [tentative invitation]

GUIDELINES

This last invitation carries a slight implication that the idea might be unbearable. The reason is that the speaker is using an unusual form of one of three informal non-assertive verb phrases which almost always take a negative form:

can't/couldn't bear *can't/couldn't help* *can't/couldn't stand*

We use them, of course, to express our negative ability:

She **couldn't bear** *to watch my son making a frightful ass of himself in public.*

Notice that *can* usually refers to present ability.

We use *could* for ability in single past events, sometimes when modified by negative words like *hardly/never/rarely/seldom*.

Charles **could** *not come.*
I **could** *never have cut a dash myself.*

More often we express past or future ability through *to be able to*:

I had not **been able to** *understand her outburst.*
We shall not **be able to** *live on investments . . .*

Permission

Can/could are both used for present permission as informal alternatives to *may/might*. Sometimes we use a sentence which looks like an act of seeking/granting/refusing permission but which has a different function, and vice versa. Consider:

Can't *we leave it for tonight?* [pained request]
I expect I **can** *take it that your father's right.* [seeking confirmation]

It's a terrible theory . . . and you **can't** *dispose of it by clamour.* [injunction]
You must dress suitably for once . . . **I can't** *possibly let you off.* [refused permission]

We use *could* to express past permission and as a reported form of *can*:

Mr March accepted the position: he **could** *do nothing more.* [agreement]
. . . agreed that Katharine **could** *be safely moved to the hotel* [agreement]

Permission for future action is usually given with *can*, not *could*:

I'll pay for the meal and you **can** *buy the tickets.* [concession]

GUIDELINE

Both *can* and *could* are used in requests, *could* being more tentative and polite. Compare:

Can *I borrow £100?* **Could** *I borrow £100?*
Of course you **can/can't**.

Opportunity

Both *can* and *could* express opportunity. We use both for the general sense:

It's the only occupation . . . where you **can** *be absolutely undistinguished and still flatter yourself a bit.*
You **could** *do so many things.*

Could alone refers to past opportunities:

You **could** *have found a more ingenious excuse.*
I have a house in Chelsea, so we **could** *go the same way.*

Future reference is usually restricted to *can*:

If I **can** *get the chance, I'll talk to him.*

There are times, however, when *could* has present/future reference. When Mr March tries to persuade his son against being a doctor, he brings up the topic of the family's opinion:

'You must know they **could** *not even begin to count,' said Charles.*

When we make statements like this, however, it is possible that we are assuming a conditional clause. If so, sentences with *could* referring to the future may well be elliptical.

Notice that we cannot replace *could* with *can* in these sentences: *can* has a meaning of ability when used of the future.

Theoretical possibility

Can carries the sense of general theoretical possibility, but we use it only in questions and negative sentences (including semi-negatives like *hardly*):

What do you think it **can** *mean?* [bewilderment]
How cynical **can** *they allow themselves to be?* [disbelief]
She **can** *hardly be expected to perform any serious function.* [disbelief]
Being ill in Venice **can't** *have had anything to do with what I ate.* [deduction]

For general statements of theoretical possibility we use *could*:

There's more security as a doctor than as anything else I **could** *take up.*
I imagined she **could** *be shy of men.*

GUIDELINE

Because of the wide range of meanings carried by *can/can't*, it occasionally gives rise to ambiguities. As it stands, the written form *Can they swim?*

could question their ability, whether they have permission, or the opportunity. It could even be a positive exclamatory question expressing admiration. Fortunately context, stress and intonation usually resolve such potential ambiguities.

> *'He who can, does. He who cannot, teaches.'*
> G. B. Shaw, *Man and Superman*

see
46 Assertion/non-assertion
72 Conditional sentences
240 Exclamatory questions

145

Modals: *may/might*

May and *might* most commonly refer either to possibility or permission. We use *might* as the past form of *may* and also to replace *may* in indirect speech. But for both possibility and permission, *might* is more tentative and polite than *may*.

Possibility

We use *may/might* to express two rather different kinds of possibility. By far the more common is that with the meaning of *possibly*:

*I **may** be away some time.* [future reference]
*We're thinking that Charles **might** become a doctor.* [future reference]
*You **may** have thought the matter was closed . . .* [past reference]
*Hannah **might** not think so.* [general reference]
*It **might** be wiser if the rest of us left you.* [tentative farewell]
*It **might** interest you.* [tentative invitation]
*I thought there **might** be a scene.* [reported anxiety]
*You **mightn't** get a second chance.* [future reference warning]

Less commonly *may/might* have the same meaning as the *can/could* possibility:

*You **might** blame me more than you do.*
*It **might** be useful.*
*It's possible I **may** be able to help.* [offer of help]

Notice that questions using *might/mightn't* are rare with this meaning.

Permission

May and *might* are both used when seeking and giving permission. But they are more formal and less common than *can/could*.

***May** I sleep on your sofa tonight?* [request]
*The able manner, if I may **say** so, in which the case has been handled* [polite formula]
*. . . asked if he **might** bring a friend* [reported request]

Except in indirect speech, *might* is rarely used today with past reference. But both *may* and *might* are used to seek permission for the future. *Might* forms tentative requests – ***Might** I use the car?* But we do not give permission or refuse it tentatively. So an answer to such a request is usually:

Yes, you **can/may**, or *No you* **can't/may not**.

Notice how we use *may/might* as well to show reluctance:

*I **may** as well tell you at once that it could turn out badly.*

*I **might** as well be civil.*

*'Ought you to be introduced?' 'I **might** as well.'*

GUIDELINES

Mayn't is no longer in use. Likewise we do not ask permission using *mightn't* – we prefer *can't/couldn't*. There is an interesting difference in the meaning of *may not*. With the meaning of possibility, the *not* negates the main verb. With the meaning of permission the *not* negates *may*. So:

*She may **not go*** (possibility) ~ *She may go, she may not.*
*She **may not** go* (permission) ~ *She has no permission to go.*

see
49 Back-shift
144 *Can/could*
110 Indirect speech

146

Modals: *must/needn't*

Must has the basic meaning of necessity, which includes obligation:

You must leave her out of it. [necessity]
I must remind you that . . . [obligation]

The two meanings have different opposites. The opposite of *must* (necessity) is *needn't*. The opposite of *must* (obligation) is *mustn't*:

*They **need** not meet again.* [no necessity]
*You **mustn't** forget.* [obligation not to]

Notice that *to need* is also a regular lexical verb as in, *You **need** to eat less*, and, *You don't **need** to drink so much*. In questions like *Need I?* it has negative bias, expecting the answer *No* – asking for a denial of necessity.

With the meaning of obligation, *must* places the obligation either on the speaker himself or another, or people in general. It can refer to present or future time. We use *must* in this sense and in a variety of functions:

*You **mustn't** worry.* [advice]
*I **must** say he sounds disagreeable.* [opinion]

You ***must*** *come to dinner.* [invitation]
I ***must*** *see if I can find you something.* [self-imposed duty]
Must *you?* [criticism]
Need *there be further bitterness?* [plea]

Notice how these refer to present and future action. *Must* with this meaning can only refer to past time when it is used in indirect speech.

I've been trying to persuade him that he ***must*** *get some advice.*

Using a heavy stress on *must*, implying unavoidable necessity, we can show sarcasm:

If I ***must*** *have an ungrateful family, the best thing they can do is not to interfere with my health.*

A secondary kind of necessity expressed by *must/needn't* is that of deduction, where we are talking about a logical necessity concerning present events:

The story ***must*** *be true.*
He ***must*** *be getting on for thirty.*
Ann ***needn't*** *be the guilty one.*

We can refer to past deductions by using the perfective aspect (*have* + *-en*):

I was afraid you ***must*** *have noticed something.*

GUIDELINES

We do not use *must* (logical deduction) in negative and interrogative clauses. Instead we use *can* (possibility). So:

You ***must*** *be mad.* ~ *I deduce you are mad.*
You ***can't*** *be sane.* ~ *It's possible you are mad.*
Can *you be sane?* ~ *Is it possible you are mad?*

'I must get out of these wet clothes and into a dry Martini.'

Alexander Woollcott, Attrib. in *Wit's End*

---

see
45 Aspect

147

Modals: *ought to/should*

These two modals (*ought to* is sometimes classified as a marginal modal because it is usually followed by *to*) have the same meaning and cover the same areas of modality as *must* – obligation and deduction. They differ from *must*, however, because they do not carry the speaker's certainty of events. Compare:

It ***must*** *be here/ It* ***ought to/should*** *be here.*

Should is more common than *ought to* and is discussed below in other senses than this.

Obligation

Notice how the obligation here is more tentative than with *must*:

We ***ought to*** *take care of him, oughtn't we?* [suggestion]
I ***oughtn't to*** *pay him compliments.* [self-criticism]
You are optimistic, as you ***ought to*** *be at your age.* [compliment]
I ***shouldn't*** *ask for anything impossible.* [self-criticism]
She ***should*** *have something better to do with her time.* [criticism]

In only one of these examples does the speaker have any certainty about his topic. Indeed with the perfective aspect, we use *ought to* and *should* to suggest that the obligation is unfulfilled:

You ***ought to have*** *chosen a more suitable time to tell me.*
She ***should*** *never* ***have*** *come with him at all.* [tentative deduction]

Deduction

Here the speaker uses *ought to* and *should* to show he does not know if what he speaks of is true, but tentatively concludes it may be. This use can have future reference:

You ***ought to*** *be pleased, oughtn't you?* [flattery]
You're paler than you ***ought to*** *be.* [criticism]
It ***should be*** *possible to stop him.* [argument]
I ***shouldn't*** *have any use for a man who did what I told him.* [supposition]

It is arguable that some examples with *should* are elliptical and therefore concealed conditions. For example, *I* ***shouldn't*** *ask for anything impossible* in another context could be a piece of advice, when it is likely to be a concealed conditional sentence with an omitted *If I were you . . .*

GUIDELINE

With *ought to* and *should* in their tentative deduction use, there is a sense of desirability or appropriateness in the speaker's mind. Compare:

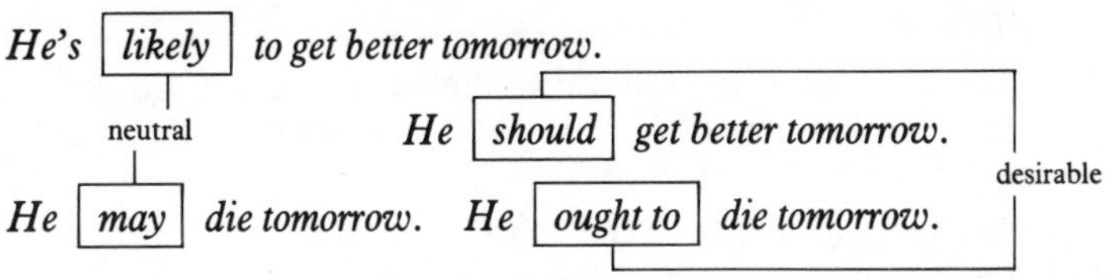

> *'I am the only person in the world I should like to know thoroughly.'*
>
> Oscar Wilde, *Lady Windermere's Fan*

Contracted forms never appear in which position?

▶ see
45 Aspect
72 Conditional sentences
88 Ellipsis
143 Modality
149, 150 *Should*

148

Modals: *will/would*

Both these modals have contracted forms as in *she'll/she'd*, though we never use either in final position. The negative forms are *will not/won't* and *would not/wouldn't*. *Would* is the past form of *will* and replaces *will* in indirect speech, but has several other non-past meanings. The two major categories of modal meaning for *will/would* are prediction and volition, each of which has three more specific areas, thus:

will/would

- Prediction
  - Pure future
  - Present predictive
  - Habitual predictive
- Volition
  - Willingness
  - Intention
  - Insistence

With all meanings, a range of functions is identifiable.

Pure future

We use will to talk about the future with all persons. (For the use of the future with *shall*, see 149). *Would* replaces *will* to talk about the future as seen from a past point in time, and in indirect speech.

I'm hoping that Ann ***will*** *marry me.* [hope]
*If she goes she'****ll*** *find it harder.* [warning]
I ***won't*** *do it again.* [promise]
If I win a scholarship that ***would*** *help me over the first years . . . I might pull through.* [prediction]
I hoped you ***would*** *come.* [reported hope]

Present predictive

This usage has a generally present meaning, similar to the deductive meaning of *must* with the sense of *It is likely that* . . . for *will*, and a more tentative *It is possible that* . . . for *would*:

That ***will*** *be Ann.* ~ *That must be/can only be Ann.* [surmise]
How ***will*** *that do?* ~ *Do you think this is adequate?*
Katharine ***will*** *know that by instinct.* [assurance]
Who ***would*** *that be?* ~ *Who might that be?*
Would *you say that he wants success?*
. . . a little more than one ***would*** *expect* ~ *might.*

Habitual predictive

This use is often found in conditional sentences and concealed conditions. Also when we describe characteristic behaviour:

It ***won't*** *get easier.*

Hannah ***would*** *say it isn't but it is.*

Florence thought she ***wouldn't*** *like it until she tried.*

The answer ***would*** *sometimes be Yes.*

Everyday . . . Mr March ***would*** *meet his brother Philip at the club. Philip* ***would*** *tell his wife, she* ***would*** *ring up her children . . .*

A less formal replacement for *would* in the last two examples is *used to*.

The three sub-categories of volition range from the weaker willingness, through intention to insistence.

Willingness

Questions (inquiries about willingness) function as offers or requests; tag question forms function as tentative commands.

*I'****ll*** *talk to him.* [promise]

Will *you dine with me tomorrow?* [invitation]

Will *you tell them to be quick.* [request]

*You'****ll*** *forgive me, won't you?* [suasion]

What ***would*** *you like to drink?* [offer]

One can't forget that, much as one ***would*** *like to.* [apology]

Intention

Intention, being a stronger form of willingness, also carries a sense of prediction.

Charles has discussed his future with me,

I ***won't*** *pretend he hasn't.*

*I'****ll*** *see if anything can be done.* [promise]

When I pressed him he ***wouldn't*** *say any more.* [refusal in past]

He ***would*** *go through with it.* [resolve]

I ***would*** *do anything for you both.* [good intentions]

Insistence

The modal auxiliary is always stressed and is never contracted to *'ll* or *'d* with this meaning. This gives even the otherwise tentative *would* a sense of determination or even stubbornness:

I ***won't*** *have the family dismissed as strangers.*
She ***won't*** *stop thinking about this affair.*
As luck ***would*** *have it, I was invited.*
He ***would*** *not have (his birthday) so much as mentioned.*
Mr March ***would*** *send for a doctor.*

GUIDELINE

There is a useful and informal use of *would(n't)* (never will) when we give it nuclear stress to show our annoyance at the wilful behaviour of someone else. The speaker is referring to a single, typical event:

*'Father has decided not to go on holiday.' 'Oh, ˇhe ˆ****would!****'*
*'Father won't go to Venice.' 'Oh, ˇhe ˆ****wouldn't****.'*

Which is the least common modal verb?

OSCAR WILDE: *I wish I had said that.*
JAMES WHISTLER: *Oh you will, Oscar. You will.*
Ingleby, Attrib. in *Oscar Wilde*.

▶ **see**
72 Conditional sentences
99 Future time
146 *must*

149

Modals: *shall/should*

Least common of all the modals, *shall* has a more limited meaning than any other and is the only one to refer solely to future events. Again it is unique because normally we use it only with *I/We*. *Shan't* is rare.

The two broad areas of meaning are prediction and volition.

Prediction

This is the pure future of traditional grammar, which we use to fulfil a range of functions:

This is the last occasion when I ***shall*** *go inside.* [regret]
We ***shall*** *be married in December.* [anticipation]
I ***shall*** *always have a slight suspicion that I ran away.* [confession]
I ***shall*** *come into his money in time.* [prediction]
I ***shan't*** *be sorry when tonight is over.* [understated foreboding]

Traditional grammar insisted on *shall* alone for *I/We*, but today we use both *shall* and *will*. Indeed all the above examples can have *will* for *shall*, with no change of meaning, except the first.

Notice also the archaic use of *shall* with the 3rd person fossilised in legal jargon:

... when I'm twenty-five ... or when I marry, 'whichever ***shall*** *be the earlier', as he insists on saying*

Volition

Affirmative and negative sentences usually show the speaker's intention, when we can alternate *shall* with *will*:

I ***shall*** *go and stay with Francis for a few days.* [intention]
I ***shan't*** *change my mind.* [determination]
I ***shall*** *marry Francis whatever happens.* [promise]
I ***shan't*** *find this easy to accept.* [threat]

Questions starting *Shall I/ Shall we/ Should I/ Should we* ... ask about the wishes of the other person. We commonly use these questions to make offers or suggestions for the future.

Shall *I carry that for you?* [offer]
Shall *I tell you something?* [offer]

What ***shall*** *I say?* [suggestion]
Shall *we tell him?* [suggestion]

The same questions with *should* are more tentative and polite. This is one of the rare occasions when we cannot use *will*. All examples above in which we use *shall* replace it with *should* in indirect speech.

I knew it was the last occasion when I ***should*** *go inside,*

and so on.

We do not use *should* as a past tense equivalent of *shall*, but we use it typically in conditional sentences:

If I married, I wonder if I ***should*** *dare to have a child . . . I* ***should*** *do the same as Katharine.*
I ***should*** *want children. I* ***should*** *start a family.*

Similarly we use *should* with hypothetical meaning:

I ***should*** *like to agree.*
I ***should*** *advise you to ignore her suggestions.*
I ***should*** *be in the way.*

GUIDELINE

We still occasionally meet the use of *shall* with 2nd and 3rd person subjects to show the speaker's wishes but it is rather old-fashioned or literary.

'They shall not grow old, as we that are left grow old:
Age shall not weary them, nor the years condemn.
At the going down of the sun and in the morning
We will remember them.'

Laurence Binyon, 'For the Fallen'

see
72 Conditional sentences
99 Future time

150

Modals: *should* in subordinate clauses

We use *should* in subordinate clauses in ways different from other modals. After *if* and *in case* we use tentative *should* to show uncertainty:

Margaret visited Mr March in case he ***should*** *change his mind.*

Compare the more probable situation which does not call for *should*:

She visited him in case he changed his mind.

When we are trying to get things done, using verbs like *ask*, *command*, *demand*, *insist*, *order*, *suggest*, or adjectives like *anxious*, *concerned*, *eager*, *essential, important, necessary, vital,* we use *should* in the subordinate clause:

He insisted that Katharine **should** *invite her.*
He suggested that we **should** *have a meal.*
. . . anxious that they **should** *not be too much alike*

For a much more formal alternative, we can use the subjunctive instead of *should. Should* is used in subordinate clauses when we are making an emotional reaction to the verb in the *that*-clause:

She was amazed that Charles **should** *want to be a doctor.*
I'm sorry that my brother **should** *be responsible for this.*
It's ridiculous that you **should** *think of it.*
It's preposterous that this man **should** *follow her.*

In the same way we can describe our reaction with nouns:

It's a comfort/disgrace/relief/scandal/shame, etc.

and adjectives:

It's absurd/disgraceful/odd/pleasing/strange, etc.

Also participial adjectives:

I'm annoyed/delighted/displeased/infuriated/surprised, etc.

Should follows all these.

The subjunctive is not available in this construction. But again, if we do not use *should,* we drop the tentative tone:

She was amazed that Charles wanted to become a doctor.

▶ **see**

72–5	Conditional clauses	260	Subjunctive
8, 186	Participial adjectives	261	Subordination

151

Modals with progressive and perfective aspects

All the modal auxiliaries may be used with progressive and perfective aspects, but not to express ability or permission:

Philip did all that Mr March **would have liked** *to do.*	[volition]
We **may** *all* **be taking** it too seriously.	[possibility]
You **can't** *possibly* **have heard,** *can you?*	[possibility]
You **must have known** *all along.*	[necessity]
You **might have known** *that it would keep me awake.*	[prediction]
Are you sure you **ought to be doing** *this?*	[obligation]
It's a position you **ought to have** *adopted.*	[obligation]
They hoped, just as they **would have hoped** *thirty years ago.*	[hypothesis]

We occasionally combine both aspects for the same modal purpose:

She **might have** *just* **been listening.**	[possibility]

▶ **see**
45 Aspect

152

Marginal auxiliaries

A number of single-word and multi-word verbs may be classed as marginal auxiliaries. Some refer specifically to time:

used to	*be about to*
be going to	*be due to*
be to	*be destined to*

They ***used to*** *call him the longest-headed man in the Stock Exchange.*

Others have modal meanings (like modal auxiliaries), several refer to more than one category of meaning. So:

have (got) to
be bound/certain/sure to
be obliged/supposed to } [necessity/obligation]

He ***had to*** *give me his telephone number.*
I was ***obliged to*** *talk to him.*

be able to
be liable to } [possibility] *be allowed to*
be permitted to } [persuasion]

Why I have never ***been able to*** *understand.*

be willing to/ would rather/ would sooner
be going to/dare (to) } [volition]

had better } [obligation]

'We'd ***better stop,****' said Katharine.*

▶ **see**
48 Auxiliary verbs
143 Modality

153

Multi-word verbs

By far the largest and commonest group of multi-word verbs are those made up of verb + particle e.g. *stand* (V.) *up* (P.), *look* (V.) *at* (P.), *go* (V.) *in* (P). *for*. They are an everyday feature of English, particularly in informal use. Most have single-word synonyms, with a more formal flavour:

to set out ~ *to embark* *to go into* ~ *to enter*

Most are idiomatic in varying degrees, in the sense that their meaning may not be clear from the meaning of their parts. Consider:

to put up with or *to look after*

We distinguish three main types of verbs + particle: phrasal verbs; prepositional verbs; phrasal-prepositional verbs.

The thousands of verb + particle combinations represent an open set in which new formations and new meanings for familiar combinations continue to appear. A small number of monosyllabic verbs come in for particularly heavy duty as the first element: *be*, *come*, *get*, *go*, *put* and *take*.

▶ **see**

154 Multi-word verbs: semantic grouping
194, 195 Phrasal verbs
196 Phrasal-prepositional verbs
221, 222 Prepositional verbs

154

Multi-word verbs: semantic grouping

Multi-word verbs represent a large class, although many of them are formed from a relatively small number of heavy-duty main verbs and particles. Within the enormous range of meanings expressed, a number of semantic groupings stand out. The commonest of these are paired opposites, transitive/intransitive pairs and subject/prepositional complement pairs.

Paired opposites are phrasal verbs with contrasting particles, and sometimes with lexical verbs in common. Examples are: *get in/get out*, *pull in/pull out*, *switch on/switch off*, *turn on/turn off*. (Others with common verbs and contrasting particles have no opposition in their meaning, only difference – *stand up/ stand down*, *turn up/ turn down*.) Conversely some pairs have contrasting verbs and particles, but strong opposite associations: *come in/ go out*, *put on/ take off*, *stand up/ sit down*.

Transitive/intransitive pairs are of two kinds. Some phrasal verbs have identical forms with and without direct objects. Consider:

The bridge ***blew up****. They* ***blew up*** *the bridge.*

Other pairs: *catch up/catch someone up*, *get up/get someone up*, *turn back/turn someone back*, *wake up/wake someone up*. Similarly, an intransitive phrasal verb may have a corresponding 'transitive' phrasal-prepositional verb. Consider:

He ***ran away****. He* ***ran away from*** *school.*

Others are: *catch up (with)*, *drop out (of)*, *fall out (with)*, *get out (of)*, *keep up (with)*.

A second kind of transitive/intransitive pairing is aspectual. Here two heavy-duty verbs have reciprocal meanings, one being intransitive and the other transitive. Consider the relationship between *come* and *bring* in:

It suddenly ***came back*** *to me. The photo* ***brought*** *it* ***back*** *to me.*

Other *come/bring* pairs are:

come in (be received as income)	*bring in* (earn)
come out (decide to strike)	*bring out* (persuade to strike)
come round (regain consciousness)	*bring round* (help regain consciousness)

Similarly each of the following intransitive *come* idioms has a reciprocal transitive *bring* phrase:

come to attention/blows/an end/life/a stop
come into action/being/contact/flower/line/the open/service/view.

Other reciprocal pairs of this kind include:
go and *put*: *go/put something/out of action* etc.
go and *send*: *go/send someone/round the bend* etc.

Subject/prepositional complement pairs are related expressions in which the subject of one is the prepositional complement of the other. Consider:
run out/ run out of

Time is ***running out****. We are* ***running out*** *of time.*

Other pairs include:

turn up (come to one's attention)
turn up with (bring to one's attention)

get behind (lose progress)
get behind with (lose progress with)
come up (arise, appear) *come up with* (bring up)

GUIDELINE

It goes without saying that a multi-word verb form may have several, very different, meanings with varying degrees of transparency. *To come in* has at least ten separate meanings as a phrasal verb.

To get up can mean not only *to rise* but *to leave one's bed, to climb something, to become more violent, to organise an event, to dress in a special way, to memorise* and more. Such richness is a gift for humorous writers –

> *'It is not twenty-four hours since she turned me down.'*
> *'Turned you down?'*
> *'Like a bedspread. In this very garden.'*
>
> P. G. Wodehouse, *Right Ho, Jeeves*

see

139	Lexical verbs	196	Phrasal-prepositional verbs
153	Multi-word verbs	221, 222	Prepositional verbs
194, 195	Phrasal verbs	270	Transitivity

155

Negative sentences

We use *not* to make negative forms of the three main types of sentences: declarative, interrogative and imperative. We also make negative sentences by using certain adverbs, determiners and pronouns.

Negative declarative

We add the *not* or *n't* to the operator to make the negative form of a declarative. In speech and informal writing, we usually use the contracted form *n't*.

He ***couldn't*** *spit as well as his brother . . .*
We ***mustn't*** *waste . . .*

If there is no operator in the affirmative sentence form, we use *do* as the operator:

I ***don't*** *care. He* ***doesn't*** *seem to care.*

We use *not* in more formal sentences; this one starts a new paragraph:

Bipti was ***not*** *in a welcoming mood . . .*

We use *not* to give emphatic stress:

'The poor boy is shy . . .' 'I am ***not*** *shy and I am* ***not*** *upset.'*

GUIDELINES

Cannot is an alternative way of writing *can not*, the uncontracted form *cannot* being more formal than *can't*, the contracted form.

The contracted form *mayn't* is obsolete in British English – use *may not*.

Notice the unusual sound change when *n't* is added to *will*: *will, won't* /wɪl/, wəʊnt/.

She ***won't*** *need these sticks now.*

Negative interrogatives

We add *n't* to the operator to make the negative form of an interrogative:

Why ***don't*** *you help them?*
Can't *you see you are waking up the babies?*

When we wish to be more formal or to be emphatic, we add the uncontracted form *not* after the subject of the question:

How can you ***not*** *believe in God after all this?*

GUIDELINES

The contracted negative form in British English of *Am I?* is ***Aren't I?*** There is nothing wrong here – the explanation is historical. The *m* has disappeared under the influence of the following *n* (*amn't* > *an't*) and the vowel change is the same as in *shall*, *shan't*/ʃæl, ʃa:nt/ and in *can*, *can't* /kæn, ka:nt/

Negative imperatives

We form negative imperatives by using *do* + *not* or *n't*:

*'****Don't*** *let him fall out.' '****Don't*** *worry.'*

We tend to use the uncontracted form *not* for more emphatic or formal commands:

Do not worry.

Occasionally, subject *you* is used in a negative command:

Don't you *worry.*

We sometimes form negative sentences by using negative adverbs like *never* and *nowhere*, and the semi-negatives *hardly*, *rarely*, *scarcely* and *seldom*:

He ***hardly*** *saw her, though she lived close.* ~ *He did not see her very often . . .*

The determiners *neither* and *no* form negative sentences:

__Neither__ Pratap __nor__ Prasad __nor__ Dehuti was married. ~ *Pratap was not married and Prasad was not married and Dehuti was not married.*

We also use negative pronouns like *none*, *no one*, *nothing* and *nobody* to form negative sentences:

Mr Biswas, his brothers and mother searched for his dead father's money in the house and furniture. They found **nothing**. ~ *They didn't find anything.*

GUIDELINES

The position in a sentence of the negative influences the meaning, by altering the scope of the negation. We can say that everything after the negative is negated. Consider Mr Biswas, who died at the age of forty-six. One of the following sentences is true, one untrue:

When he died he was not still a journalist. (~ he had been one)

When he died he was still not a journalist. (~ he never had been one)

The first sentence of Naipaul's novel tells us, *Ten weeks before he died, Mr Mohun Biswas, a journalist . . . was sacked.*

The first of the two sentences is true, then. But the difference between true and false here depends on the position of the negative.

see
109 Imperatives
184 Operator
254 Sentence types

156

Nominal clauses

A finite clause introduced by a *wh-* word, *if* or conjunction *that*, and taking the role of a noun or noun phrase, is a nominal clause. We may omit introductory *that* except when the *that*-clause stands in front-position. Compare:

He knew △ *he hated Dalmire.*

obligatory

That *he hated Dalmire was undeniable.*

Nominal clauses commonly function as sentence subject, direct object, complement, adjective complement, prepositional complement and can stand in apposition:

It would be a miracle **if he lasted beyond Christmas**.	[subject]
What he didn't like so much *was the deadening familiarity*.	[subject]
She knew **that I loved her**.	[direct object]
The problem was **that they hated each other**.	[complement]
It was uncanny **how it happened**.	[complement of adjective]
. . . told him of **what they had achieved**	[complement of preposition]

The thought came to him ***that she was not entirely indifferent.***
[apposition]

GUIDELINES

Other subordinate clauses are disposable in a way that nominal clauses are not. We can usually omit other subordinate clauses without loss of meaning or grammatical sense. Compare the undeletable nominal *that*-clause with the deletable relative *that*-clause below:

essential

The position was [*that they hated each other.*] [nominal]

non-essential

It was an understanding [*that they had both reached*] *as if it was some unique genetic accident.* [relative]

see

66 Adjective complement
37 Apposition
61 Clauses
76 Conjunctions
110 Nominals in indirect speech
247 Relative clauses
261 Subordination
252 Verbs + *that*- clauses

157

Non-finite verbs

The finite verb, one essential part of every sentence, has a recognisable subject and tense, as in *It* (s.) *broke* (v. past). The four non-finite verbs rarely stand alone and have no obvious subject or tense. The non-finite forms are:

the bare infinitive – *break*
the *to*-infinitive – *to break*
the present participle – *breaking* – the *-ing* form
the past participle – *broken* – the *-en* form.

These are the simple forms. But in parallel with simple and complex tenses, we use *be* and *have* to make complex infinitives and participles: active and passive.

complex infinitives:
to be broken passive
to be breaking progressive active
to be being broken progressive passive
to have broken perfect active
to have been broken perfect passive
to have been breaking perfect progressive active

Complex participles:
having broken perfect active
have been broken perfect passive
having been breaking perfect progressive active
being broken progressive passive

The simple non-finites in particular are a major group of building blocks in framing English sentences. We use the participles in one major role for forming complex tenses:

I'm **coming** *with you.*
Jackson had **driven** *from Paris.*

Another major role for the infinitives and the participles is with catenative verbs:

He watched the car **go**.
The lines seemed **to vanish** *from his face.*
I like **beating** *them.*
Get yourself **settled** *in.*

Here the essential verbal nature of the non-finites remains clear, yet we regularly use non-finites for every part of the sentence – subject, object, complement, adverbial – and these most flexible of verb forms frequently function as nouns, adjectives and modifiers:

I can still hear the **screaming**.	[*-ing* as nominal]
The **commanding** *officer*	[*-ing* as adjectival]
Damned *cold out tonight*	[*-en* as modifier]

In non-finite clauses we use the *to*-infinitive and participles for a variety of meanings:

He retired to bed early, not to sleep, but to work.	[reduced purpose adverbial]
a chandelier hanging from the ceiling	[reduced relative clause]
two of the windows shown on the photograph	[reduced relative clause]

Notice also non-finite comment clauses like:

That would make sense, knowing our Tony.

▶ **see**

117	Bare infinitive	185	Participles
51	Catenative verbs	186	Participles as other word classes
63	Comment clauses	187	Pseudo-participles
94	*-en*	118	*to*-infinitive
123	*-ing*	264	Tenses

158

Nouns: general

Nouns refer to or name people, things and concepts:

Iris   Bruno   man   head   bell   sea   sovereignty   time   good

Nouns are typically used after the articles: *a bell*, *the sea*. We often modify a noun in order to be clearer about which person, thing or concept we mean:

A Severed Head   Bruno's Dream   An Accidental Man
The Sovereignty of Good   The Time of the Angels

These groups are all noun phrases. We usually use nouns and noun phrases as the subjects, objects and complements of verbs:

noun phrase as subject — noun phrase as object

The novels of Iris Murdoch include these titles.

▸ **see**

38	Articles	168–73	Nouns: plural
161–6	Common nouns	174–7	Noun suffixes
159	Nouns: features	183	Objects
160	Noun classes	167	Proper nouns
178	Noun phrases	276	Word classes

159

Nouns: some semantic features

Like adjectives, adverbs and verbs, nouns include a number of paired opposites:

age/youth	*honesty/dishonesty*	*start/finish*
arrival/departure	*joy/sorrow*	*top/bottom*
front/back	*love/hate*	*war/peace*
height/depth		

> *'People at the top of the tree are those without qualifications to detain them at the bottom.'*
>
> Peter Ustinov, Attrib.

Like adjectives and adverbs, nouns may be gradable or non-gradable. A man can be *a bit of an idiot*, *something of an idiot*, *rather an idiot*, *quite an idiot*, *a ninety-nine per cent idiot* or *a total, unmitigated, complete idiot*. *Idiot* is gradable, whereas words like *death*, *algebra* and *sausage* are non-gradable.

Like adjectives and verbs, nouns can be organised into sets. *Buttercup*, *cowslip*, *daisy*, *poppy* and *primrose* are members of the wildflower set. *Cello*, *drum*, *horn*, *oboe* and *piano* are members of the musical instrument set.

Like adjectives, adverbs and verbs, nouns can stand in serial relationship; the following list of names for centres of population is a series, with each centre being larger than the one before:

hamlet village town city conurbation

Traditional grammar distinguished between concrete and abstract nouns, but this notional division is not a good guide to grammatical usage, nor is it easy to apply.

▸ **see**

105 Gradable/non-gradable

160

Noun classes

Nouns may be proper nouns or common nouns.

Proper nouns refer to a unique person, thing or concept:

Margaret Drabble   *Whitehall*   *Easter*

They always start with a capital letter; they are almost always singular and they usually have no article. All other nouns are common nouns.

Common nouns are either count nouns or non-count nouns. Count nouns can be counted, have plural forms and usually follow a form of the article:

boy   *flower*   *house*   *shoe*   *zoo*

Non-count nouns have no plural forms, are not used with the definite article and are followed by singular verbs:

furniture   *fun*   *information*   *salt*   *water*

> *'Sorrows are not known: love is not learnt.'*
>
> Rainer Maria Rilke, 'Die Sonette an Orpheus'

▸ **see**

161–6 Common nouns
80 Count/Non-count
158 Nouns
159 Nouns: features
178 Noun phrases
168–73 Nouns plural
174–7 Nouns suffixes
167 Proper nouns

161

Nouns: five kinds of common nouns

It is useful to identify five kinds of nouns. This helps us to be more exact in naming things. These are group nouns, part nouns, unit nouns, measure nouns and species nouns.

Notice these are typically followed by *of* + another noun.

▸ **see**

162 Group nouns
165 Measure nouns
163 Part nouns
166 Species nouns
164 Unit nouns

162

Nouns: group nouns

Group nouns name a set of objects and can be both singular and plural. They are also called collective nouns. We often use a particular group noun with certain objects to form a fixed phrase.

Some common examples are:

an army (of soldiers)	*a gang* (of workmen/thieves)
a band (of musicians)	*a herd* (of cattle/elephants/goats)
a bunch (of flowers/grapes)	*a litter* (of puppies/cubs)
a clump (of trees)	*a pack* (of cards/wolves)
a crew (of sailors)	*a shoal* (of fish)
a fleet (of cars/ships)	*a swarm* (of bees/insects)
a flock (of birds/sheep)	*a team* (of players)

Several group nouns name a group of people with a special relationship; these rarely havè the *of* + noun construction. Common examples are:

audience	*congregation*	*government*	*population*
choir	*couple*	*jury*	*staff*
class	*crowd*	*orchestra*	*trio*
committee	*family*	*party*	*union*
company	*generation*		

Notice that group nouns like *audience*, *jury*, etc. can be followed by both singular or plural nouns and pronouns:

> *An* (sing.) *English jury* (sing.) **consists** (sing.) *of twelve people.*
> *The jury* (sing.) *leave* (pl.) *the court to consider their* (pl.) *verdict.*

We use singular forms when we are thinking of the group as a whole and plural when we are thinking of individual members.

GUIDELINES

When the group is very large or indivisible (*administration*, *company*, *council*, *crowd*, *department*, *firm*, *generation*, *population*, *union*) singular forms are more likely. When the group is small (*couple*, *trio*, *quartet*) plural forms are more likely.

> *'The worst government is the most moral. One composed of cynics is often very tolerant and humane. But when fanatics are on top there is no limit to oppression.'*
>
> H. L. Mencken, *Notebooks*

see
71 Concord
160 Noun classes
161 Nouns: five kinds

163

Nouns: part nouns

Part nouns name parts of things. Common examples are:

half   *part*   *a quarter*   *the remainder*   *the rest*

Notice that we use these nouns when we are thinking of the part in relationship to the whole. When we are thinking of separate pieces of a large mass or number, we use unit nouns.

▶ **see**
164 Unit nouns

164

Nouns: unit nouns

Unit nouns name individual bits and pieces. We use them to turn lumps of mass into units. The most common unit noun is *a piece*; it is used with many non-count nouns:

a piece of cloth/coal/metal/paper/poetry/wood
a piece of advice/gossip/information/news

Other general unit nouns are *bit* and *item*.

a bit of cloth/fun/nonsense/wood
an item of clothing/expenditure/news

Many unit nouns form fixed phrases with non-count nouns. Common examples are:

a block of ice/wood
a drop of oil/rain/water
a flash of inspiration/light/lightning
a grain of corn/rice/sand
a heap of coal/dirt/rubbish
a lump of coal/sugar
a puff of smoke/wind
a sheet of ice/metal/paper
a speck of dust
a stick of celery/chalk
a strand of hair/wool
a strip of cloth/paper/wood

Notice an interesting small group of unit nouns which are usually only used with the negative. We use these fixed phrases when we want to stress the absence of even the smallest amount of something:

There was not a glimmer of hope/light.
There was not a grain of truth in the statement.
There was not a scrap of information to be had.
There was not a shred of evidence available.
There was not a speck of colour in her face.
There was not a wink of sleep for anyone that night.

> *'I have not slept one wink.'*
> William Shakespeare, *Cymbeline*

▶ **see**
80 Count/non-count
161 Nouns: five kinds

165

Nouns: measure nouns

These measure units of length, weight, volume and area:

Length	*inch foot yard mile*
	centimetre metre kilometre
Weight	*ounce pound stone ton*
	gramme kilogram tonne
Volume	*pint gallon litre*
Area	*acre hectare*

'Give him an inch and he'll take a mile.'

Proverb

see
161 Nouns: five kinds

166

Nouns: species nouns

Species nouns divide sets of objects or masses into types or species. These nouns are both singular and plural. Common examples are:

brand breed class kind make sort species type variety

We talk about:

a brand of chocolate/flour/petrol/sugar/whisky
breeds of cat/cattle/dog/horse/rabbit
a class of accommodation/animal/person/service
kinds of behaviour/fuel/humour/music/stone
sorts of coat/fruit/furniture/weather/wood
a species of bird/fish/monkey/moth/whale
types of entertainment/hobby/person/qualification/vehicle
a variety of apples/butterfly/lettuce/potato

The most general species nouns are *kind*, *sort* and *type* which can premodify most nouns. *Brand* and *make* are used about manufactured items. *Breed*, *species* and *variety* are used about living things which have evolved into categories.

Notice in the above examples all the count nouns are singular. We can use the plural form but it is more likely after a plural species noun, and it is more informal:

many kinds of dogs   *different makes of batteries*   *several species of monkeys*

GUIDELINE

Usually there is no article before the final noun, so: *a different kind of jacket* rather than **a different kind of a jacket*. When you add a premodifier, place it before the species noun: *an early variety of apple*, not **a variety of early apple*.

> *'The Republican form of Government is the highest form of government; but because of this it requires the highest type of human nature – a type nowhere at present existing.'*
>
> Herbert Spencer, *The Americans*

▸ see

38	Articles	161	Nouns: five kinds
80	Count/non-count	204	Premodifiers

167

Nouns: proper nouns

Proper nouns usually name an individual person (*Henry Moore*); place (*York*); work of art (*The Lotus Eaters*); ship (*the Titanic*) or a fixed part of the calendar (*Monday*, *September*).

Proper nouns usually start with a capital letter.

Proper nouns are usually singular and usually do not follow an article.

Personal names

In English we can informally call someone by their first (Christian or given) name: *Samuel*. Or by a familiar form of that name: *Sam*, *Sammy*.

We can, more formally, call men by their surname (last or family name): *Johnson*. Or we can use their full name: *Samuel Johnson*.

All first names and surnames start with a capital letter and have no article.

Titles come before the name(s) and also have a capital letter: *Dr Samuel Johnson*/*Dr Johnson*.

The normal titles are *Mr*, for men, and *Mrs*, *Miss* or *Ms* for women. Other titles show royalty (*Queen Victoria*), nobility (*Lord Peter Wimsey*), conferred honour (*Sir Alec Guinness*), military rank (*Sergeant Pepper*) or academic status (*Professor Quirk*).

Calendar items

These include festivals and religious periods, names of months and days of the week:

New Year's Day	*Christmas*	*March* etc.
Easter	*Boxing Day*	*Monday*
Good Friday	*January*	*Tuesday*
Easter Sunday	*February*	*Wednesday* etc.

These proper nouns are used rather like common nouns, because we sometimes use them in the plural (though not months) –

Where is the stress in **Park Street** and **Park Lane**?

> *'I always love to begin a journey on Sundays.'*
> Jonathan Swift, *Polite Conversation*

– and because we sometimes use the genitive form:

Monday's child is fair of face,
Tuesday's child is full of grace,
Wednesday's child is full of woe,
Thursday's child has far to go,
Friday's child is loving and giving,
Saturday's child must work for a living,
And the child that is born on the Sabbath day
Is fair and wise and good and gay.

Nursery Rhyme

We often use both definite and indefinite articles with calendar items:

the Easter before last   *the Christmas after next*
the Saturday before Christmas   *It was on a Monday morning*

We occasionally premodify them with an adjective:

Black Monday   *Pancake Tuesday*   *Ash Wednesday*   *Maundy Thursday*
Good Friday   *Holy Saturday*   *Remembrance Sunday*

Geographical names

These include names of continents:

Africa   *Asia*   *Australia*   *Europe*   *South America*

names of countries:

England   *Northern Ireland*   *Scotland*   *Wales*

names of counties:

Avon   *Humberside*   *Staffordshire*   *Sussex*

names of cities, towns and villages:

Bath   *Durham*   *Great Dunmow*   *Kilmarnock*

names of lakes, mountains and rivers:

Loch Ness   *Lake Windermere*   *Ben Nevis*   *Snowdon*   *the Thames*

Notice that some geographical names take the definite article:
the Netherlands   *the Alps*   *the Thames*   *the Atlantic*

Place names

The names of places like streets, squares and buildings are often formed from a name followed by a common noun – but both start with capital letters:

'Oxford Street   *Park 'Lane*   *Leicester 'Square*   *Regent's 'Park*
Westminster 'Bridge   *Kew 'Gardens*   *Sherwood 'Forest*

Notice that names ending in *Street* have the main stress on the first word. The others have the main stress on the last word. Some place names include the definite article: *the Albert Hall*, *the South Bank*, *the Mall*.

GUIDELINE

Most place names do not include the definite article. But if the name has postmodification with a phrase starting *of*, it must start with the: *the House of Commons*, *the Place of Westminster*, *the University of London*.

see
39 Articles with proper nouns
160 Noun classes
200 Postmodifiers
204 Premodifiers

168

Nouns: singular and plural

In English singular means one and plural means more than one. The nouns which normally take singular verbs are:

singular count nouns	*a man*	*the sky*
non-count nouns	*meat*	*the weather*
proper nouns	*June*	*Chester*

The nouns which are plural, and therefore take a plural verb, are:
plural count nouns *men* *girls*
nouns which only exist in the plural *jeans* *binoculars*

A few nouns can be singular and plural, and take both singular and plural verbs:
nouns with only singular forms *one/two Japanese* *one/two sheep* *one/many offspring*
nouns with only plural forms *a/many crossroads* *one/two series*

GUIDELINE

The exceptional use of plural proper nouns, e.g. *the Smiths*, is discussed under articles with proper nouns.

see
39 Articles with proper nouns
71 Concord
80 Count/non-count
167 Proper nouns

169

Nouns: regular plurals

The usual way to make a noun plural in writing is to add *-s* to the singular:
cat/cats *dog/dogs* *horse/horses*

Nouns ending in *-s*, *-ss*, *-sh*, *-ch*, *-x* and *-z* take the suffix *-es*:

bus/buses	*loss/losses*	*brush/brushes*
church/churches	*tax/taxes*	*buzz/buzzes*

Nouns ending in a consonant + *-y* change the *-y* to *i* and add *-es*:
ally/allies *family/families* *lady/ladies* *ferry/ferries*

Notice, however, that proper nouns ending in *-y*, when plural, do not do this:

Aldous and Julian Huxley ~ the Huxleys
the Orkney Islands ~ the Orkneys

Nouns ending in *-o* have plurals in either *-os* or *-oes*. These are the commonest *-os* plurals:

dynamos	*memos*	*radios*	*studios*
kangaroos	*photos*	*solos*	*videos*
kilos	*pianos*	*sopranos*	*zoos*

These are the commonest *-oes* plurals:

dominoes echoes heroes potatoes tomatoes vetoes

These can be spelt in either way:

buffalo(e)s cargo(e)s halo(e)s motto(e)s tornado(e)s volcano(e)s

Nouns ending in *-f* often change the *-f* into *-v* and add *-es*:

calf/calves	*loaf/loaves*	*thief/thieves*
half/halves	*self/selves*	*wife/wives*
knife/knives	*shelf/shelves*	*wolf/wolves*
life/lives		

Notice these exceptions: *beliefs*, *chiefs*, *roofs*: and three may be spelt in either way: *handkerchiefs/handkerchieves*, *hoofs/hooves*, *scarfs/scarves*.

GUIDELINE

The pronunciation of the regular plural endings *-s* and *-es* depends on the sound before the plural suffix. The pronunciation is:

after sibilants /ɪz/ – e.g. *horses roses wishes watches bridges garages*

after all other voiced consonants and vowel sounds /z/ – e.g. *beds bells days eyes* etc.

after voiceless consonants other than sibilants /s/ – e.g. *lips streets bricks beliefs cloths*

see
170 Irregular plurals
171 Plurals of compounds

170

Nouns: irregular plurals

The following common nouns are completely irregular:

man/men	*foot/feet*	*mouse/mice*	*ox/oxen*
woman/women	*tooth/teeth*	*louse/lice*	*penny/pence*
child/children	*goose/geese*		

Several Latin and Greek words in English keep their original plural forms. Others use regular English plurals in *-s*. Some have both forms, the foreign plural for technical use, the *-s* plural for general, everyday use: radio shops sell *antennas*; biologists talk about insects' *antennae*.

The commonest words that have kept their Latin/Greek plurals are: *-us*

cactus – *cacti* but also *cactuses*
focus – *foci* but also *focuses*
fungus – *fungi* but also *funguses*
locus – *loci*
nucleus – *nuclei* but also *nucleuses*
radius – *radii* but also *radiuses*
stimulus – *stimuli*
syllabus – *syllabi* but also *syllabuses*
terminus – *termini* but also *terminuses*

Most other words ending in *-us* have regular plurals: *circuses*, *viruses*.

-a

alga/algae *antenna/antennae* (but also *antennas*) *larva/larvae* *vertebra/vertebrae*

Most other nouns ending in *-a* have regular plurals: *arenas*, *diplomas*.

-um

addendum/addenda *aquarium/aquaria* (but also *aquariums*)
bacterium/bacteria *curriculum/curricula* (but also *curriculums*)
datum/data *erratum/errata* *maximum/maxima* (but also *maximums*)
memorandum/memoranda (but also *memorandums*)
minimum/minima (but also *minimums*)
referendum/referenda (but also *referendums*)
spectrum/spectra *stratum/strata* *ultimatum/ultimata* (but also *ultimatums*)

Notice some of these have become so anglicized that people use plural forms as though they were singular:

one agenda/ two agendas, *an insignia/ many insignias*.

Borrowed Greek nouns ending *-is* form their plurals with *-es*:

analysis/-es *diagnosis/-es* *parenthesis/-es*
axis/-es *hypothesis/-es* *synopsis/-es*
basis/-es *oasis/-es* *thesis/-es*
crisis/-es

The one exception is *metropolis/metropolises*.

Other plurals to note:

appendix/appendices (in books), but *appendixes* (in medicine)
index/indices (in maths) but *indexes* (in books)
criterion/criteria *phenomenon/phenomena*

▶ **see**
171 Plurals of compounds
169 Regular plurals

171

Nouns: plurals of compound nouns

Most compound nouns form their plural by making the second word plural in the normal way:

photocopy/photocopies *toothbrush/toothbrushes* *weekday/weekdays*

(But notice the plurals *lay-bys* and *stand-bys*.)

When the compound includes a postmodifier, the first word usually is made plural:

man-of-war/men-of-war   *son-in-law/sons-in-law*   *passer-by/passers-by*

GUIDELINE

Don't expect a lot of logic here. Irregular plurals are irregular and must be learned as individual items.

see
200 Postmodifiers

172

Nouns which always have a plural form

Some nouns have a plural form, but take a singular verb:

news

The main news is on BBC1 at 9 o'clock every night.

names of subjects ending in *-ics*

athletics   *classics*   *economics*   *linguistics*   *mathematics*   *physics*   *politics* etc.

names of some diseases

measles   *mumps*   *shingles*

names of some games

billiards   *darts*   *dominoes*   *draughts*

Some nouns only have a plural form and take a plural verb:

names of clothing having two equal parts joined together

braces	*pants*	*suspenders*
briefs	*pyjamas*	*tights*
jeans	*shorts*	*trousers*
knickers		

***Jeans were** first made by Levi Strauss, a San Francisco sail-maker, in 1850.*

names of tools or instruments having two equal parts joined together

binoculars	*pincers*	*scissors*
compasses	*pliers*	*spectacles*
dividers	*scales*	*tongs*
glasses		

*The golden **scales** over the Old Bailey **are** a symbol of justice.*

other nouns (although they may have a singular form with another meaning) include

barracks	*innings*	*savings*	*thanks*
clothes	*golf links*	*shambles*	*tropics*
congratulations	*oats*	*spirits*	*wages*
customs	*odds*	*stairs*	*wits*
goods	*outskirts*	*steps*	

*Wellington **Barracks are** in Birdcage Walk.*

Some nouns always have a plural form and can take both singular and plural verbs. Some common examples are:

crossroads *headquarters* *means* *oats* *offspring* *series* *species*

173

Nouns with zero plural form

Non-count nouns usually do not have a plural form and take singular verbs.

Names of nationalities ending in *-ese*

Burmese *Japanese* *Maltese* *Sudanese*
Chinese *Lebanese* *Portuguese* *Vietnamese* etc. take plural verbs

The ***Portuguese*** *are Britain's oldest ally.*

Nationality adjectives ending in other sibilants also have a plural form, but are used with generic meaning – all the people, followed by a plural verb:

British *Flemish* *Polish* *Swedish*
Dutch *French* *Scots* *Swiss*
English *Irish* *Spanish* *Welsh*
Finnish

The ***Welsh*** *are great singers.*

Animal names

Most animal names have regular plurals: *cat/cats*, etc. But – *cod*, *deer*, *plaice*, *reindeer*, *salmon*, *sheep*, and *trout* have no other form and take both singular and plural verbs.

Fish has two plural forms – *fish* and *fishes*. We use the regular plural when thinking about individual creatures/species: *deep-sea fishes*, *fresh-water fishes*. We use *fish* when we are thinking of catching or eating them: *fish and chips*. In the same way we can count numbers of *ducks*, *herrings*, *partridges* and *pheasants*. But hunters shoot *duck*, etc. and fishermen catch *herring*, etc.

3RD FISHERMAN: *I marvel how the fish live in the sea.*
1ST FISHERMAN: *Why, as men do a-land; the great ones eat up the little ones.*

William Shakespeare, *Pericles*

Quantity nouns like *dozen* and *hundred* have regular plural forms. But when they are premodified, they keep the singular form: *three dozen eggs*, *two hundred years*.

Other examples:

a few thousand pounds *eight million people* *three score years and ten*

Notice the singular form in:

a six-inch nail *a seven-stone weakling* *the fifty-metre dash*
a ten-foot ladder *a two-furlong post* *a ten-kilo weight*
a five-mile race

How are **bride** and **widow** unusual?

GUIDELINE

You may hear people informally say:
He's six foot tall and weighs twelve stone. In these cases the plural forms of the nouns are more correct.

see
39 Articles with proper nouns
80 Count/non-count
277 Zero forms

174

Nouns: male and female suffixes

Some pairs of nouns have male–female meaning without any gender sign:

boy/girl	*husband/wife*	*nephew/niece*
brother/sister	*king/queen*	*uncle/aunt*
father/mother	*man/woman*	etc.

Other pairs use suffixes to mark gender:

actor/actress	*god/goddess*	*prince/princess*
bridegroom/bride	*hero/heroine*	*steward/stewardess*
duke/duchess	*host/hostess*	*waiter/waitress*
emperor/empress	*manager/manageress*	*widower/widow*

Notice that *bridegroom* and *widower* add the suffix to the female noun.
Also notice these pairs: *businessman/woman*, *policeman/woman*, *salesman/woman*.

> *'Detectives are only policemen with smaller feet.'*
> Marlene Dietrich, *Stage Fright*

see
142 Marked/unmarked

175

Nouns: affixes describing size

Affixes meaning *small*. English has fewer diminutives than several other languages.

-ette
cigarette kitchenette launderette maisonette

-let
booklet leaflet piglet starlet

-ling
duckling hireling underling weakling

micro-
microbiology *micro-chip* *micro-computer* *micro-processor* *microwave*
mini-
mini-bus *mini-cab* *miniskirt*

Affixes meaning *large*.

macro-
macro-economics *macro-linguistics*

176

Nouns: suffixes naming people

-ant (added to verbs ~ *one who . . . s*)
accountant *assistant* *attendant* *consultant*

-ee (added to verbs ~ *one who is the object of the verb*)
addressee *appointee* *employee* *examinee*

-eer (added to nouns ~ *engaged with . . .*)
auctioneer *engineer* *mountaineer* *mutineer*

-ent (added to verbs ~ *one who . . . s*)
correspondent *resident* *superintendent*

-er (added very often to verbs ~ *one who . . . s*)
baker *driver* *lender* *singer* *writer*

also compounds: *bloodsucker*, *fire-eater*, *sword-swallower*.

Notice some of these nouns do not refer to people: *grasshoppers* and *leafcutters* are insects; *ant-eaters* and *retrievers* are animals; *flycatchers* and *woodpeckers* are birds.

-(i)an (added to nouns naming areas of knowledge ~ *one concerned with*)
historian *librarian* *mathematician* *musician*
(added to names of places ~ *coming from*)
Bermudan *Georgian* *Lancastrian* *Neapolitan*

-ist (added to nouns ~ *skilled in . . .*)
artist *cellist* *economist* *journalist* *physicist*
(added to nouns ~ *supporter of -ism*)
activist *communist* *feminist* *monetarist*

-or (added frequently to verbs ~ *one who . . . s*)
conspirator *director* *editor* *professor*

Also common forms with no verb base: *author*, *doctor*, *tailor*.
Also non-personal nouns like: *accelerator*, *projector*.

-ster (added to nouns ~ *one involved in . . .*)
gamester *gangster* *shyster* *trickster*

Notice all these are contemptuous.
Others (not contemptuous) include: *barrister*, *chorister*, *pollster*, *tipster*.

▶ **see**
70 Compound nouns

177

Nouns: suffixes naming abstractions

-age (added to verbs ~ *action or example of . . .*)
breakage carriage drainage marriage

-al (added to verbs ~ *the action of . . .*)
arrival denial dismissal proposal refusal

-ation (added to verbs ~ *the action/state of . . .*)
alteration education exploration imagination

GUIDELINES

Beware of changing stress patterns. The stress is usually on the first syllable of the *-ation* suffix: *'educate/edu'cation, 'magnify/magnifi'cation*.

-dom (added to nouns and adjectives ~ *the quality of being . . .*)
freedom martyrdom stardom wisdom

-(e)ry (added to nouns ~ *the condition, behaviour or place of . . .*)
archery bakery heraldry nursery

-ful (added to nouns naming measures/containers)
eyeful fistful cupful pocketful
(Notice that *earful* and *eyeful* when used metaphorically in a slang way are never plural.)

-hood (added to nouns ~ *the state of . . .*)
childhood manhood neighbourhood parenthood

-ism (added to nouns ~ *the teaching/practice of . . .*)
communism conservatism defeatism optimism
(Compare corresponding entries in *-ist*.)

-ity (commonly added to adjectives ~ *the state of being . . .*)
ability density elasticity equality falsity hilarity

GUIDELINE

The main stress is placed on the syllable before the suffix. This often means a changed stress pattern from the adjective: 'vulnerable/vulnera'bility, and sometimes change in the final vowel of the adjective: *pomp**ous**/pomp**os**ity*, *simil**ar**/*simil**ar**ity.

-ment (usually added to verbs ~ *the state of being . . .*)
amusement argument arrangement estrangement

-ness (commonly added to adjectives ~ *the quality of being . . .*)
gladness happiness kindness meanness readiness

-ship (commonly added to nouns and sometimes adjectives ~ *the role or state of . . .*)
chairmanship dictatorship friendship hardship

-ssion/ -sion (commonly added to verbs ~ *the act of . . .*)
conversion corrosion erosion explosion impression

-tion (commonly added to verbs ~ *the act of . . .*)
conversation deception information perfection

> *'Every form of addiction is bad, no matter whether the narcotic be alcohol or morphine or idealism.'*
>
> C. G. Jung, *Memories, Dreams, Reflections*

178

Noun phrases

A noun phrase (N.P.) is one or more words which we use in a sentence as subject, direct object, indirect object, complement or as prepositional complement.

Cordelia gave her instructions slowly.

N.P. as subject

(Proper names and pronouns usually stand alone as noun phrases.)

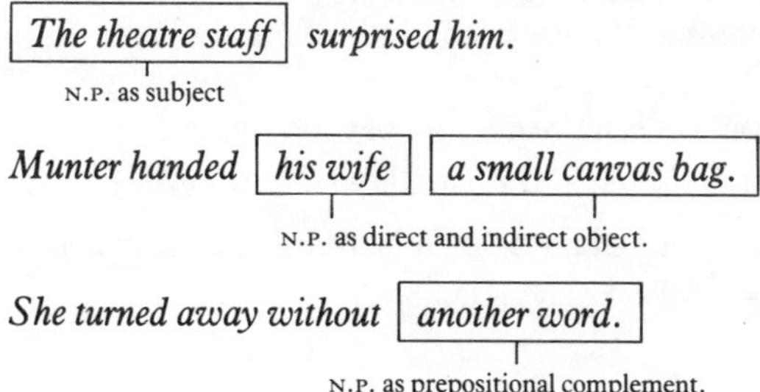

We call it a noun phrase because it is doing the work of a noun, and its most important part, the head, is usually a noun. The heads of the noun phrase above are: *Cordelia*, *staff*, *wife*, *bag*, *word*. Occasionally we use pronouns and adjectives as heads of noun phrases:

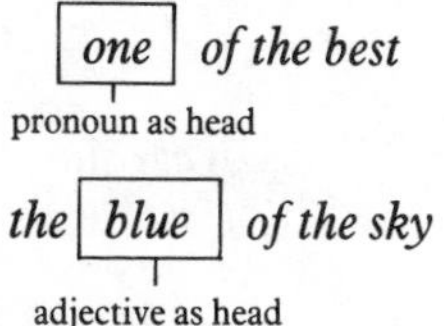

The simplest noun phrase with a common noun has a determiner and noun head:

a murder *the police*

Many noun phrases also have one or more modifiers; those we put in front of the head are premodifiers: those after the head are postmodifiers:

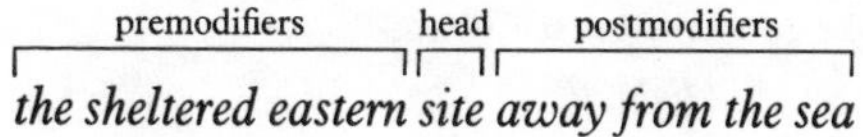

When can a noun phrase include a whole clause?

GUIDELINE

Yes, a noun phrase can include a whole clause – for example when the head is postmodified by a relative clause e.g.

premodifier | head | relative clause

a stone archway which led to a formal walled garden.

see
84 Determiners
200 Postmodifiers
204 Premodifiers

179

Numbers

Cardinal numbers, like *one*, *two*, *three*, which we use for counting, have a direct one-to-one relationship with ordinal numbers, like *first*, *second*, *third*, which we use for ranking. We use both kinds of numbers as determiners and pronouns:

I'm not the only one (pron.). *There are twenty-five* (det.) *others*.
I found the second (det.) *trial game easier than the first* (pron.).

With cardinal numbers and ordinal numbers it is useful to consider the related group of general ordinals.

see
180 Cardinal numbers
84 Determiners
182 General ordinals
181 Ordinal numbers
228 Pronouns

180

Cardinal numbers

Apart from *one*, which can only refer to a single count noun, all cardinals refer to plural count nouns:

one *of us here*
for ***two*** *minutes*
three *games of snooker*

GUIDELINE

We make a nice distinction of meaning by using the lower cardinals with or without *the*. Consider:

one *person you can trust* ~ *this person and possibly more*
the one *person you can trust* ~ *the only person*

Quantity nouns like *dozen*, *gross*, *hundred*, *thousand* and *million* do not take a plural form when we use a numeral determiner before them to refer to definite numbers:

You see . . . ***five thousand*** *in letters and in numbers*

On the other hand, when we want to talk about indefinite numbers we use these in their plural forms, followed by *of*: ***scores*** *of people*, ***hundreds*** *of spectators*, ***thousands*** *of pounds*.

Quantity nouns usually need *a* or *one* in front of them in the singular: *one dozen*, *a score*, *one hundred*, *a million*, etc.

Notice that for numbers over 100, in British English we use the word *and* between the last two spoken items, unless they are zero: 120 ~ *a hundred and twenty*, 2096 ~ *two thousand and ninety-six*. American English does not use *and* here.

GUIDELINE

If we do not want to be very precise about number – for instance in telling our age – there are several devices available to express approximate numbers. Talking about someone's age, we can say:

she's fiftyish ~ round about 50 years old
she's in her thirties ~ between 30 and 40
she's 30-plus ~ more than 30 years old

Talking about numbers of things, we can say:

30 odd/ 30 or so/ a good 30/ some 30 ~ 30 or maybe more

see

80 Count/non-count
84 Determiners
179 Numbers
181 Ordinal numbers

181

Numbers: ordinal numbers

These (determiner or pronoun) refer to singular and plural count nouns and non-count nouns. Ordinals as determiners usually follow another determiner:

to make a ***second*** *approach . . .*
the ***first*** *thought I had . . .*
I never felt so exhausted and relieved as after that ***first*** *match.*

Both cardinals and ordinals tend to follow other determiners, rather than stand before them:

that ***first*** *weekend*
our ***second*** *appearance*
another ***five*** *matches to play*

When we use both cardinals and ordinals together, we usually put ordinals first:

After his ***first four*** *trial games, Machin was given a contract.*

Ordinals commonly have pronoun use in dates. In British English *the* and *of* are obligatory: in American English they are not used.

August 26 ~ *August* ***the twenty-sixth***
26 August ~ ***the twenty-sixth of*** *August*

With kings and queens the article is also obligatory before the ordinal:

Elizabeth II ~ *Elizabeth* ***the Second***
Henry VIII ~ *Henry* ***the Eighth***

▸ **see**

180 Cardinal numbers
84 Determiners
182 General ordinals
179 Numbers
228 Pronouns

182

Numbers: general ordinals

These are words like *another*, *other*, *next*, *last* (determiners and pronouns), *others* (pronoun only), *past* (determiner only).

Another as pronoun refers to a singular count noun:

Wade jumps from one foot to ***another****.*

But as a determiner we use it to refer to plurals also (with the meaning *a further*):

another *part of the ruins*
Another *ten minutes pass.*

With cardinals, *another* always stands first:

another *three matches to play*

Other and *past* (determiners) may refer to both singular and plural count nouns and non-count nouns:

Some ***other*** *night, Dad. She's on edge at the moment. Has been for the* ***past*** *week. We'll try some* ***other*** *time.*

As a pronoun *other* may refer to singular nouns only:

He's neither one side nor the ***other****.*

next and *last* (determiners and pronouns) may refer to both singular and plural:

I was too busy for the ***next*** *few weeks.*
The trainer gave us his ***last*** *instructions.*
. . . ***last*** *of all . . .*

others (pronoun only) refers to plurals only:

I followed the ***others*** *into the small unheated dressing room.*

Notice that we can use *last*, *next* and *past* after their nouns: *Monday* ***last****, Friday* ***next****, for the whole month* ***past***. But this is less common than the determiner position.

GUIDELINE

Some general ordinals can go either before or after ordinal numbers:

*our **other** two children* *our two **other** children*
*on the **last** three occasions* *on the three **last** occasions*
*your **next** four meetings* *your four **next** meetings*

In these examples there is little difference in meaning; the first sequence is more common.

> *'Die, my dear Doctor? That's the last thing I shall do!'*
> Viscount Palmerston, last words

see

180 Cardinal numbers
80 Count/non-count
84 Determiners
179 Numbers
181 Ordinal numbers
200 Postmodifiers
228 Pronouns

183

Objects, direct and indirect

Like subjects, objects – direct and indirect – are either a noun phrase or a nominal clause:

noun phrase
Ralph shaded ***his eyes*** (D.O.).

noun phrase — noun phrase
I'll give ***the conch*** (D.O.) *to* ***the next person to speak*** (I.O.).

We've found out ***what we wanted to know****.*
[nominal clause as direct object]

But only nominal relative clauses may stand as indirect object:

Piggy asked ***whoever he met*** *his name.*
[nominal relative clause as indirect object]

Generally the direct object names the person or thing affected by the action of the verb: the indirect object names the receiver of the action:

Give [*him*] [*a fourpenny one.*]
person receiving D.O.–I.O. — that which is given – D.O.

Notice that a noun phrase (in this case a single word) can be a joint object of more than one verb:

. . . busy finding and devouring [*food*]
object of both verbs

Similarly a string of coordinate objects can stand after a single verb:

We're on an island . . . We saw ***no houses, no smoke, no footprints, no boats, no people.***

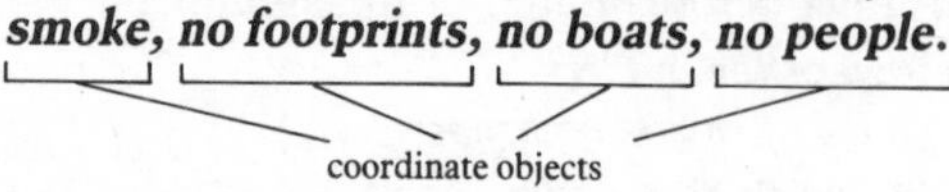

As above, a single object stands immediately after its verb, in the common pattern S. + V. + O., although for emphasis or other stylistic reasons we can front an object:

fronted D.O.

Shirts, shorts and different garments, they carried in their hands . . .

When both objects are present, the indirect object stands between verb and direct object in the pattern S. + V. + I.O. + D.O.

I'll (S.) *give* (V.) *him* (I.O.) *the conch* (D.O.).

Alternatively the indirect object is represented by a prepositional phrase in final-position. William Golding rephrases the above sentence only two lines later, when he uses the more expansive alternative pattern for the indirect object:

I'll (S.) *give* (V.) *the conch* (D.O.) ***to the next person to speak*** (I.O.).

Personal pronouns take the objective case where it exists for both direct and indirect objects:

They used to call **me** *Piggy.*

objective case

The heat . . . had given **them** *the complexions of newly washed plums.*

Reflexive pronouns have objective forms which we use for both direct and indirect objects when they refer to the same person or thing as the subject. (We say they are co-referential.)

Piggy hauled ***himself*** *up.*
Ralph found ***himself*** *a sapling.*

When we make an active sentence passive, it is the active direct object which becomes the subject of the corresponding passive sentence.

D.O. — subject

Ralph was doing something. ~ *Something was being done.*

I.O. — D.O. — subject

I'll give him the conch. ~ *The conch will be given to him.*

GUIDELINES

Sometimes we can omit one of the objects. Usually it is the indirect object which can be dropped:

He held out the conch [*to Piggy*]

You write a letter [*to your auntie.*] — indirect objects which we could drop

He'd never have got [*us*] *meat.*

Sometimes, however, we cannot drop the indirect object:

Piggy handed Ralph (I.O.) *his glasses* (D.O.) . . .

The sun . . . reminded him (I.O.) *how time was passing* (D.O.).

And with at least three common verbs we omit the direct rather than the indirect object:

Tell him △ *Teach me* △ *Pay the cashier* △

▶ **see**

77	Coordination	156	Nominal clause
269	Di-transitive verbs	178	Noun phrases
98	Fronting	246	Reflexive pronouns

184

Operator

The operator and the predication are the two parts of the predicate:

```
          ┌ Subject ........................................... I
Sentence ─┤
          └ Predicate ─┬─ Operator ........................ must
                       └─ Predication ..................... go
```

The operator is the first, or the only, auxiliary verb in a sentence. For example, in the following sentence, the two auxiliaries are *may* and *have*. *May* is the operator:

I ***may*** *have just killed Rachel.*

The predication is always the rest of the predicate, in this case, *have just killed Rachel*. The operator is important in the forming of interrogatives, negative declaratives and other constructions. Where there is no operator in a simple declarative sentence, like *I know*, we use the verb *do* as a dummy operator to form questions – ***Do*** *you know?* – and negatives – I ***don't*** *know*.

We change the order of the subject and operator to make other kinds of sentences from declaratives. This inversion is found in:

Yes/No questions

Have you *parted company?*

wh- questions, when the *wh*- word is not the subject

But what ***were you*** *saying?*

negative questions

Can't you *understand that?*

question tags

'I'll pack them, ***shall I?****'*

response questions

'I gave Julian a water buffalo . . .' 'Oh, ***did you?****'*

fronting of negative and semi-negatives

Nor ***is there*** *anything like one's hatred for an ex-spouse.*

fronting of *so* (meaning *me too*) etc.
'I feel shy now.' 'So ***do I.'***

hypothetical conditions with omitted *if*
What I wanted to do was to kiss her in the lift going down, ***should we*** *chance to have that momentary love to ourselves.*

The operator is important in the process of ellipsis. We often omit the subject and operator, for example, in:

statements
'Where's Arnold?' '△Gone to the library.'

questions
'... it's far more likely she will laugh.' '△Laugh?'

coordinate clauses
There were murmurs from the bedroom, then△ silence.

sub-clauses
(The market resembled) a seedy eighteenth-century barracks, though△ quiet at this time and sombre as a cloister.

We sometimes omit the operator alone in:

questions
'△You understand me?'

We usually omit the predication in

short answers
'Why have you taken up with Rachel?' 'I haven't△.'

response questions
'She agrees.' 'Does she△?'

question tags
'You still love Arnold, don't you△?'

sub-clauses
'So you want to be a writer?' 'I feel I can△.'

The operator and predication also figure in the process of substitution. Substitutes for the predication include:

do
'I couldn't get on the train. At least, I could have ***done*** *if I didn't mind being squashed, but I* ***do,*** *I'm a bit of a claustrophobe.'*

so
'So *am I.'* (the emphatic agreement following the above.)

do this
And if it means running two establishments, it means running two establishments. Other men have ***done this.***

do so
The mind is always sensitively filing and sorting the ways in which self-esteem (vanity) has been damaged. In ***doing so*** *it is at the same time industriously discovering methods of making good the damage.*

The operator is important in three other ways:

We add *not* or *n't* to the operator to form negative declaratives and interrogatives:

*'You **don't** understand.'*
*'Why **shouldn't** you have a private place?'*

In affirmative sentences with an operator, the mid-position for adverbs is immediately after the operator:

*I **should** instantly* (adv.) *have been sick.*

When we want to put emphasis on the modal meaning of a spoken sentence, we put the intonation nucleus on the operator, whether the meaning is positive or negative:

'Well I think it ˋwas like that!'
'How ˋcould you have told her?'
'I ought to see Priscilla,' I said, I think, aloud. But I knew that I just ˋcouldn't.'

GUIDELINES

The division of the predicate into operator and predication is an important feature of grammar. If you still have a problem identifying the operator, remember this – not all statements have an operator; but in an affirmative sentence, if one is present, it is normally the first word after the subject. In a *Yes/No* question, it is the first word.

see

86	*to do*	136, 137, 138	Inversion
88–92	Ellipsis	155	Negative statements
98	Fronting	235–44	Questions
74	Hypothetical conditions	263	Substitution

185

Participles

These are non-finite verb forms, the *-ing* participle (*breaking*) and the *-en* participle (*broken*). We use them most commonly in forming verb tenses: the *-ing* participle is used in all progressive tenses and carries the meaning of action in progress, the *-en* participle is used in all perfect tenses and carries the meaning of action occurring in the period before-then or before-now:

*You'll be **staying** in your apartment . . .?*
*He had already **discussed** the problem with her.*

The *-en* participle is also used to construct passive forms of all tenses:

*. . . he was often **photographed** . . .*

We use both participles in the following roles:

in catenative use

*he saw Stavrou **running** down the slope.*
*Stavrou saw his men **killed**.*

as other word classes

*. . . forgetting his **aching*** (adj.) *limbs . . . his **numbed*** (adj.) *hands*
*I heard some **shooting*** (N.).

When is an unattached participle acceptable?

in reduced relative clauses

. . . *the clothes* ***worn by the four women*** [defining]

. . . *a suicide note,* ***regretting his involvement*** [non-defining]

in reduced adverbial clauses

. . . *folded her arms,* ***as if holding herself together***

as sentence adverbials

Talking about Tony, *what's happening there?*

in absolute clauses

Wanda, ***a blanket wrapped round her,*** . . . *peered down.*

GUIDELINES

Most non-finite clauses are subordinate and have a grammatical relationship to their main clause. When a participle clause has no stated subject, we assume it is the same as the main clause subject. So, in the sentence: ***Coming*** *past Mary's, he noticed the hall light was on* – we assume that the *-ing* clause means, ***As he was coming*** *past.* But when we say: **Coming past Mary's, the hall light was on* – we cannot relate the participle to the subject of the main clause (i.e. the light was not coming past . . .). In this case we have used an unattached participle (or dangling participle). This is usually bad grammar, and sometimes ludicrous:

**Dipped in sugar, the children loved it.*

The unattached participle is, however, acceptable in comment clauses, sentence adverbials and absolute clauses. Another situation where an unrelated participle is acceptable is when we assume an impersonal subject. So in informal conversation, we can say, ***Coming*** *past Mary's house, there's a sharp corner* ~ *As one comes past/As you come past . . .*

Public notices may also escape the accusations of bad grammar for the same reason:

**When entering the Mosque
shoes should not be worn**

Perhaps we use unattached *-ing* participles in daily conversation more than we realise (*-en* clauses are more literary in style). Certainly, when both partners in a conversation fully understand what is meant, the utterance has passed the first test of all pieces of language: intelligibility.

Jack Higgins' Argentinian hero offers the half-French heroine a drink:

'Champagne?' he said. 'Being French I would presume it to be your drink!'

Both characters, no less than the reader, ignore the technical error.

see

2 Absolute clauses
24 Adverbial clauses
51 Catenative verbs
63 Comment clauses
94 *-en* participle
123–9 *-ing* form
157 Non-finites
3 Passive
186 Participles as other word classes
201 Participles as postmodifiers
247 Relative clauses
257 Sentence adverbials
264 Tenses

186

Participles as other word classes

The *-ing* and *-en* participles commonly stand in for word-classes other than verbs. The separate roles of the two participles are discussed elsewhere.

Here we examine participles as adjectivals and nominals. Some participles, like *surprising/surprised* are fully adjectival:

... *an* ***appalling*** *prospect*
... *a* ***depressing*** *air of poverty*
... *thoroughly* ***pleased*** *with himself*

These are participial adjectives. Other participles may appear adjectival, being used in post-position, but they cannot stand in attributive position:

the matters ***arising*** but not **the* ***arising*** *matters*
the men ***involved*** but not **the* ***involved*** *men*

These are clearly verbal participles, reduced relative clauses. But there are others we use attributively:

the ***pouring*** *rain* *a* ***passing*** *waiter* *a* ***parked*** *car*

Despite their adjective-like position, these participles still constitute reduced relative clauses. (We cannot say **a very parked car* or **the most pouring rain.*)

There are some participles which we only use attributively, and then only when compounded or qualified:

*a state-****owned*** *industry* *a diesel-electric* ***powered*** *submarine* Never **an* ***owned*** *industry*, etc.

For those adjectives which look like participles, yet have no corresponding verb, see Pseudo-participles.

We use *the* + participle as a singular nominal, to refer to a class of people:

It was no place for the ***faint-hearted.***

Other examples are:

the dead and the dying	*the bereaved*	*the handicapped*
the living	*the diseased*	*the injured*
the aged	*the disabled*	*the uneducated*
the afflicted	*the disfigured*	*the unemployed*

We use participles with this generic meaning in exactly the same way as common adjectives – *the old and the young*.

Notice how the passive *-en* participle lends itself to naming groups of people who have been afflicted in some way.

> *'There are more dead people than living. And their numbers are increasing. The living are getting rarer.'*
> Eugène Ionesco, *Rhinoceros*

▶ see

8 Adjectives and participles
94 *-en* participle
7 Generic use of adjectives
123–9 *-ing* form
156 Nominals
187 Pseudo-participles

187

Pseudo-participles

Several adjectives and compound adjectives look like participles from their *-ing* and (more often) *-en* endings, yet are not participles from verbs. For instance,

Beautiful women, exquisitively ***gowned****. (*to gown)*
. . . a shotgun ***crooked*** *in his right arm (*to crook)*

-en forms are particularly common in pseudo-participles meaning *having*, when the noun identifies a personal feature:

. . . herding cows, ***barefooted***
. . . a handsome, ***full-bodied*** *woman*
. . . he had a ***flat-boned*** *face . . .*

Other pseudo-participles include:
oncoming, *ongoing*, *outgoing*, *ingrowing*, *ingrown*, *overgrown*, *overhanging* and similar adverb + participial compounds. Also prefixed participles which have no complementary prefixed verbs: *uninspiring*/*uninspired*, *uninviting*/*uninvited* and *undismaying*/*undismayed*, etc.

Hence the humorist's play on words:

> *'He spoke with a certain what-is-it in his voice, and I could see that, if not actually disgruntled, he was far from being gruntled.'*
>
> P. G. Wodehouse, *The Code of the Woosters*

▶ see

69 Compound adjectives

188

The past perfect tense

This tense uses *had* in conjunction with the *-en* form, as in:

They ***had heard*** *the story before.*

It is marked for both past time and for perfectiveness, meaning that the state, event or habit had occurred before the point in the past we are thinking of. Just as the present perfect refers to before-now, the past perfect refers to before-then. The point in the past is either stated or implied:

He knew that he ***had been*** *lucky.*

Hazel ***had eaten*** *various roots in his life, but only once before* ***had*** *he* ***tasted*** *carrot.*

Sometimes it makes little difference whether we use the past simple or the past perfect:

*This had exactly the effect that Hazel (**had**) **intended**.*

It does not matter whether the intention was a single action at a before-then point (therefore needing *had intended*) or whether the intention continued up to the time of the effect (no *had* needed).

We particularly need the past perfect when we wish to emphasise the previousness – partial or otherwise – of the earlier action. This typically happens in back-shifted and other subordinate clauses:

I found ***I'd run*** *down to the edge of the wood.*

Things ***had*** *not* ***looked*** *better since they had first set out.*

He felt as he ***had (felt)*** *when they crossed the river.*

He sat on a bank until the light ***had*** *quite* ***faded****.*

(After *before* the past perfect clause refers to a later event than the main clause.)

Before they had left the farmyard, *the dog began to bark.*

Notice that to report verbs both in the past simple and in the past perfect, we use the past perfect. Therefore we do not know exactly which form was used for an original piece of direct speech when it is reported in this tense. Richard Adams writes:

Hazel . . . told them about the predicament of his warren in having no does, and how he ***had come*** *to look for some.* (Hazel may have said: *. . . and so I* ***came/have come*** *to look for some.*)

There is one occasion, however, when we must use the past perfect. Two events in the past may be described in the order that they occurred, using the past simple.

The doe died in the night, as Hazel learned next morning.

But in fact Adams puts the events into reverse order and is compelled to write:

Hazel learned next morning that she ***had died*** (past perfect).

GUIDELINES

We often combine modal auxiliaries with the past perfect in hypothetical clauses:

Without Fiver's encouragement, he ***would have lain*** *down . . . and given up.*

Pity it's going to be dark – we ***could have taken*** *him:* ***he'd have*** *enjoyed it.*

If it had not been for the metal staple, he ***might have*** *fallen.*

As with other tenses, the past perfect is incompatible with certain adverbials. Remember that the commonest uses of the past perfect are in back-shifted situations. Where we use it as 'one tense further back' from the past simple, or present perfect, we also back-shift the adverbs. For details see Indirect speech.

Explain: **Well, I ˇwas going shopping!**

> *'If I had had to choose between him and a cockroach as a companion for a walking tour, the cockroach would have won by a short head.'*
>
> P. G. Wodehouse, *Very Good, Jeeves*

▶ **see**

49	Back-shift	143	Modal auxiliaries
74	Hypothetical clauses	191	Past simple tense
110–15	Indirect speech	223	Present perfect tense
142	Marked/unmarked		

189

The past progressive tense

This tense uses *was/were* and the *-ing* form, as in *He* ***was singing.*** The *was/were* marks the tense for past and the *-ing* form gives it the sense of ongoing activity. We use it for a single past activity or a series of repeated actions happening at the past moment being thought about. Often the past progressive is a background tense to the past simple mirroring the relationship between the present progressive and simple tenses:

Two rabbits ***were sitting*** *together.*
What ***was*** *I* ***saying****?*
The sun ***was sinking ahead.***
They ***were*** *just* ***telling*** *me, before you came.*
. . . Hazel suddenly woke . . . something ***was attacking*** *him.*

The long-term past

In parallel with the use of the present progressive with certain frequency adverbs, we use the past progressive in the same way for repeated actions:

He ***was forever having*** *visions of the future.*
Bluebell ***was always telling*** *stories.*
He ***was constantly having*** *to urge them on.*

Past plans for the future

With a meaning similar to that of the present progressive, we also use the past progressive to indicate an intended action in the future (from a past moment):

I ***was going*** *out to get lettuces that morning . . .*
When it was clear that the rain ***was going*** *to stay . . .*

Notice a special use of this form. By giving emphasis to the past auxiliary, we mean that the projected event is not going to take place:

'Come and play tennis.' 'Well, I ˇ***was spending*** *the day in the garden . . .'*
~ gardening had been my intention, but you've persuaded me . . .

Back-shift

We use the past progressive as the back-shifted form of the present progressive:

Time they ***were going*** *to bed.* [after *it's time* . . .]

. . . *asked him what he* ***was doing*** *there* [in indirect speech]

As with the past simple, we use the past progressive for distancing ourselves from people, when a more direct approach would call for a present tense.

A bold *Watership Down* character says:

We ***ought to*** *stop here.*

Less aggressive members of the party select:

(past simple for politeness: *thought*; past simple for tentativeness: *might*)

We ***thought*** *we might stop here.*

Even more politely:

(past progressive for extra politeness: *were thinking*; past simple for tentativeness: *might*)

We ***were thinking*** *we* ***might*** *stop here.*

For further details see Back-shift.

GUIDELINES

The typical use of the past simple and progressive tenses together is when a single event (past simple) interrupts or co-occurs with an ongoing action (past progressive):

Fiver ***found*** *what they* ***were looking*** *for – a cowslip.*

He ***was getting*** *old, but his wits* ***were*** *still clear.*

In this last statement the ageing process is ongoing at the past moment being discussed, and clearly continues. The major contrast between the two tenses is the completeness of the action in the past simple and the incompleteness of the past progressive. Compare:

Schubert wrote five symphonies. ~ *he completed them.*
He was writing his last symphony. – did he finish it?

see

49 Back-shift
22 Frequency adverbs
142 Marked/unmarked
191 Past simple tense
225 Present progressive tense

190

The past perfect progressive tense

This tense uses *had been* followed by the *-ing* form, as in *She* ***had*** already ***been*** *working*. It is marked for a state, activity or series of actions at least partially completed before a point in the past. Like the past perfect it refers to before-then. The point in the past may be implied by the context, or stated.

Recent activity – before-then

When we use the tense without a time adverbial, we mean that the activity is recent:

They ***had been moving*** *in a group . . . they* ***had been trying*** *to maintain a steady pace . . .*

Longer activity

Sometimes the before-then activity is assumed to continue beyond the past moment:

Bigwig's shoulder ***had been hurting*** *him a good deal during the afternoon and he felt low.*
It ***had*** *now* ***been raining*** *for several hours.*

Notice that we can still use *now* for greater immediacy, for a past point in time. *Then*, of course, is also correct and more usual. Sometimes we imply that the earlier activity may finish at the past moment:

I don't know what ***I'd been expecting.***
They ***had been watching*** *every evening since he had left* (and now he was back).

As with other progressive tenses, we use the past perfect progressive as a framework of activity for a single past event. It is a narrative tense which authors often use in a flashback technique and otherwise is commonly used in hypothetical statements – *If Hazel and his companions* ***had been living*** *in their home warren, they would all have been killed.*

GUIDELINE

Even this remotest of tenses is used for distancing. But we use it to express a degree of diffidence which is almost forlorn. Compare:

Can I come?	most direct
Could I come?	politer, tentative
I hoped I could come.	uncertainty creeping in
I was hoping I could come.	Even more polite/tentative
I had hoped I could come.	Acknowledging unlikelihood
I had been hoping I could come.	Politely giving up hope

see
49, 188, 191 Distancing by back-shift
142 Marked/unmarked
188 Past perfect tense

191

The past simple tense

This tense uses the *-ed* form of the verb, as in *I came, I saw, I conquered.* The *-ed* marks the tense for past time. Most often we use the past simple to refer to events, states and habitual actions completed at some time in the past. But just as the present simple refers to events other than present ones, so the past simple is used to refer to events other than past. Thus we use it to refer to the present and occasionally the future when a verb is back-shifted in indirect speech, in wishing and hypothetical clauses. We also use it referring to the present time for the purpose of distancing ourselves.

Past events, states and habits

The event or state may be short or long, and a number of happenings in the distant past may be thought of as a single event.

*I **was** scared stiff that night.*
*I **knew** your mother well.*
*The gate **led** into the lane.*
*He never **let** himself become excited by . . . danger.*
*A plover **called** three or four times and was silent.*

Back-shift

*It's time we **got** back.* [after *it's time* . . .]
*I wish it **would** rain.* [after *wish*]
*Still, he thought, this **was** no time to pick and choose.* [indirect speech]
*I wouldn't care if my legs **weren't** so tired.* [in hypothetical clause]

We sometimes use a simple past form to refer to the present time as a marker of social distance or politeness:

***Could** you just go and try the rope, Hazel?*
*You **wanted** me, Hazel?*

These are alternatives for the less polite/deferential *Can you just go . . .? You want me?*

Future in the past

This is when we refer to a past event predetermined at a point in the future from an earlier one:

*She felt that she **was** going to die.*
*It was clear that the rain **was** going to stay.*

GUIDELINE

Notice how *perfect* adverbials (*already*, *since*, *yet*, etc.) are (in British English) incompatible with the simple past tense, just as *past* adverbials are incompatible with perfect tenses. The commonest *past* adverbials include: *ago*, *last week/month/year/yesterday* and dates.

Present adverbials like *this week/month/year*, *today* can stand with both perfect and past tenses.

see
49 Back-shift
74 Hypothetical clauses
110–15 Indirect speech
142 Marked/unmarked
275 Wishing

192

Performative verbs

These are verbs in which the speaking of the verb with the first person in the present simple tense performs the action itself. (With other persons and tenses, the verb describes the function.)

When we say *I forbid it*, the speaking of the verb is our act of forbidding.

To say *I apologise* is to make the actual apology.

Other performative verbs include:

advise	*challenge*	*offer*	*resign*
agree	*declare*	*predict*	*swear*
bequeath	*defy*	*promise*	*vow*
bid	*guarantee*	*request*	*warn*

We can use **hereby** before the verb to indicate that the act named by the verb is performed by its utterance: *I hereby promise*.

Notice how the events signalled by performatives are instantaneous:

I ***name*** *this ship Ark Royal.* *We* ***thank*** *you.* *I* ***baptise*** *this child Alexandra.* *I* ***congratulate*** *you.* *I* ***declare*** *the meeting closed.*

This is the use of the present simple tense with instantaneous meaning.

▸ **see**
226 Present simple tense

193

Personal pronouns

Those pronouns which are used as subjects and objects of verbs and typically refer to animate beings are personal pronouns. They are:

Subject		**Object**
I	1st person singular	*me*
you	2nd person singular	*you*
he	3rd person singular	*him*
she	3rd person singular	*her*
it	3rd person singular	*it*
we	1st person plural	*us*
you	2nd person plural	*you*
they	3rd person plural	*them*

We can also include as personal pronouns *one* and the reflexive *-self* series.

The subject forms are always used in subject position:

We *were so weary.*
Bengt and I *launched the dinghy.*

Object pronouns are used not only in object position and to complement prepositions:

It had worn ***them*** *apart.*
All four of ***us*** *took hold of the line.*

But modern grammar prefers to regard *as* and *than* as occasional prepositions to sanction phrases like: *as strong as* ***him****; better than* ***them***.

Purists, who prefer the subject pronoun here, argue that these are really examples of ellipsis, in which the operator has been omitted. To avoid awkwardness, do not use the subject forms without the operator. So:

either *as strong as* ***him****/better than* ***them***
or *as strong as* ***he is****/better than* ***they are***.

However, the object pronoun is fully accepted as subject complement, particularly in response utterances:

It's only **me**. *It wasn't* **us**. *That'll be* **him** *at the door.*

GUIDELINES

When personal pronouns are part of a coordinated noun phrase, we use the same subject or object pronoun form as we would if the pronoun were used alone. So:

George and I *are both older than* ***them***.
She and Val *are older than either* ***George or me***.

With coordinated personal pronouns, we have a preferred order both in subject and object form. So, use first person pronouns last, or if they do not occur, third person last. So:

you and I	*she and I*	*you and they*
you and me	*them and me*	*you and him* etc.

With two third-person pronouns, we prefer *he and she/ him and her* as sequence.

Two interesting points of usage concern *it* and *we*. *It* refers not only to inanimate subjects (***It's*** *quite interesting, that book*) but to non-count nouns (*Better weather, isn't* ***it****?*), to singular abstractions (*the break of day*) and whole sentences (*I didn't say what I felt about her, but* ***it*** *wasn't flattering*).

It also has other useful functions – empty *it* and introductory *it*.

We also has special uses. The editorial *we* occurs in newspaper journals to give anonymity to a writer:

We *believe the government is attempting a show of strength.*

The authorial *we* occurs in books:

We *now turn to a more difficult aspect.*

The rhetorical *we* is used in a collective sense:

We *have a preferred order of pronouns.*

The so-called royal *we* has disappeared from a democratic society and past examples are sources of amusement.

'We are not amused.'

Queen Victoria, *Notebooks*, 1900

What is unusual about **to eke out** and **to egg on**?

▶ **see**
77 Coordination
93 Empty *it*
134 Introductory *it*
228 Pronouns
246 Reflexive pronouns

194

Phrasal verbs: intransitive

These multi-word verbs have a verb + spatial adverb particle.

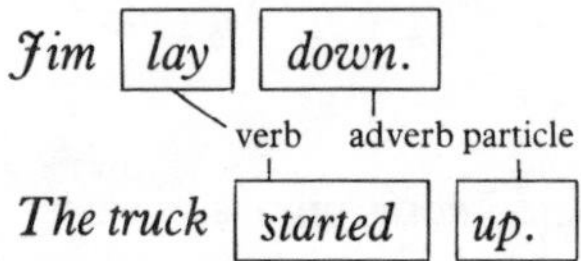

The particle cannot be separated from its verb: adverbs precede or follow the phrasal verb.

The truck suddenly started up, or *The truck started up suddenly.*

The adverbial particle is always fully stressed in speech and we frequently give it dynamic intonation:

He turned a'way.
They ran 'on past the 'stadium.

Some phrasal verbs are more idiomatic than others. Consider how we can fairly easily infer the meaning of the combinations: *sit down*, *sit up*, *sit back*. By contrast, *set out*, *take off* or *give in* are much more opaque, and we must learn their meanings as a single unit, almost without association with the common verbs *set*, *take* and *give*. In extreme cases the verb does not exist alone and only has meaning in combination with its particle, for example *to peter out*.
Common phrasal verbs include certain uses and meanings of:
break down/ out/ in/ up   *clear off/out*   *come about/ on/ off/ out/ to/ round/ up*   *fall off/ out/ through*   *get off/ on/ out/up*   *give in/ out/ up*   *go off/ out/ round*   *look back/ in/ round/ out*   *pull in/out*   *set off/ out*   *show off*   *turn out/up*   *wake up*

▶ GUIDELINES

Sometimes the difference between a phrasal verb and an ordinary verb + adverb is not too clear. Let us compare two meanings of *to fall out*:
A *The money* (s.) *fell* (v.) *out* (adv.).

B *The couple* (s.) *fell out* — phrasal verb

A carries the literal meaning, B the metaphorical, idiomatic meaning.
A can take an intervening adverb – *fell* ***right*** *out*,
B cannot.

A can tolerate inversion – ***Out fell the money***,
B cannot.

A is subject + verb + adverb. B is subject + phrasal verb.

▸ see

136 Inversion
153 Multi-word verbs
195 Phrasal verbs: transitive

195

Phrasal verbs: transitive

These multi-word verbs have a verb + spatial adverb particle + the direct object of the verb:

They were (v.) *taking off* (adv.) *their overcoats* (o.).
Jim switches (v.) *on* (adv.) *the car radio* (o.).

In these examples the sequence is subject + verb + adverbial particle + object (SVAO)

We can also say: *Jim switched the car radio on*, the order being SVOA. In most examples we can, in fact, put the direct object before or after the particle. But there are certain occasions when there is no choice.

We use the SVAO order:

when the object is a long one. To place it between verb and particle would disrupt their unity.

The Shanghai police had given up | *any attempt to control the crowd.* |
long object

in certain fixed phrases

. . . *as if to keep up* ***appearances***

when the object is an *-ing* clause, however short

He kept on ***running***.

and when the phrasal verb is strongly idiomatic.

The verb/particle unity must be maintained, whereas the identical (but non-idiomatic) forms for verb and adverb can be separated by an adverbial. Compare:

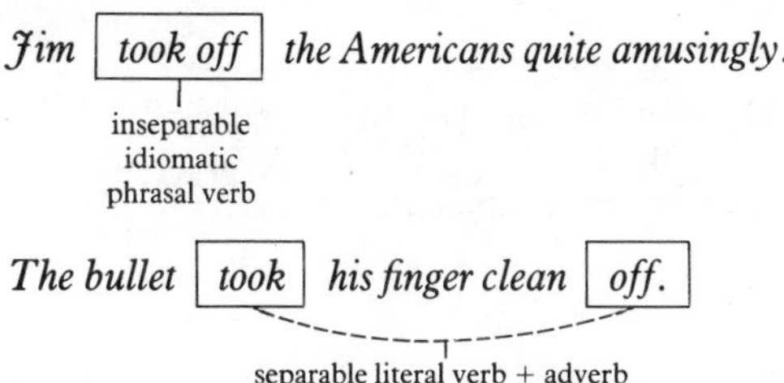

We use SVOA

when the direct object is a pronoun or a proper name

Jim pulled **himself** *away.*

He pushed **Dr Ransome** *back.*

in certain conventionalised idiomatic fixed phrases

We have to put **our heads** *together.*

to keep **one's eye/hand** *in*

to keep **one's hair/shirt** *on . . .*

and to avoid ambiguity:

. . . forever running the street down. ~ *forever disparaging their neighbours* (*running down the street* is likely to be taken literally)

Most transitive phrasal verbs have passive forms:

Jim's mother was cut off from him.

But where the phrasal verb has a fixed object, we never turn the idiomatic phrase into the passive:

. . . people gave up the ghost, not **the ghost was given up*

Common transitive phrasal verbs include:

back up   break down/in/off/up   bring about/in/off/out/round/up
call off/in/up   carry on/out   clear out/up   cut down/off/out/up
get back   give away/back/in/up   let down/off/out
make out/up   pay back/in/out   pull down/up   put across/down/off/on
ring off/up   run down/in/over/up   take in/off/on/over/up   try on/out
turn down/off/on/out/up

GUIDELINES

Notice that some phrasal verbs, like *get in* and *take off*, may be both intransitive and transitive. In the case of *get in* there is little change in meaning (*she got in/he got her in*). With *take off* the meanings are quite different (*the plane took off/he took his hat off*).

As with intransitive phrasals, transitive forms often have multiple and very different meanings. Consider *put off a decision* (postpone) *put off one's friends* (discourage) *put someone off by an action* (displease) *be put off by an interruption* (distract) *put someone off at the station* (allow them to alight) *put someone off to sleep* (anaesthetise) . . . and there are more!

> *'Never put off until tomorrow what you can do today.'*
>
> Proverb

see

153 Multi-word verbs

183 Objects

194 Phrasal verbs: intransitive

196

Phrasal-prepositional verbs

These multi-word verbs have a verb + adverb particle + prepositional particle + its complement:

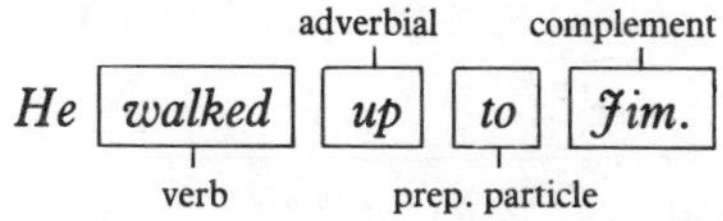

A few cases also require a direct object:

Basie put *Jim* *up to stealing . . .*
D.O.

These verbs constitute a smaller group than the others, are usually found in informal English and are idiomatic in varying degrees. Consider, for instance, how *to look down on someone* in its metaphorical sense (despite) is far less idiomatic than *to put up with someone* (tolerate) whose meaning is totally inexplicable from its components. Such verbs are strongly cohesive. Others are less so. In the case of verbs like *drop out of* and *get away from*, we feel that the prepositional particle has been added to a phrasal verb: indeed in such cases a cognate phrasal verb exists. Compare:

set off (leave) *set off for* (leave for)
fall out (argue) *fall out with* (argue with)
go in (enter) *go in for* (enter as a candidate)

Notice how the underlying phrasal verb may have a one-word synonym, but the phrasal-prepositional definition may need to repeat the prepositional particle. In other cases a phrasal verb exists, but the formally similar phrasal-prepositional verb is not similar in meaning. The phrasal verb *to stick up* is fairly transparent in meaning, whilst we feel that the formally similar phrasal-prepositional verb *to stick up for* (to take someone's side in a quarrel) is quite unrelated in meaning, and fully idiomatic.

Common phrasal-prepositional verbs include:

carry on with *catch up with* *do away with* *drop out of* *face up to* *fall out with* *get away with* *go back on* *go in for* *keep up with* *look forward to* *make up for* *put up with* *stick up for*

Transitive *fix* (N.) *up with* *put* (N.) *down to* *put* (N.) *in touch with* *put* (N.) *up to* *take* (N.) *out of* *throw* (N.) *back on* *turn one's nose up at*

▶ GUIDELINES

Phrasal-prepositional verbs in passive and relative structures can sound awkward, but we meet some in conversation:

It was recently done away with.
It's something I look forward to. (Or more formally, *It's something* **to which** *I look forward.*)

Here it is the prepositional complement which becomes the new subject. When we use a passive or relative with a transitive phrasal-prepositional verb it is the direct object we choose as the new subject. Consider:

They fixed him (D.O.) *up with a new suit.* ~ *He was fixed up with a new suit.*

Put the bill (D.O.) *down to my account.* ~ *The bill that they put down to my account.*

'If you don't like people, put up with them as well as you can. Don't try to love them; you can't, you'll only strain yourself.'

E. M. Forster, *Two Cheers for Democracy*

▶ **see**

153 Multi-word verbs
194, 195 Phrasal verbs

197

Possessives

There are two kinds of possessives. One group are determiners which stand before nouns, the other group act as pronouns and stand alone. Both groups show possession by persons or connection with impersonal nouns.

▶ **see**

84 Determiners
198 Possessives as determiners
199 Possessives as pronouns
228 Pronouns

198

Possessives as determiners

These are sometimes called possessive adjectives.

Here is the full list:

my *I'd left* **my** *shoes on the bus.*
our *Baba saw* **our** *friend, Tod Mead.*
his **His** *long face had an odd expression.*
her **Her** *cheeks looked flushed.*
its *(There was) a shoot of winter jasmine,* **its** *spare yellow flowers giving hope and brightness.*
your **Your** *fashions are original – rubber boots and a feather hat.*
their *The other couple sipped* **their** *port wine.*

All possessives as determiners may refer to count nouns, singular and plural, and non-count nouns. We can add *own* after the possessive determiner for extra emphasis or contrast:

Passing ***my own*** *gateway I expected to see my father with a shotgun.*
. . . each washed ***his own*** *half of the floor on Saturdays.*

But it is possible to omit the noun after *own*, when it becomes a pronoun:
It was her make-up, as I had forgotten my ***own****.*

▶ GUIDELINES

When we are talking about parts of the body in English, unlike some other languages, we usually use a possessive:
My *legs began to tremble.*
There were black circles under ***her*** *eyes.*
(They) turned to the door with ***their*** *hands to* ***their*** *ears.*

But with prepositional phrases, particularly when talking about injuries, we use *the*:
When Eugene was attacked, they kicked him on ***the*** *shin, hit him on* ***the*** *mouth and punched him on* ***the*** *nose. He also had a cut over* ***the*** *eye.*
He pulled me up by ***the*** *hand to show me the view.*

▶ **see**
80 Count/non-count
84 Determiners
100 Genitive

199

Possessives as pronouns

The corresponding pronouns are similar in form to the determiners. Here is the full list, with examples:

mine *He put out his hand for* ***mine****.*
ours *In the village next to* ***ours***
his *My face was almost on a level with* ***his****.*
hers *The Body was a friend of* ***hers****.*
yours *You can wash her hair; she can wash* ***yours****.*
theirs *Everyone had invitation cards: Kate and Baba pretended they had lost* ***theirs****.*

Notice that spoken possessive pronouns are usually stressed:
*(His tea) tasted of hair shampoo, ˌso did ˈ****mine****.*

We use the possessive pronoun in the same way as the double genitive. Compare:
a friend of ***John's*** *a friend of* ***his***
a decision of the ***government's*** *a decision of* ***theirs****.*

▶ GUIDELINE

Its is never used as a pronoun. When used as a determiner, it is never spelt with an apostrophe (*It's* ~ *It is* or *It has*).

We do not use possessive determiners with certain other determiners. Instead we use the appropriate possessive pronoun. Compare:

this + my + idea > this idea of ***mine***
a + your + brother > a brother of ***yours***
several + their + silly ideas > several silly ideas of ***theirs***

'The world is too much with us; late and soon
Getting and spending, we lay waste our powers:
Little we see in Nature that is ours.'

William Wordsworth, 'Sonnet'

▸ see
84 Determiners
104 Double genitive
228 Pronouns

200

Postmodifiers

These are single words, phrases or clauses which stand after the head in a noun phrase, giving more precise meaning to the head.

head
a man ***of strong passions***

head
its composition, ***which was two years ago***

Postmodification may consist of one or more of the following: prepositional phrases, relative clauses, non-finite clauses, adverbials and adjectives.

Prepositional phrases

This is the commonest kind of postmodifier. Most prepositional phrases consist of preposition + noun:

near (prep.) *Rome* (N.)

But other word classes may follow the preposition:

pronoun: *for* ***him***
wh-clauses: *on* ***what he was paid***
-ing clauses: *for* ***resuming his studies***

The major function of prepositional phrases is as adjectival postmodifier in a noun phrase:

two youths ***on white horses***
authors ***of today***

Relative clauses

We introduce relative clauses by one of the relative pronouns, *who*, *whom*, *whose*, *that*, *which* and *what*, and also the relative adverbs *when* and *where*. The *wh-* relative points back to the noun head of the noun phrase, its antecedent:

head

The proudest boast of men **who had served under my father** *was . . .*

head

(I couldn't) criticise the Emperor Augustus, **who was my maternal grand-uncle**.

The first of these two postmodifiers is a defining clause, the second non-defining.

Usually, as above, the relative immediately follows the head, unless it is the object of a preposition. Then, the preposition stands between head and relative:

head prep. relative

a dull affair, by which I set little store

head prep. relative

a garrison town through which he passed

The relative may be omitted in defining clauses when it is in the objective case. This zero pronoun produces a contact clause:

head relative clause

the drunken nonsense △ they deliver

head relative clause

the only truth △ he spoke

Non-finite clauses

Non-finite clauses may be regarded as reduced forms of relative clauses. There are three forms of non-finite clauses: *-ing* participle clauses, *-en* participle clauses and *to*-infinitive clauses:

. . . a lofty promontory **overlooking the sea**

Antony, **incited by Cleopatra,** *sent Octavia a bill of divorce.*

. . . made no attempt **to conceal his . . . depravity**

The *-ing* participle clauses and *-en* participle clauses are particularly close in form and function to full relative clauses, even to the extent of having the defining/non-defining distinction. Compare:

Among the people **removed from Rome** *during the famine were the sword-fighters.* [defining non-finite clauses]

There is a popular ballad, **still sometimes sung by old people** *. . .* [non-defining non-finite clause.]

Postmodifying infinitive clauses may be both active and passive:

nothing **to eat**
nothing **to be done**

Unlike *-ing* and *-en* clauses, infinitive clauses as postmodifiers have parallels with relative clauses where the relative pronoun can be subject, object and adverbial:

a trick **to win** *popular affection* ~ *a trick which would win . . .* [subject]
no knife **to cut** *(his food) up with* ~ *with which he could cut . . .* [object]
time **to pay** *her the last offices* ~ *when he could pay . . .* [adverbial]

Notice that where the head of the noun phrase is the object of the infinitive verb, we often add *for* + subject:

very little water (**for him**) *to drink, and none* (**for him**) *to wash in.* [head: *water*]

Adverbials as post-modifiers

We use certain adverbials as postmodifiers. A few single adverbs can postmodify:

Augustus **alone**
the crowd **outside**
the long march **back**

Finite clauses starting with *wh-* words may have an adverbial relation with the head word (of time/place/manner) as clauses of time, place or manner etc.:

the President's box **where Caligula sat** [place]
that stormy day **when he had sailed** . . . [time]

Also adverbial clauses introduced by zero pronoun or *that* or *to*-infinitive:

the weeks **I spent in Capua** [time]
the day **that my sword-fighter was beaten** [time]
a means ***to escape death*** [purpose]

Adjectives as postmodifiers

Adjectives normally precede their nouns, but in certain cases postmodify them. For example, as a (written) stylistic device we place a string of adjectives after the noun head:

She was a typical Roman matron of ancient legend – ***strong, courageous, modest, witty, pious, fertile and chaste.***

We always place adjectives after *some-* and *any-* compounds:

something **particular**

and in certain official fixed phrases:

cipher **extraordinary**
heir **presumptive**

Notice also:

astronomer **royal** *chairman* **elect** *courts-***martial** *director* **designate**
lords **temporal** *lords* **spiritual** *postmaster* **general**

'Time present and time past
Are both perhaps present in time future,
And time future contained in time past.'

T. S. Eliot, *Four Quartets*

GUIDELINE

In some languages the adjective follows the noun far more often than in English. If in doubt, put the single adjective first.

see

201	Adjectives	200	Postmodifiers
19	Adverbials	220	Prepositional phrases
82	Defining/non-defining	249	Relative clauses
118, 157, 187	Non-finite clauses	277	Zero forms
178	Noun phrase		

201

Post-position adjectives

These are adjectives which follow the nouns they modify (postmodifiers).

Adjectives must follow: *some-/any-/no-/every-* series words. We dislike ***anybody rude***, we avoid ***something menacing***, we don't go ***anywhere dangerous. Someone new***, ***something unusual*** or ***somewhere different*** are all attractive.

Obviously adjectives which are only used attributively cannot take this position: **nobody mere* **anybody elder* **something sheer* are nonsense.

> *'Nothing great was ever achieved without enthusiasm.'*
> Ralph Waldo Emerson, *Essays*

Many *a*-series adjectives are used after their nouns. In a hospital we may find some *patients awake* and other *patients asleep*, but all the *nurses alert*. In an accident at sea, there may be *ships ablaze*, *boats adrift*, *ropes alight*, *decks awash*, but, we hope, most *seamen alive*.

Some *a*- adjectives as postmodifiers are commonly found with certain nouns in almost fixed phrases:

with arms akimbo   ***with feet astride***   ***man alive!***   ***a race apart***
the watch ashore

When a writer uses several adjectives in a description, he may place some after the noun as part of his literary style:

> *Riordan, an abnormally tall, abnormally thin man,* ***black-haired, deeply tanned and dressed*** *in a near-ankle-length black raincoat, . . . was literally shaking with rage as he stood facing his audience, his fists* ***ivory-knuckled*** *on the table before him.*
> Alistair MacLean, *Floodgate*

Adjectives with complements cannot stand in attributive position but can follow their nouns. Consider:

The landrover is a ***suitable*** *vehicle.* [attributive – no complement]
The landrover is a vehicle ***suitable for rough roads****.* [postmodifying complement]

The landrover is a* **suitable for rough roads *vehicle.*
[attributive complement – unacceptable]

There are many adjectives which may take a complement. The complements include prepositional phrases, *to-* infinitive clauses or *that*-clauses:

India was **desperate for independence**. [prep. phrase]
India was **desperate to be independent**. [*to*-infin clause]
Indians were **desperate that they should become independent**. [*that*-clause]

All three kinds of complement can follow the noun: *A country desperate for independence. A country desperate to be independent. People desperate that they should become independent.* The post-modifier may be an *-en* or *-ing* participle:

Men and women **selected** *to be Air Force officers train at Cranwell.*
Men and women **chosen** *for training as Royal Navy officers go to Dartmouth.*
Men and women **training** *at Sandhurst become Army officers.*

> *'A floor so cunningly laid that no matter where you stood it was always under your feet.'*
> Spike Milligan and Eric Sykes, *The Goon Show*

Adjectives ending in *-able* or *-ible* are usually attributive: *a possible answer, available tickets.* But a few can stand after the noun:

There's no answer **possible**. *There are no tickets* **available**. *Tell us about the work* **obtainable**. *Take us to the people* **responsible**.

More commonly, *-able/-ible* adjectives can follow the noun when it is restricted, e.g. by a superlative adjective: *only, first, last, single,* etc.

the latest **possible** *time/the latest time* **possible**
the only **recognisable** *feature/the only feature* **recognisable**
the last **available** *seats/the last seats* **available**

Notice, however, that we do not say **the earliest typewriter* **portable**, **the rarest snail* **edible** or **a single book* **readable**.

▶ GUIDELINE

No clear explanation for this is available. Treat the examples above as fixed phrases.

▶ **see**

1	*a-* series words	200	postmodifiers
47	Attributive adjectives	218–20	Prepositional phrases
65–8	Complementation of adjectives	119	*to*-infinitive
185	Participles		

202

Participles as postmodifiers

-ing participles and *-en* participles are frequently used before the noun in attributive positions (see adjectives and participles). Some may also be used as postmodifiers, with no change of meaning:

*before the **following** Sunday/before the Sunday **following***
*during the **approaching** season/during the season **approaching***
*within the **agreed** time/within the time **agreed***
*on the **appointed** date/on the date **appointed***

Others appear in both positions but with a different meaning – the difference is largely that the attributive position carries a permanent meaning, and post-position a more temporary one:

the '***spoken*** ˌ*language*	*the language* ˌ***spoken***
the ***re'corded*** ˌ*message*	*the message* ***re'corded***
the '***used*** ˌ*stamps*	*the stamps* ˌ***used***
the ***per'forming*** ˌ*dog*	*the dog* ***per'forming***

Here, the post-modifier is much more like a verb. Notice also that the stress is even in the first column, but on the participle in the second the focus has moved from the thing to the action. Finally, a number of participles appear only in the post-modifying position: Consider: '*Among the places **visited** . . .*' We do not say **the **visited** places*. Other examples:

*items **left/taken***
*kindness **shown/received***
*money **sent/spent***
*people **involved/questioned***
*permission **granted/obtained***
*persons **objecting/waiting***
*victims **found/discovered***

Customers will be charged for any items broken

Notice in china shop

GUIDELINE

Reading the above notice, a customer will interpret the last two words as *items (which get) broken*. This is a relative clause which has been reduced by having certain words omitted. It is useful to think of all examples of adjectival postmodifiers as being reduced relative clauses.

> *'A child mis-educated is a child lost.'*
>
> John F. Kennedy, Attrib.

see

8 Adjectives and participles
5 Adjective positions
200 Postmodifiers
247 Relative clauses

203

Predicative adjectives

a- series adjectives normally take the predicative position.

Aloof and *alert* are the exceptions, and can take both positions:

the ***aloof*** *men sounded* **alert**   *the* **alert** *woman sounded* **aloof**.

Two small groups of adjectives usually take the predicative position only: health adjectives and three emotional adjectives: *faint*, *ill*, *poorly*, *well* and *unwell* are always predicative, when referring to health. They can all follow *She looks* . . . But * *a faint/poorly/well person*, * *an ill/unwell person* are unacceptable.

Notice that *healthy* and *sick* take both positions. *Glad*, *content* and *upset* are always predicative: *she looks* **content**, *she sounds* **glad**, *she seems* **upset**. But never * *a content lady* * *a glad man* * *an upset person*.

A large group of adjectives take complements. With their complements they can only stand in predicative position. For example, *able* and *fond* as regular adjectives are used in both attributive and predicative position – *an able man*, *a fond glance*. But when they take a complement, they must follow the verb.

> *'At bottom, Carlyle was probably fond of the Americans, but he was able to conceal it.'*
>
> Mark Twain, *My First Lie*

GUIDELINE

Think of adjective + complement phrases as verbs. *To be crazy/mad/wild about* ~ *to adore*; *to be nervous/afraid/timid about* ~ *to fear* etc.

see

1 *a*-series words
4 Adjectives: general
65–8 Complementation of adjectives

204

Premodifiers

These are usually single words which stand between any determiners and the head in a noun phrase making its meaning more precise:

determiners	premodifiers	head
the two	*leading social*	*orders*.

Premodifiers are commonly adjectives, participles, other nouns, compounds and adverbs.

Adjectives as premodifiers most often combine with one or more determiners:

her (det.) *real* (adj.) *feeling*
this (det.) *curious* (adj.) *history*

We join two or more adjective premodifiers with *and*, as in any listing sequence:

the ***secret and illegitimate*** *pride*
a ***suspicious, jealous, reserved, and melancholy*** *temperament*

And we may premodify the adjectives themselves e.g. by adverbs:

a far (adv.) *greater* (adj.) *appetite* (head) *for blood*

GUIDELINES

We only use *and* between the last two premodifiers of a list if they are attributes of the same kind. Notice how neither Crispus nor Posthumus use *and* in the following:

A simple Roman Knight, Crispus? Then you had better take a few simple Roman riding lessons.

Participles, both *-ing* and *-en* forms, may be used as premodifiers:

ordinary, ***easy-going*** *people*
the ***insulting*** *remark*
the ***established*** *custom*
the ***armed*** *rebellion*

Nouns in attributive use including the genitive are common premodifiers:

the ***frontier*** *provinces* *a* ***soldier's*** *life*
sovereign *power* *a* ***fool's*** *errand*

GUIDELINE

In the examples above, the genitive form has a generic or non-specific meaning: *a soldier's life* ~ *the life of a soldier, a fool's errand* ~ *one appropriate for a fool.*

When, however, we use the genitive with a specific meaning, as in *Augustus's oldest friend*, the genitive is functioning as a determiner (= *his*). Most genitives therefore are determiners and only premodifiers when we use them with a generic meaning. Compounds of various kinds may act as premodifiers:

a tall, dark-haired, fair-skinned, heavily-built *man*
seven-months *children* ***free-born*** *Romans*
petty ***jack-in-office*** *oppression*

We use only a few adverbs as premodifiers. These are usually focusing adverbs like *just*, *only*, *exactly*, *very*, *purely*, *simply*, *chiefly*, *especially* and *even*; or intensifiers like *merely*, *fairly*, *quite*, and *rather*:

some were ***even*** *honest shepherds*
merely *a matter of routine*
rather *a problem* ***quite*** *a surprise*

GUIDELINES

It is worth remembering that premodifiers are only part of the noun phrase, which is likely to have one or more determiners and may also have some post-modifiers. Then the premodifiers and post-modifiers may have (adverbial) modifiers:

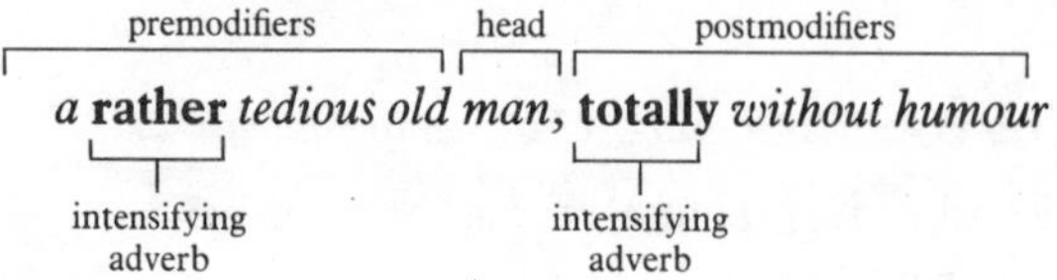

see

4 Adjectives
8 Adjectives and participles
11 Adjective order
47 Attributive adjectives
69 Compounds
14 Focusing adverbs
130 Intensifiers
7 Nouns as adjectives
178 Noun phrase
185 Participles
200 Postmodifiers

205

Prepositions

Prepositions are, as the name suggests, words which we typically place before other word classes, most frequently noun phrases, e.g. ***on** the road*, ***before** the ending of the day*.

They are a minor word class in that their function in a sentence – showing relationships – is often more important than their actual meaning: they are structural words as opposed to content or lexical words. Like other minor word classes they are a closed class. That is, we can write a complete list of prepositions in English, one that is unlikely to change or be added to.

Most prepositions are simple in that they consist of one word. Common examples are:

above	*down*	*off*	*to*
after	*for*	*on*	*under*
at	*from*	*over*	*until*
before	*in*	*past*	*up*
below	*into*	*since*	*with*
by	*of*	*through*	*without*

Complex prepositions consist of more than one word, but function in the same way as simple ones:

*The love shone **out of** her face.*
*She kissed the baby on the top of its head **by way of** punctuation.*

Common complex prepositions include:

according to	*due to*	*in front of*	*on top of*
as well as	*except for*	*in spite of*	*out of*
away from	*by means of*	*in relation to*	*up to*
because of	*in comparison with*	*on account of*	*with reference to*

Notice the difference between:

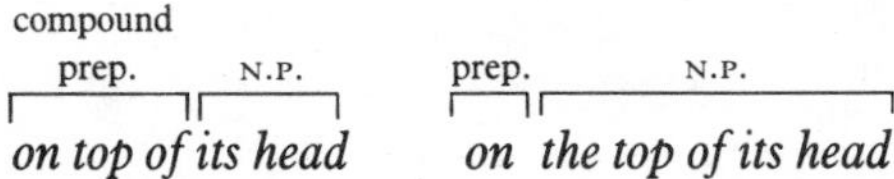

Many nouns, verbs and adjectives have fixed prepositional complementation. Consider: *independence* ***from***, *to depend* ***on***, *independent* ***of***. When in doubt, consult a good dictionary. However, the commonest prepositions do have a certain consistency of meaning.

GUIDELINE

There is no such complex preposition as *off of*. Expressions like *Get off of my back* are only heard from uneducated speakers.

see

65	Adjectives and prepositional phrases	215	Prepositions in relative clauses
206	Prepositions and overlap	218	Prepositional phrases: form
207	Prepositions: meaning	219	Prepositional phrases: function
208–13	Prepositions: types	220	Prepositional phrases: position
		276	Word classes

206

Prepositions and overlap with other word classes

Many prepositions also function as adverbs, participles and conjunctions. Compare:

Paul's mother came to (prep.) *tea.* ~ *She visited and had tea.*
Paul's mother came to (particle). ~ *She regained consciousness.*
The ship went under (prep.) *the bridge.* ~ *It passed beneath the bridge.*
The ship went under (adv.). ~ *It sank.*
. . . after (prep.) *her arrival . . . after* (conj.) *she had arrived*

The following are both prepositions and adverbs:

aboard	*beneath*	*less*	*since*
about	*besides*	*near*	*through*
above	*between*	*off*	*throughout*
across	*beyond*	*on*	*under*
along	*by*	*opposite*	*underneath*
around	*down*	*over*	*up*
before	*in*	*outside*	*within*
behind	*inside*	*past*	*without*
below			

The following are both prepositions and conjunctions:

after as before but for than since till until

Some prepositions have related forms as adverbs and conjunctions:

Preposition	**Adverb**	**Conjunction**
after	*afterwards*	*after*
because of		*because*
before	*beforehand*	
beside/besides	*besides*	
except for		*except*
in case of		*in case*
in front of	*in front*	
instead of	*instead*	
on top of	*on top*	
out of	*out*	

Sometimes words which we use as both preposition and adverb are called particles. It is less confusing, however, to reserve the term particle for the second element of prepositional and phrasal verbs.

The following are prepositions only:

against	*beside*	*in front of*	*towards*
at	*during*	*into*	*with*
among	*for*	*on top of*	*without*
amongst	*from*	*toward*	

GUIDELINE

For anyone who finds this confusing, you can explain that the important thing to understand about prepositions is that they show the relationship between things, people or events:

one ***after*** *the other*   *him* ***instead of*** *her*

sheltering ***on account of*** *the rain*

see
194, 195 Phrasal verbs
221, 222 Prepositional verbs

207

Prepositions: meaning

The meaning of prepositions is diverse. Some, like *during*, have a fairly clear meaning; others are less easy to define. *Of*, for example, has seventeen different entries in the Shorter Oxford Dictionary. However, we can identify a large class which refers to relationships of space and place, another overlapping class which refers to relationships of time and a number of smaller classes. Many members of each class also have metaphorical meanings.

In another dimension we can group prepositions according to their orientation, whether they help us to think of static relationships to:

a fixed POINT in space or time (***at*** *home/night*).
a LINE or SURFACE in space or time (***on*** *the river/that day*).
an AREA or VOLUME in space or time (***in*** *the field/the air/the future*).

or a relationship of motion to a POINT or LINE etc. in space or time (***towards*** *the wall/evening*).

or a pervasive relationship within an AREA or DISTANCE of space or time (***throughout*** *the house/day*).

This gives five major types, with several minor ones. Prepositions may belong to more than one type, according to their range of meanings, several having spatial, temporal and metaphorical meanings.

▸ see
208 *At*-type prepositions
209 *On*-type prepositions
210 *In*-type prepositions
211 *Towards*-type prepositions
212 *Throughout*-type prepositions
213 Other prepositional meanings

208

At-type prepositions

These identify a static relationship with a fixed point in space or time and also have related metaphorical meanings:

Preposition	Space/Place	Time	Metaphorical
after	*'n' is after 'm'*	*after lunch/the bell*	*after all/consideration*
around	*around the table/us*	*around the clock/noon*	*around seventy*
at	*at home/the market*	*at night/ten/Easter*	*at a glance/rest*
away from	*away from school*	*a year away from now*	*take two away from ten*
before	*before the end/the corner*	*before midnight/ Friday*	*before you could blink*
beyond	*beyond Mars/the hill*	*not beyond 6 p.m. tomorrow*	*beyond tears/the grave*
by	*by the fire*	*by now/midsummer*	*keep it by you*
far from	*far from London*	*not far from now*	*far from easy/the truth*
near	*near the centre/the shops*	*near closing time/ death*	*near exhaustion/ perfection*
off	*off centre/limits*		*off key*
on	*on page 2/horseback*	*on Tuesday/one occasion*	*on receipt/reflection*
round	*round my wrist/the sun*	*round the clock*	*talking round the subject*

Notice that *after*, *before* and *off* are largely time prepositions. *Beyond* in time expressions is usually non-assertive.

> *'He fell in love with himself at first sight and it is a passion to which he has always remained faithful.'*
> Anthony Powell, *The Acceptance World*

▸ see
46 Assertive/non-assertive

Beneath can have metaphorical meaning – but **underneath**?

209

On-type prepositions

These identify a static relationship with a line or surface in space or time. They also have related metaphorical meanings:

Preposition	Space/Place	Time	Metaphorical
above	*above the horizon/clouds*	*above an hour*	*above suspicion/ reproach*
across	*across the equator/sea*	*across the centuries*	*across my mind/the board*
against	*against the wall*		*against the light*
along	*along the seam/ground*		
behind	*behind the curtain/melody*		*my family is behind me*
below	*below the waist/ground*		*below average/the belt*
beneath	*beneath the ridge/skin*		*beneath one's dignity/ social position*
beside	*beside the hedge/lake*		*beside the point*
beyond	*beyond the highway/lake*	*beyond next week/ death*	*beyond help/reason*
off	*off the road/the map*		*off his head/off colour*
on	*on the edge/floor*	*on Friday/time*	*on the way/strike*
on top of	*on top of the cupboard*		*on top of one's work/the world*
onto	*onto the edge/floor*		*onto a good thing*
opposite	*opposite the coast/ the wall*		
over	*over the frontier/Spain*	*over the years/ the weekend*	*over age/a kilogram*
past	*past the tape/village*	*past midnight ten past two*	*past expectations/caring*
under	*under ground/your hat*	*under two hours*	*under age/£10/the weather*
underneath	*underneath your arm*		

210

In-type prepositions

These identify a static relationship with an area or volume in space or time and also have related metaphorical meanings.

Preposition	Space/Place	Time	Metaphorical
about	*about the floor/the house*	*about six o'clock/ a week*	*has his wits about him*
around	*around the garden/city*	*around two/1 January*	
during		*during the week/ childhood*	

Preposition	Space/Place	Time	Metaphorical
in	*in the square/building*	*in 10 minutes/in time*	*in public/danger/ general*
inside	*inside the lines/car*	*inside a week/a decade*	
outside	*outside the fence/room*	*outside working hours*	*outside my responsibility*
within	*within the perimeter/ the college*	*within minutes/ a year*	*within limits/reach*

Notice that *during* refers to time only.

211

Towards-type prepositions

These identify a relationship of motion to a point, line, area, etc. They also have related temporal and metaphorical meanings.

Preposition	Space/Place	Time	Metaphorical
across	*(go) across the road*	*across the years*	
against	*against the wind/tide*	*against our old age*	*against my wishes*
along	*(go) along the passage/ street*		
around	*(go) around the tree/ island*	*around midday*	*look around you*
at	*aim at the target*		
away from	*(get) away from him/ home*		
beneath	*beneath a stone/the moon*		*beneath his guidance*
beside	*(walk) beside the river*		
down	*down the stairs/hill*	*down the years/ages*	*down the hatch/down wind*
into	*into the circle/bed*	*into the future*	*into existence/oblivion*
off	*(get) off the road/bus*		*getting off the subject*
onto	*onto the track/green*		*getting onto someone*
out of	*out of line/bed*	*out of hours*	*out of order/spirits/ temper*
over	*over the side/Japan*	*over the weekend*	*over my dead body*
round	*round the track/town*	*round the clock*	
since		*since birth/March*	*since sliced bread*
through	*through the window/ forest*	*Monday through Friday*	*through an ordeal/exam*
to	*to London/the 21st century*	*10 to 3/Monday to Saturday*	*worry us to death*
towards	*(go) towards home/the light*	*towards dawn/9*	*towards peace/the truth*
under	*(go) under a bridge/bus*	*in under an hour*	*under discussion*
until		*until night/now*	*until I drop*
up	*up a ladder/slope*	*up to then/New Year*	*up the pole/upwind*
with	*with the wind/tide*	*with winter/the passing years*	*with the crowd*

Would you rather be **shouted at** or **shouted to**?

Notice that *since*, *till* and *until* refer to time only. Compare *into/onto* which are marked for motion, with *under/over*, with which the idea of motion or no motion is carried by the verb.

212

Throughout-type prepositions

These identify a pervasive relationship with an extent of space or time. They also have related metaphorical meanings.

Preposition	Space/Place	Time	Metaphorical
all over	*all over the country/ his face*		*all over the place*
all round	*all round the house/sky*		
all through	*all through the book/city*	*all through the night/ life*	*all through the friendship*
for	*for miles/a distance*	*for ages/a month*	*for better, for worse/not for long*
throughout	*throughout the world*	*throughout summer/ one reign*	*throughout the profession*

213

Other prepositional meanings

Prepositional phrases referring to spatial and temporal relationships answer the questions *Where?* and *When?/ How long?* We can identify several minor groups in the same way.

The question *Why?* identifies prepositional relationships of cause, reason, motive and purpose:

She overslept **because of** *too many late nights.* [reason]
He resigned **on account of** *ill-health.* [cause]
All **for** *love* [motive]
Take something to read **for** *the journey back.* [purpose]

The questions *Where?/Who?* + prep. identify prepositional relationships of goal, target, recipient:

Throw it **to** *me.* [goal]
Throw it **at** *me/the wicket.* [target]
It's a present **for** *her mother.* [recipient]

GUIDELINE

Several pairs of prepositional verbs with *to/at* carry a meaning of aggression for *at* and friendliness with *to*. Compare:

come at/to *grumble at/to* *run at/to*
fly at/to *nod at/to* *shout at/to*
gesture at/to *point at/to*

The question *How?* identifies relationships of manner, similarity and means/instrument:

He answers **with** *a smile.* [manner]
She spoke **without** *a trace of an accent.* [manner]
You're behaving **like** *an idiot.* [similarity]
She wants to fly **by** *Concorde.* [means]
I'll pay **by** *credit card.* [instrument]

The question *Who/What by?* identifies the role of agent.

A river swollen **by** *rain . . .*
This book is published **by** *Penguin Books.*
'Trial by Jury' **by** *Gilbert and Sullivan.*

Yet however we classify prepositional meaning, there will always be at least one odd man out. You may have noticed that *of*, the commonest preposition, does not figure in any of the above types of preposition. This is largely because of its diversity of meaning and partly because in some contexts we cannot give a paraphrase for it: what does *of* mean in *it's good* ***of*** *you* apart from a grammatical relationship?

Here is a selection of meanings for *of*, drawn from *Alexa*, by Andrea Newman.

husbands **of** *friends* ~ *belonging to*
a bag **of** *sweets* ~ *containing*
a litter **of** *toys on the floor* ~ *made from*
the back **of** *the car* ~ *part of the whole*
some **of** *our former friends* ~ *from among*
a wave **of** *nostalgia* ~ *consisting of*
the emergence **of** *the adult* ~ *done by subject*
the salvation **of** *the human race* ~ *done to object*
the fact **of** *another baby* ~ *that is, equal to*
a horror **of** *fields* ~ *caused by*
a matter **of** *life and death* ~ *connected with*
ashamed **of** *my good luck* ~ *by*
a life **of** *sin* ~ *with*
remind us **of** *the narrow path* ~ *about*
that was nice **of** *you* ~ *after adjective*
to tire **of** *sherry* ~ *after verb*

GUIDELINE

Despite the variety of meanings we can find for *of*, its most basic and productive use is in noun phrases which have an underlying subject + verb pattern:

day breaks ~ *the break of day*
the dog barks ~ *the barking of the dog*

'This is on me.'

Dorothy Parker, suggested epitaph for her own tombstone,
Attrib. in J. Keats, *You Might as Well Live*

Only two relative pronouns complement prepositions – which?

▶ **see**
103 The genitive and *of*-construction
178 Noun phrases

214

Prepositions and reduced adverbial clauses

We use a number of prepositions to introduce non-finite *-ing* adverbial clauses:

Erin finds herself . . . ***by*** *writing about other people.* [manner]

Despite *spending country weekends in childhood . . . I have a horror of fields.* [concession]

Without *discovering where you are an alien, you cannot know for certain where you belong.* [circumstance]

She took out her typewriter, ***instead of*** *first unpacking her clothes.* [contrast]

Other prepositions used in this way include *on* (time), *in spite of* (concession), *with* (circumstance).

> *'You can't make an omelette without breaking eggs.'*
>
> Proverb

▶ **see**
23 Adverbial clauses
25 Adverbial reduced clauses
125 *-ing* clauses

215

Prepositions in relative clauses

In some relative clauses we have a choice between two constructions:

. . . plays he had read ***of***
plays ***of*** *which he had read*

The first construction is less formal than the second. We have this choice when the relative clause contains a prepositional phrase or a prepositional verb. Then, the relative pronoun (*which*, *that*, *who*, etc.) acts as complement of the preposition:

the bloom of youth, which she has lost little ***of***
the bloom of youth, ***of*** *which she has lost little*

But only *which* and *whom* can stand immediately after a preposition. Sometimes, therefore, we have to change the relative pronoun from zero, *that* or *who* to *which* or *whom* in framing the more formal expression:

the social ostracism that widows complain ***of*** [informal]
the social ostracism ***of*** *which widows complain* [formal]

The preposition + *which/whom* construction is avoided by many people, sometimes regarded as pedantic and at best as the most formal on a scale of choices of expression:

They talked about people they'd been at college **with**. [least formal]
. . . *that they'd been at college* **with**
. . . *who they'd been at college* **with**
. . . *whom they'd been at college* **with**
. . . **with** *whom they'd been at college* [most formal]

With prepositional verbs, themselves usually informal, the preposition + *which/whom* construction is sometimes incongruous. Consider:

. . . *something you needn't* **worry about** ~ . . . *something about which you needn't worry*(?)

. . . *people you* **bump into** ~ . . . *people into whom you bump*(!?)

There are some prepositions, however, which never take end- position: *during* and most complex prepositions:

There was a pause **during** *which we both thought about it*, never **There was a pause which we both thought about it during*(!)

. . . *the pills* **by means of** *which she attempted suicide*, never *. . . *the pills which she attempted suicide by means of*(!)

GUIDELINES

Sometimes a writer selects the preposition + which construction for stylistic reasons. Andrea Newman is a popular writer who is not afraid of final prepositions. But here she uses *of which* in order to give end focus to an adjective:

. . . *cunning disguises*, **of which** *I felt quite proud*

Elsewhere she uses the same strategy to avoid the awkwardness of too great a gap between a preposition and its complement:

. . . *the occasions* **on which** *we had previously met* . . .

. . . *the uneasy second* **in which** *I might have been supposed to kiss the children* . . .

see

97 Focus
218–20 Prepositional phrases
221–2 Prepositional verbs
247–50 Relative clauses
251 Relative pronouns
277 Zero forms

216

Prepositions in final position

Traditional grammar taught that prepositions must always stand before their complement – 'Never end a sentence with a preposition.' But this rule can give rise to very stilted English. We would never say * *Like what do mangoes taste?* And without using other words we have no alternative way of saying *I know what you are talking* **about**.

What's exceptional about **a thing I'm in favour of...?**

In everyday English we regularly use prepositions in final position in:

relative clauses

This would explain . . . the social ostracism that widows complain ***of.***

wh- questions

What are you working ***on?***

wh- clauses

I doubt if you realise what you're taking ***on.***

indirect speech

I often wonder where all the money comes ***from.***

infinitive complementation

It's marvellous to have someone to talk ***to.***

passive form of prepositional verbs

I do not mind being stared ***at.***

exclamations

What a state Christine had got ***into!***

Most complex prepositions, however, stand before their complements: ***Apart from*** *hermits . . .*

Exceptions to this include *in front of*, *next to*, *up to*, *in favour of*.

GUIDELINES

During never takes final position. We cannot say **What year was it during?* but ***During*** *what year was it?* Whilst we use a final preposition in many *wh-* questions, like *Who with?* we cannot do so when a noun follows the *wh-* word. **Which person with?*

> *'This is the sort of English up with which I will not put.'*
>
> Winston Churchill's written comment in the margin of a state document written by a civil servant who tortuously avoided final prepositions, Quoted in Sir Ernest Gowers, *Plain Words*

see

205 Complex prepositions
95 Exclamations
110–15 Indirect speech
67 Infinitive complements
247 Relative clauses
273 *Wh-* clauses
236 *Wh-* questions

217

Omission of prepositions

Before certain time adverbials we usually omit prepositions. *Today*, *yesterday* and *tomorrow* never have *at*, *on* or *in* before them. Nor do time expressions like *next week*, *last March*, *this month*, *all day*, *the week before last*, *tomorrow evening*.

Paul meant to go . . . ***last night.***

Another evening *she and I went to the pub.*

But non-static prepositions are necessary, and are never omitted – *during the day*, *before last month*.

In nominal clauses with *that* and *to*- infinitive we drop prepositions before *that* (or zero *that*) and *to* (usually the prepositional part of a prepositional or phrasal prepositional verb).

Paul insisted ***on*** *her going.*
Paul insisted △ (that) she went.
She was delighted ***with*** *the letter.*
She was delighted △ to receive the letter.

In non-reported *that*-clauses, we keep the preposition, but insert a phrase like *the fact/idea/thought*.

She was depressed ***about the fact that*** *Christine had withdrawn.*

In indirect questions we often omit prepositions before *wh*- words:

Tell me ***about*** *your ideas.*
Tell me △ what you think.

With other reporting and thinking verbs in indirect questions the omission of the preposition is optional.

*I've no idea (****of****) what* happened.

In a few cases, as in *question about*, *worry about*, *be concerned about*, the preposition is obligatory:

I'm most concerned ***about*** *how you'll manage to work.*

Prepositions are in fact obligatory before all *wh*- nominal clauses, whether reported or not:

She hates being reminded ***of*** *how good she used to be.*
They're so carried away ***with*** *what they're saying.*

▶ GUIDELINE

We do not use prepositions before *if*. Where necessary we replace the *if* with *whether*:

I wondered if she would pass.
I was wondering ***about*** *whether she would pass.*

▶ see

110	Indirect questions	252	Reporting verbs
156	Nominal clauses	274	*Wh*- words
196	Phrasal-prepositional verbs	277	Zero forms
221, 222	Prepositional verbs		

218

Prepositional phrases: form

A prepositional phrase consists of a preposition followed by its complement. This is usually:
A noun phrase or a pronoun

I felt a wave ***of pity*** (N.P.).
Are they pleased ***with it*** (pron.)?

a nominal *wh-* clause

I did a rough estimate of **what my outfit had cost** (*wh-* clause)

She questioned Christine closely about **what she really wanted** (*wh-* clause).

an *-ing* clause

He put a glass of sherry in my hand, **without offering me a choice** (*-ing* clause).

. . . by **suggesting a solution** (*-ing* clause)

and very occasionally, adverbs

from (prep.) *below* (adv.)

and adjectives

just above (prep.) *sub-normal* (adj.)

Normally the preposition stands in front of its complement.

▸ see

125 *-ing* clauses
156 Nominal clauses
178 Noun phrases
216 Prepositions in final position
228 Pronouns

219

Prepositional phrases: function

Prepositional phrases do not function in the same way as prepositions, in the way that noun phrases work as nouns. Prepositional phrases typically are attached to nouns and verbs. They may function as:

postmodifiers in a noun phrase

. . . the school **Paul's at**

. . . a generous letter **about my work**

adverbials

Behind her *. . . was a two-year-old.*

I earned my living **with my brain.**

complements of verbs

I go **to infinite trouble.**

. . . listening **to the silence**

complements of adjectives

Full **of buildings and people**

What's wrong **with that?**

(rarely) noun phrases as subject, object, complement, etc.

Between engagement and marriage *is a difficult time.* [subject]

Back in **less than five minutes.** [complement of another preposition]

logical subject to a *to-* infinitive

. . . an arrangement **for her** *to have a holiday*

'A gifted small girl has explained to me that pins are a great means of saving life, "by not swallowing them".'

C. E. Montague, *Dramatic Values*

▶ **see**
23 Adverbials
65 Complementation of adjectives
178 Noun phrases
200 Postmodifiers

220

Prepositional phrases: position

Prepositional phrases typically follow the words they are attached to:

nouns . . . ***the aftermath*** *of some infectious disease*
verbs . . . ***loaded*** *with flowers*
adjectives . . . ***lost*** *for words*

But as adverbials, prepositional phrases can stand in front- mid- and end-position, like adverbs themselves. For adverbials of time, place and manner, front- and end-position are commonest, though mid-position is possible:

after a little thought . . . at first . . . at once [time]
At the top . . . in the corridor . . . in a shop [place]
Without a pause . . . with satisfaction . . . but not in a hostile way [manner]

But for sentence adverbials or linking adverbials front- and mid-position is common:

At the same time*, it would be dishonest to pretend.* [linking adverbial in front-position]
A train might ***in fact*** *have been quicker.* [adverbial in mid-position]

> *'The least pain in our little finger gives us more concern and uneasiness than the destruction of millions of our fellow-beings.'*
>
> William Hazlitt, *American Literature*

▶ **see**
23 Adverbials
35 Adverbial position
140 Linking adverbials
200 Postmodifiers
257 Sentence adverbials

221

Prepositional verbs: intransitive

These multi-word verbs have a verb and prepositional particle which is followed by a complement:

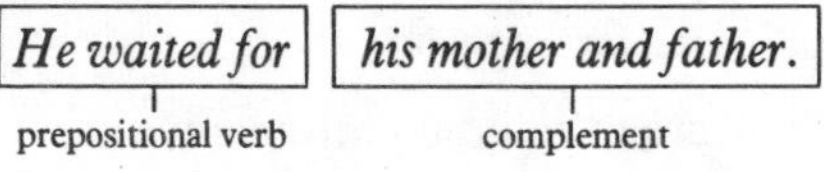

The link between particle and verb is less strong than the link between particle and complement: we often split particle and verb, but never particle and complement. Consider:

He waited (v.) *patiently* (adv.) *for* (prep.) *them* (c.).
He waited (v.) *for* (prep.) *them* (c.) *patiently* (adv.), but never
* *He waited for patiently them.*

For this reason alone it is more useful to regard the noun phrase (or pronoun) following the prepositional particle as a complement of the preposition, rather than as an object of the prepositional verb. Common prepositions used in prepositional verbs include:

against	*for*	*of*
among	*from*	*onto*
at	*into*	*upon*
beside	*like*	*with*

The above particles are prepositions only, but the following can stand as both prepositional and adverbial particles:

about	*below*	*over*
above	*by*	*past*
across	*down*	*round*
after	*in*	*through*
along	*inside*	*under*
around	*near*	*up*
before	*off*	*without*
behind	*on*	

How, then, can we distinguish a transitive phrasal from a prepositional verb if they may use the same construction? Consider *to cut down* which can be either: *Jim* ***cut down*** *the avenue* (prepositional) or *Men were* ***cutting down*** *the panels* (phrasal).

There are three clear differences:

i) Prepositional particles always stand before their noun phrase complement, phrasal particles can follow their noun phrase objects.
Jim cut down the avenue (prepositional).
Men were cutting the panels down (phrasal).
But * *Jim cut the avenue down.*

ii) Prepositional pronoun complements always follow the particle, phrasal pronoun objects stand before the particle.
Jim cut down **it**. *Men were cutting* **them** *down.*

iii) In speech any pauses we make keep the unity of preposition and complement, and verb and adverb particle.
Jim cut ( ) down the avenue.
Men were cutting down ( ) the panels.

There are hundreds of prepositional verbs in English.

A small group uses verbs which cannot stand alone:

account for *amount to* *consist of* *long for* *rely on*

A much larger group uses verbs which are in common intransitive use without the particle, like *look/look at*. Examples of such pairs are:

agree (to/with) *care (about/for)* *come (across/by/into/off)*
complain (about/of) *cope (with)* *depend (on)* *go (for/into)*
look (after/at/for/into/to) *object (to) succeed (at/in)* *talk (about/of)*

A large group of prepositional verbs are members of a pair, where the verb alone is also in transitive use but with a different meaning, like *worry/worry about*. Compare:

Jim ***worried*** *the beggar.*
Jim ***worried about*** *the beggar.*

Examples of such pairs are:

approve (of) *argue (about)* *ask (about/for)* *break (into)* *call (for)*
dream (about/of) *refer (to)* *take (after/to)* *think (about/of)* *wait (for)*

GUIDELINES

How can we tell the difference between a prepositional verb and an ordinary verb followed by an adverbial prepositional phrase? The prepositional verb has a complement, which is either an object or a person and answers the question *what?* or *who?*

The prepositional phrase after an ordinary verb is adverbial and answers the questions *where? when? how?* Compare:

prep. verb c.
I came by a lot of money. *What?*

v. prep. phrase
I came by taxi. *How?*

Notice how prepositional particles associated with a verb are often found in association with cognate nouns and adjectives:

to succeed at/with *success at/with* *successful at/with*

> *'The court will now stand for Judge Schnower – and if you'll stand for him, you'll stand for anything.'*
>
> Spike Milligan, *The Goon Show*

see
153 Multi-word verbs 222 Prepositional verbs: transitive
205 Prepositions 270 Transitivity

222

Prepositional verbs: transitive

These multi-word verbs have verb + direct object + prepositional particle + its complement.

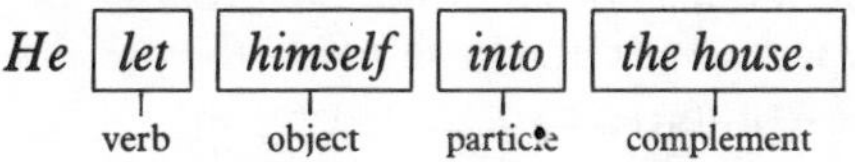

These verbs tend to use the same prepositional particles listed in 221 above. Having direct objects, most have a passive form:

Forgotten scents reminded him of the period before the war.

He was reminded of the period before the war.

Notice, however, that we cannot form a passive with the same meaning when the direct object is a reflexive pronoun. Consider:

Chinese conjurors turned **themselves** *into birds.*
They (themselves) were turned into birds (presumably by someone else!).

In all the above cases, the verb selects a fixed preposition, but object and complement are free. The verbs are, for example, *to let N. into N., to remind N. of N.*, and are only partially idiomatic. More idiomatic groups are those verbs which have fixed prepositional complements, like *to set N. in motion*, or fixed direct objects, like *to set eyes on N.*, or full idioms with every component fixed, like *to set the Thames on fire*. Some of these may appear in passive forms, others not:

They made a fuss of them.	*A fuss was made of them.* But,
They made a go of it.	**A go was made of it.*
He put my mind at rest.	*My mind was put at rest.* But,
We see eye to eye.	**Eye is seen to eye.*

As a general rule, the more idiomatic a phrase, the less flexible it is.

Common transitive prepositional verbs include:

accuse N. of   *blame N. for*   *catch sight of*   *cross swords with*   *give way to*
keep pace with   *lose touch with*   *make fun of*   *pay attention to*
prevent N. from   *protect N. from*   *remind N. of*   *save N. from*
take care of   *take notice of*   *take pity on*   *thank N. for*

▶ **see**
153 Multi-word verbs
221 Prepositional verbs: intransitive
246 Reflexive pronouns

223

The present perfect tense

This tense uses *has/have* before the *-en* form of the verb, as in *I have fallen*. In speech we usually use the contracted forms *'s* and *'ve*. The tense is marked for the perfective aspect which indicates that the event has occurred in the period before-now and is at least partially completed. The event may be completed (*I've broken my leg*) but it still has present significance. A repetitive or extended action may be partially completed at the present time (*I've read three of the five novels*) and continue into the future. But whenever we use this tense we are thinking of now.

We use the present perfect to refer to the long-term present stretching back into the past and the short-term present including the recent past.

In each case the length of the period may be identified adverbially, but we think of the period as seen from the present. (In all cases, the present is the moment of speaking/thinking/writing.)

The long-term present

Here we are thinking of states or repeated actions that extend into the present:

*We'**ve had** a very bad time.*
*I'**ve forgotten**.*
*I'**ve** always **found** there was something in what he said.*
*You'**ve** never **learnt** to obey orders, have you?*
*Not one of us **has** ever **helped**.*
*Our stories **haven't changed** in generations, you know.*

Two useful words help us to mark the beginning of the state or activity – *for* and *since*:

*It's the best news **I've heard for** a long time.*
*And rabbits **have stolen** vegetables **since** that day.*

The short-term present

Here we have in mind a recent action which has present significance.

*It's really **been** extremely good of you to come and see me. (~ and now you can go!)*

*He'**s convinced** me. (~ I'm now convinced.)*

A very recent action can be marked by *just*, *recently*, *lately*:

*I'**ve** just **had** an idea.*
*There **has been** too much rain lately.*

As with long-term present meanings we often use *since* and *for* with short-term present reference. With *since*, the period of time is measured from a fixed point before-now. With *for* the time is measured in periods up to now.

*We'**ve learned** a few things **since** we left.*
*Holly'**s been** more or less himself **since** he woke up.*
*I'**ve been** forced to live with him **for** the last two months.*

GUIDELINES

Because the present perfect includes the present moment in its meaning, we only use with it adverbials which include the present: *today*, *this month*, *this year*, *up to now*, *not long ago*, *recently*.

But those adverbials with no inclusive present meaning, like *yesterday*, *last month*, *on Friday last*, are obviously not compatible.

We combine some modals with the present perfect in a number of idiomatic expressions:

*I **might** have guessed! I **could** have died laughing.*
*You **ought to** have known better.*
*You **shouldn't** have been so careless.*

> *"'I dunno," Arthur said. "I forget what I was taught. I only remember what I've learnt."'*
>
> Patrick White, *The Solid Mandala*

Explain: **He has been making up his mind all the week**

▶ **see**
45 Aspect
142 Marked/unmarked
264 Tenses

224

The present perfect progressive tense

This tense combines the *have/has* of the present perfect with *been* and the *-ing* form of the progressive, as in *She* ***has been swimming***. We use it about events or states which are relatively short though not necessarily complete. If complete they have only recently finished and still have current significance. It is the current impact of the activity that concerns us rather than its completion. In the fairy tale, 'Goldilocks and the Three Bears', the bears look at half-eaten porridge and ask *Who* ***has been eating*** *my porridge?* whilst rumpled blankets prompt, *Who* ***has been sleeping*** *in my bed?* We use the present perfect progressive for short-term activity, when no adverbial is present, and for activity still in progress, the length of which is stated by an adverbial.

Short-term recent activity

*I'****ve been thinking*** *about what you said.*
I hope your friends ***have been looking*** *after you.*
*We'****ve been talking*** *to another mouse . . .*

Incomplete activity

A range of adverbials is available except for those which – like *yesterday* – do not include the present in their meaning.

*We'****ve been digging*** *all the afternoon.*
*I'****ve been living*** *with him for the last two months.*
*They'****ve been travelling*** *all night, you know.*

This use may refer to a single action or a series of habitual acts.

Notice that we can only interpret verbs describing momentary actions in this and other progressive tenses with a habitual meaning or as slow motion. Consider:

I opened my eyes. I have been opening my eyes.
He fired one shot. He has been firing one shot.

The tense is normally incompatible with such verbs since it gives a meaning of duration to actions which do not have duration. The other occasion we make use of this incompatibility is for sarcasm:

He's been getting out of bed all this week. ~ *He's been claiming to be about to get out of bed all this week.*

▶ GUIDELINES

In a few situations the two present perfect tenses carry the same meaning. For example:

Indians have lived/have been living in Mauritius for generations. Their ancestors must have travelled/have been travelling for weeks.

Usually the two tenses carry contrasting meanings – complete actions with the present perfect and continuing activity with the present perfect progressive.

Present Perfect	**Present Perfect Progressive**
*She's **stayed** here twice.*	*She's **been staying** here. (Twice* etc. are incompatible.)
*We **have visited** her occasionally.* (but not **We **have visited**,* which does not state a completed action.)	*We **have been visiting**.*
***Have** you (ever) **smoked**? (~ **Have** you ever **been** a smoker?)*	***Have** you **been smoking**? (~ Your breath smells.)*
*Who **has cut** this string?* (one cut)	*Who **has been cutting** this string?* (series of cuts)
*I've **been robbed**.* (passive common)	**I've **been being robbed**.* (Passive clumsy and usually avoided.)

▶ **see**
45 Aspect
223 Present perfect tense
264 Tenses

225

The present progressive tense

This tense uses *am/is/are* followed by the *-ing* form of the verb, as in *He **is reading**.* The two parts of the verb are both markers; the auxiliary marks it for present time, the *-ing* form for action in progress. This action may not be complete and it is often relatively short. We use the present progressive to talk about the actual present moment, about the short-term present, the long-term present and for certain future events already planned.

The actual present

We use the present progressive here to refer to an incompleted single action in progress at the moment of speaking:

*It's **getting** dark.*
*What **are** you **doing** here?*

The speaker is not concerned about when the event started or when it will finish, but that it is happening now.

The short-term present

In this meaning we may refer to a single event or a repeated habitual action taking place over a relatively short period which spans the present moment:

***I'm trying** to explain . . .*
*We'**re waiting** for you and **getting** wetter every moment.*

The long-term present

When we use the present progressive with a frequency adverb (*always*, *continually*, *forever*, etc.) we are talking about repeated events occurring in the immediate past and likely to continue into the immediate future:

The Council **are** *always* **watching***.*
He'**s** *always* **doing** *things like that.*

This last example could be said petulantly to function as a complaint – and complaining is a common function for this usage. But, in fact, here the sentence is an expression of a mother's pride in her offspring.

Present plans for future

We use the present progressive, often with a future time adverbial to express our plans and expectations:

I'm going *to speak to him.*
It'**s going** *on raining all night.*

When no future adverbial is present, we are thinking of an imminent event.

Notice how the present progressive has greater immediacy than the present simple. Compare:

Present simple – general habit

They | *take* | *no notice of us.*

Present progressive – now

They | *are taking* | *no notice of us.*

We often use the present progressive to refer to background events to a single event:

While **you're doing** *that, I'll run down to the fields.*

GUIDELINE

We do not usually use verbs with stative meaning in the present progressive. We do not say:

**I am understanding you. *Are you hearing the radio?*
**He is being handsome. *The box is holding 40 matches.*

Yet Pipkin says,

I **am being** *silly.*

He is using the verb *to be* in a dynamic sense. When we use stative verbs with progressive tenses, we are giving them a temporary, unusual meaning. So:

I **am** *silly.* ~ *I am habitually silly.*
I **am being** *silly.* ~ *I am being uncharacteristically silly at this moment.*

This useful strategy helps us to imply subtle differences of meaning:

He **is** *British.* ~ *He comes from Britain.*
He **is being** *British.* ~ *He is pretending to be British.*
or *He is behaving at the moment in a typically British way.*

*She **has** a headache.* ~ *Her head is aching.*
*She **is having** a headache.* ~ *She is pretending to have a headache.*

▶ **see**

45	Aspect	226	Present simple tense
87	Dynamic/stative meaning	264	Tenses
22	Frequency adverbs		

226

The present simple tense

This tense uses the base form of the verb, inflected with *-s* for the 3rd person singular: *I know*, *he knows*. We use it – despite its name – to refer to timeless states or events, the present time, past and future time.

The timeless present

This is also called the state present, since we use it with verbs of stative meaning.

*Wood **floats**.*
*It never **rains** but it **pours**.*

In this meaning of the present simple we talk about the timeless, eternal truths of the physical world, including the generalised folk wisdom expressed in proverbs.

The habitual present is used to talk about habits, repeated actions and states covering the long-term present.

*You **know** me perfectly well.*
*He**'s** generally there about this time.*

This meaning of the present simple also includes a sense of timelessness, but unlike the timeless present we often include a frequency adverbial, and the verb may not refer to the present moment (as in *He's generally there*).

The actual present

We often use verbs with a stative meaning in this way:

***I'm** in a fine temper, I can tell you.*
***It's** safe enough . . . it**'s** not exactly danger I feel about this place: I **can't** tell what, but it **worries** me.*

This meaning is sometimes called the instantaneous present, a reminder that we use it for the shortest kind of action as described by a sports commentator, or someone demonstrating a process:

*Now we **swim** over.*

We also use the present simple with this meaning with the first person of performative verbs which perform the act named by actually being spoken:

*I **admit** I hadn't any idea.*
*I **apologise** for the mistake.*

Explain the newspaper headline: **England Crumble**

Present simple for fixed future

When we name a future time for an event, we often use the simple present to show we are certain about it.

Wherever we **settle** *down in the end . . .*
The day I **call** *you Chief Rabbit, Hazel, that will be the day.*

This use with future meaning is also common in subordinate clauses; particularly after *if* and *when*:

If I **start** *feeling there's anything dangerous, I'll tell you.*
We shall come back one night, and when we **do** *. . .*

Present simple for past meaning

One, rare, use of this, sometimes called the historic present, is found when an author switches into the present to give his description greater reality:

Odysseus **brings** *not one man to shore with him. Yet he* **sleeps** *sound beside Calypso and when he* **wakes** *thinks only of Penelope.*

Similarly writers of newspaper headlines, cartoon captions and chapter headings use this present simple. Three chapters of *Watership Down* are entitled *The Thunder* **Builds** *Up*, *The Thunder* **Breaks** and *Hazel* **Comes** *Home*. Just as titles are a kind of resumé of a longer content, we often write a summary of a play or book in the present. The inside cover of *Watership Down* starts:

One dim moonlight night, a small band of rabbits **leave** *the comfort and safety of their warren and* **set out** *on a long and dangerous journey . . .*

More commonly, we report past events when using verbs of communication in the present simple to imply that what was said or heard still applies:

Now he **says** *he can sense . . . danger.*
I **hear** *you've come a long way.*

Other verbs of communication include:

learn see talk tell understand

GUIDELINE

Although *Watership Down* was written in 1971 we can talk and write about it in the present simple to suggest that the work is still alive:

Richard Adams **tells** *the story of Hazel and his followers . . .*

We refer in the same way to the available works of all creative artists:

> *"'It's like the question of the authorship of the* Iliad,*"*
> *said Mr Cardan.*
> *"The author of that poem is either Homer, or, if not Homer, someone else of that name."'*
>
> Aldous Huxley, *Those Barren Leaves*

▶ **see**

87	Dynamic/stative meaning	264	Tenses
192	Performative verbs	265	Tense and time
261	Subordination	271	Verbs

227

Pronames

Most languages have informal words which are used in place of the correct name, when the speaker cannot or will not recall that name. The following are all used in English to replace proper names:

how-d'you-do *so-and-so*
thingummy/thingamajig/thingumbob/thingummybob *whatnot* *whatsit*
whatsername/whatsizname/whatsyourname/whatyoucallem/whatyoucaller/ whatyoucallim/whatyoucallit *youknow*

So we can talk about *Mr How-d'you-do*, *Mrs Whatsername* and *President Whatnot* when we genuinely cannot remember the names of absent people. It is not polite to speak directly to someone in this way: *Hey, you, whatsyourname* is deliberately impolite.

Notice how two pronames can be varied

for number
whatyoucallit (singular)/*whatyoucallem* (plural)
whatsizname (singular)/*whatstheirname* (plural)

for gender
whatsizname (male)/*whatsername* (female)
whatyoucallim (male)/*whatyoucaller* (female)

The non-personal forms are used to replace common nouns for which we have forgotten the word: *I can't find the what-not/thingummybobs* (most pronames are nouns). Occasionally people who are shy use a proname instead of a taboo word: *He's a wicked old so-and-so*. Or even instead of words like *lavatory*: *Where's the how-d'you-do/whatsit/you know?*

At best pronames are informal, usually humorous and sometimes impolite.

'He would answer to "Hi!" or to any loud cry
Such as "Fry me!" or "Fritter my Wig!"
To "What-you-may-call-um!" or "What-was-his-name!"
But especially to "Thing-um-a-jig!"'

Lewis Carroll, *The Hunting of the Snark*

228

Pronouns: general

Pronouns are a closed, minor word class.

Formally, many pronouns are closely related to determiners, between which there are many look-alikes:

Have a **little** (det.) *whisky? A* **little** (pron.), *then.*

Quantifiers like *little* have common forms for determiners and pronoun use. So do demonstratives (*these*) and interrogatives (*which*). Personal and possessive pronouns have related forms to determiners (*me*, *mine*, *my*) as does the *some-any-no-* series of pronouns.

Pronouns by definition are substitute words for nouns/noun phrases, though they often replace whole clauses:

No one/She/Mine *arrived.*
The man who met us at the airport – ***he*** *arrived.*

Interrogative pronouns take the place of unknown subjects and objects: ***Who*** *arrived?*

The richness of pronoun use is demonstrated in the number and complexity of individual entries.

▶ **see**

83	Demonstratives	246	Reflexive pronouns
84	Determiners	251	Relative pronouns
179	Numbers	258	*Some-/any-/no-* series
193	Personal pronouns	274	Interrogative pronouns
199	Possessive pronouns	274	*wh-* words
229	Quantifiers	276	Word classes

229

Quantifiers: general

These are determiners and pronouns which show quantity or amount:

. . . a large family with several (det.) *children still at school*

Quantifiers often have the same form for determiners and pronouns:

By all (det.) *means.*   *Is that all* (pron)?

There are five groups of quantifiers, most containing both determiners (det.) and pronouns (pron.)

▶ **see**

84 Determiners
228 Pronouns
230–4 Quantifiers: meaning

230

Quantifiers of inclusive meaning

The full list of these is:

determiners *all both each half every*
pronouns *all (of) both (of) each (of) half (of) everybody everyone everything*

All (det. and pron.) refers to count nouns (both singular and plural) and non-count nouns:

What is it all (det.) *about? Is that all* (pron.)*?*
all (det.) *the letters all* (pron.) *worked hard . . .*
all (det.) *her concentration knows all* (pron.) *about them*

Both (det. and pron.) refers to plural count nouns only, referring to two:

with both (det.) *hands same again, both* (pron.) *of you*

Each (det. and pron.) refers to singular count nouns only and takes a singular verb:

each (det.) *morning each* (pron.) *of these couples*

Notice that we can use *all*, *both* and *each* after nouns or pronouns when they are subjects or indirect objects:

They all set off for the church.
they both felt . . . nostalgia.
Dorothy and Adrian each take it.

We can also use *all* and *both* after direct objects, but not *each*:

Her marriage . . . made it all public.

Half (det. and pron.) refers to count nouns (both singular and plural) and non-count nouns:

half (det.) *the patients half* (pron.) *of them*
half (det.) *that number half* (pron.) *of the wine*

Every (det. only) refers to singular count nouns only.

at every opportunity

Everybody/everyone (pron. only) substitute for singular personal nouns only:

. . . talking in the porch, holding everybody up
Everyone agreed that it was a very nice wedding.

Everything (pron. only) substitutes for singular impersonal nouns only:

They took everything so seriously.

▶ see
80 Count/non-count nouns
84 Determiners
228 Pronouns

231

Some- and *any*- words as quantifiers

The full list of these is:

determiners *any* *some* *either*
pronouns *any (of)* *some (of)* *either (of)* *somebody/-one* *something* *anybody/-one* *anything*

Some (det. and pron.) and *any* (det. and pron.) have two meanings:

1 Indefinite quantity or amount referring to plural count nouns and non-count nouns. This is the more common meaning. The determiners are unstressed and *some* is pronounced /səm/. The pronouns are usually unstressed, but *some* is pronounced /sʌm/. We use *some* (det. and pron.) in assertive contexts, that is, in affirmative sentences and questions which have positive bias (expecting a positive answer).
We use *any* in non-assertive contexts, that is, in negative statements, open questions (expecting either positive or negative answers) and in statements showing doubt or uncertainty.
plural nouns
for any (det.) *other students* *some* (pron.) *of her pupils*
non-count nouns
some (det.) *fresh air* *some* (pron.) *of his enthusiasm*

2 Identification, referring to count nouns (singular and plural) and non-count nouns. Here both *some* and *any* have some stress and *some* is pronounced /sʌm/. *Some* (det.) in this meaning, identifying particular one/ones, can be used in negative and interrogative sentences. *Any* (det.), identifying some unnamed person or thing, can be used in positive sentences:
singular nouns
any (det.) *other Sunday* *any* (pron.) *of the other nuns*
plural nouns
some (det.) *people left* *some* (pron.) *were lengthier*
non-count nouns
with some (det.) *difficulty* *the distress, if any* (pron.)

GUIDELINES

We use stressed *some* as a determiner in one special and informal way. It suggests an emotional appraisal meaning *extraordinary* either positive or negative. Sometimes only the context can show which meaning we intend:

Did you enjoy 'How Far Can You Go'? Yes, that's ***some*** *book.*
Isn't David Lodge a strict Catholic? Huh! ***Some*** *Catholic!*

Either (det. and pron.) refers to singular count nouns only, meaning one or other of the two.

on either (det.) *side* *either* (pron.) *of his parents*

Somebody/one and *anybody/one* (pron. only) refer to people only, not to things, and have a genitive form: someone's.

Something and *anything* (pron. only) usually refer to things only, not to people. We use the *some-* compounds in affirmative sentences and questions which have positive bias (expecting a positive answer). We may use *any-* compounds in negative sentences, questions with no bias (expecting positive or negative answers) and in statements showing doubt and uncertainty.

affirmative statement
Somebody came round with a collecting-box.

question with positive bias
Why be a Catholic . . . rather than something else?

negative statement
None of them said anything.

question without bias
How else would anyone know?

uncertain statement
Sultry afternoons were occasions for sin, if anything was.

GUIDELINE

In informal speech, we occasionally use *something* to refer to people in phrases of admiration:

That man's really **something**!
Isn't she **something**!
He's **something** *quite different!*

see

42	Articles and meaning	84	Determiners
46	Assertive/non-assertive	228	Pronouns
80	Count/non-count nouns	234	Negative quantifiers
		258	*Some-/any-no-* series

232

Quantifiers: degrees of quantity/amount

The full list of these is:

determiners

many	*(a) few*	*enough*	*(a) little*
more	*fewer*	*several*	*less*
most	*less*	*much*	*least*
	fewest		

pronouns

many (of)	*(a) few (of)*	*(a) little (of)*	*(a) lot (of)*
more (of)	*fewer/less (of)*	*enough (of)*	*lots (of)*
most (of)	*fewest (of)*	*several (of)*	*plenty (of)*
	much (of)		

Compare: **A few ideas/Few ideas**

Many, *more*, *most*, *few*, *fewer/less*, *fewest*, *enough*, and *several* (dets. and prons.) refer to amounts of plural count nouns.

so many (det.) *friends*
most (det.) *things in life*
few (det.) *Catholics*
enough (det.) *cups with handles*
several (det.) *Papal announcements*

most (pron.) *of the things she read*
enough (pron.) *of this philosophising*
many (pron.) *who disobeyed*
a few (pron.) *have been switched on*
fewer (pron.) *and fewer* (pron.) *of them.*

Notice how *few* and *little* without *a* have negative bias. Compare:

few friends ~ *not many friends*
a few friends ~ *some friends*

little fun ~ *not much fun*
a little fun ~ *some fun*

Enough is a rather unusual determiner in the positions it takes. We can use it before or after a plural count noun or a non-count noun, though the front-position is more usual: ***enough** plates/food*; *drinks/drink **enough** for twenty*.

But with a singular count noun we only use *enough* after it: *He's fool/man **enough** to do it.*

A lot, *lots (of)*, *plenty (of)*, (dets. and prons.) refer to amounts of plural count nouns or non-count nouns:

*They didn't mean **a lot**.*
*He was missing **an** awful **lot**.*
***lots of** young men*
*He had **plenty of** leisure.*

GUIDELINES

In informal English, we meet both *fewer* and *less* referring to plural nouns: *fewer/less people*. In fact, *less* is the comparative form of *little* and should only be used before non-count nouns: *little Latin and less Greek*. It is more correct to use *fewer* only before plural count nouns: *fewer children/people/animals/things*.

Much, *more*, *most*, *(a) little*, *less*, *least* and *enough* (dets. and prons.) refer to amounts of non-count nouns:

could not rouse much (det.) *enthusiasm*
You are not going to hear much (pron.)
with more (det.) *caution than usual*
Dennis put in more (pron.) *than he could afford.*
embraced with little (det.) *contact*
most (pron.) *of the time*
surprised how little (det.) *envy he felt*
enough (pron.) of the Protestant in her

> *'Money may not buy happiness but with it you can rent enough.'*
>
> Dick Richards, *Ginger, Salute to a Star*

▶ **see**
80 Count/non-count nouns
84 Determiners
228 Pronouns

233
Unitary quantifiers

One (det. and pron.) has a number of uses, other than as a number, as in:

__one__ or two of those things

As a determiner we use it with indefinite meaning:

in the hope that __one__ day his faith would be restored

As a pronoun, *one* can substitute for singular count nouns and noun phrases:

After that first __one__, things became easier. one ~ birthday
Angela . . . was __one__. one ~ one of two matrons of honour

> *'The woman who is really kind to dogs is always one who has failed to inspire sympathy in men.'*
> Max Beerbohm, *Zuleika Dobson*

Ones is the plural form of this use of *one* (a contradiction in terms?):

One does not kill off characters lightly, I assure you, even __ones__ like Anne.

We also use *one* as an indefinite personal pronoun, meaning people in general, with a genitive form *one's*:

Whether __one__ prayed in church or in __one's__ living room seemed unimportant to her, as long as __one__ prayed.

▶ GUIDELINES

We can use three other quantifiers in front of *one of*: *any*, *each* and *every*.

any one of us *each one of you* *every one of them*

We can omit *one* in the first two cases, but not in the third, since *any* and *each* can stand as both determiner and pronoun, but *every* is never used as a pronoun.

any one of us ~ any of us
each one of you ~ each of you
*every one of them ~ *every of them*

▶ **see**
84 Determiners
179 Numbers
228 Pronouns

234

Negative quantifiers

The full list of these is:

determiners *no neither*
pronouns *none (of) neither (of) nobody no one nothing*

No (det. only) can refer to singular and plural count nouns and non-count nouns:

No woman is worth it, not even Angela.
No more distinctions between . . . male and female . . .
*Disasters happen with **no** apparent reason or justice.*

Neither (det. and pron.) refers to singular count nouns only, meaning not one and not the other of two:

Neither (det.) *man gives a thought*
Neither (pron.) *of them seemed to think.*

None (of) (pron. only) refers to singular and plural count nouns and to non-count nouns:

None of *the group had any experience . . .*
None of *her confessors looked particularly shocked.*
None of *the food . . .*

Nobody/No one (prons. only) mean the same thing – no person – and refer to people only:

No one *could say for certain when this happened.*

Nothing (pron. only) refers to single things and never people:

*There was **nothing** that priest, bishop or Pope could do to stop them.*

GUIDELINES

Have you noticed how several quantifiers make up contrasting pairs: *more/less, one/all, many/few*. David Lodge is one of many writers who often use such contrasts for stylistic purposes:

***All** these things or **none** of them.*
*. . . the conclusion that religion was **all** form and **no** content*
*You've **everything** to gain and **nothing** to lose by being sorry.*

'Nothing matters very much and very few things matter at all.'

Lord Balfour, Attrib.

see
80 Count/non-count nouns
84 Determiners
228 Pronouns

235

Questions: general

There are two main classes of question, one which expects an open answer, *wh-* questions, and the other expecting closed answers from a limited choice, often either *yes* or *no*, *yes/no* questions. Tag questions are an important special kind of *yes/no* question. Alternative questions and exclamatory questions are also a kind of *yes/no* question. Response questions are an elliptical form of tag questions and declarative questions are similar in function to tag questions.

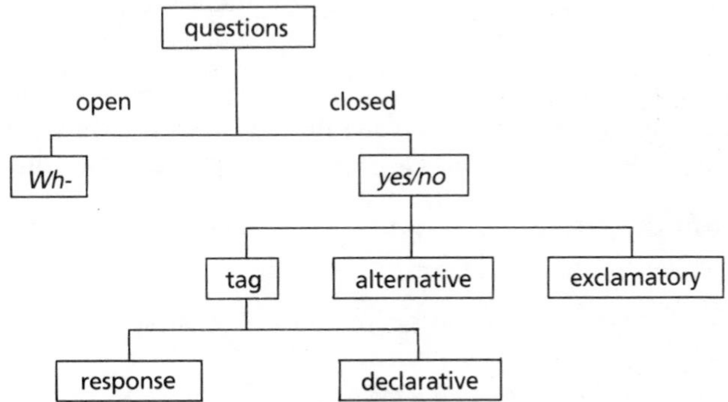

Two minor question types, echo questions and rhetorical questions, may take the form of *wh-* questions or *yes/no* questions.

▶ **see**

239	Alternative questions	241	Response questions
242	Declarative questions	244	Rhetorical questions
243	Echo questions	254	Simple sentences
240	Exclamatory questions	238	Tag questions
110	Indirect questions	236	Wh- questions
132	Interrogatives	237	Yes/no questions

236

Wh- questions

These are sometimes called content questions or information questions, because they are usually seeking answers of substance. (Exceptions include formulas like *How do you do?*)

Wh- questions start with one of the following *wh-* words:

who whom whose what which when where why how

(all of these can be given greater emphasis by adding *-ever* – *why-ever*, etc.)

Wh- questions are normally pronounced with a falling intonation:

What's 'that?

We form *wh-* questions in one of two ways:

If the *wh-* part is the subject of the verb, the order of words is the same as in a similar statement

Who (s.) *had* (op.) *the key of the garage?*

if the *wh*- part is object, complement or adverbial, we put the operator in front of the subject

What are (op.) *you* (s.) *doing here?* (*what* = object)
What is (op.) *it* (s.)? (*what* = complement)
Why do (op.) *people* (s.) *who have enough money try to get more money?* (*why* = adverbial)

GUIDELINE

Usually the question word beginning with *wh*- is the question element, or *wh*- part, as above. But sometimes the *wh*- part is longer than one word. (In the following sentence *What hope* is the *wh*- part.)

***What hope** was there for her as an old woman?*

Sometimes the *wh*- part is the complement of a preposition, and we have a choice between a formal and an informal structure. In speech and informal writing, we separate the *wh*- part from its preposition, which remains trailing at the end of the question:

***What** did he suspect you **of**?*
***Where** did you start **from**?*

The more formal – and less common – alternative is to place the preposition before its complement:

***Into which** country will it lead . . .?*

Wh- questions are sometimes negative. Usually the negative is formed by adding *n't* to the operator:

*Why **hasn't** he told us?*

But for special emphasis, or in very formal writing, we may use the full form of *not*:

*Why has **not** England a great mythology?*
*Why do you **not** marry?*

This last question is asked by a younger brother of his older sister, and is more of a suggestion than a question. In fact we often use *Why don't you* . . . to give instructions and make suggestions:

He had only one suggestion . . . Why don't you tell Mr Wilcox?
Why not give him the money?

The elliptical positive question with *why* followed by the bare-infinitive usually carries the force of an instruction:

Why be so polite to servants? ~ *Don't be so polite . . .*

Similarly we often say *Why bother? Why worry?* meaning *Don't bother*, *Don't worry*.

GUIDELINES

wh- questions are the only questions which do not typically have rising intonation. Nine times out of ten they take falling intonation. But their status as questions is immediately obvious from the initial question word.

▶ **see**
117 Bare infinitive
184 Operator
216 Prepositions in final position

237

Yes/no questions

Yes/no questions are so called because they expect either *yes* or *no* as their answer. We form a positive *yes/no* question by placing the operator before the subject of the corresponding statement:

Is (OP.) *Helen* (S.) *all right?*

In speech we always give a rising intonation to *yes/no* questions:

Have (OP.) *you* (S.) *been there 'long?*

If there is no operator in the underlying affirmative verb phrase, we use *do* as with negative sentences:

Do (OP.) *you* (S.) *know where it 'is?*

As with negative sentences, we often use main verb *have* as operator in British English, though in informal conversation *Have . . . got* is more common:

Have (OP.) *you* (S.) *any ideas?*
How much have (OP.) *you* (S.) *got?*

American English prefers . . . *do you have . . .?* in both these sentences.
As with *wh-* questions, we use *yes/no* questions to fulfil functions other than seeking information. For example:

May I help you in? [offer to help]
Won't you have something to eat? [invitation]
Could you possibly lower your voice? [polite command]

Sometimes we use positive *yes/no* questions to show the answer we expect – we give them positive or negative bias:

Mr Wilcox asked, 'Is there ***anything*** *wrong . . .?'*
*Jacky asked, '****Anyone*** *been round to our place?'*

These two questions are neutral, without bias: the speakers are not being suspicious. But if they were suspicious that something was wrong/someone had been round, they would use a biased form of question to show they expected a positive answer:

Is ***something*** *wrong?* ~ *Surely something is wrong.*
Someone *been round . . .?* ~ *Surely someone has been round.*

▶ GUIDELINE

In asking someone to have a drink, our invitation is stronger and more polite if the question has positive bias and expects *yes* as the answer.

Therefore *Would you like* ***anything*** *to drink?* is less inviting than *Would you like* ***something*** *to drink?*

We form negative *yes/no* questions by adding *n't* to the operator or by using some other negative form. All such sentences have a strong bias:

Don't *you agree?* ~ *Surely you agree.*
Has ***nobody*** *asked you?* ~ *Surely somebody asked you.*

We use such questions to press people to agree with us:

Margaret Schlegel, unexpectedly invited to make an uncomfortable journey to see Mrs Wilcox's house, tries politely to refuse and completes her excuses with a negative question designed to make Mrs Wilcox agree with her: *'Later on I should love it, but it's hardly the weather for such an expedition, and we ought to start when we're fresh.* ***Isn't*** *the house shut up, too?'*

We also use such questions to press people into positive action:

Margaret Schlegel, newly engaged to marry the successful Mr Wilcox, finds he is reluctant to tell her his income. She uses two negative questions with very strong positive bias: *'****Don't*** *you know your income? Or* ***don't*** *you want to tell it to me?'*

The bias of such questions often communicates their speaker's annoyance, disbelief, surprise, disappointment or pleasure:

But ***hasn't*** *she any address?*
Didn't *she send me a message or something?*

When we use a falling intonation with *yes/no* questions, they are exclamatory questions. Compare:

Isn't *that 'beautiful?* ~ *Surely you think that is beautiful.*
Isn't *that `beautiful?* ~ *How beautiful that is!*

▶ GUIDELINE

Certain other languages answer negative questions in a different way from English. The English reply does not follow the positive or negative form of the question:

Have you finished yet? No (I haven't), Yes (I have).
Haven't you finished yet? No (I haven't), Yes (I have).

▶ **see**
240 Exclamatory questions
155 Negative sentences
184 Operator

238

Tag questions

A question-tag is a kind of *yes/no* question which is added to a statement. The statement may be positive or negative. The two parts, statement and tag, form one sentence, a tag question. Most tag questions consist of a simple statement followed by a tag. This is usually a two-word question consisting of operator and personal pronoun. The operator is repeated from the statement and the pronoun refers to the subject of the statement:

That (s.)*'s* (op.) *the problem, isn't* (op.) *it* (s.)*?*

As with negatives and yes/no questions, if there is no operator in the affirmative we use *do* as a dummy operator:

Wickham Place faced north, didn't (op.) *it* (s.)*?*

If the statement is positive, the tag is usually negative and vice versa:

You like (pos.) *them, don't you* (neg.), *Eric?* [pos. + neg.]
You don't (neg.) *mind them coming, do you* (pos.)*?* [neg. + pos.]

Occasionally we use the uncontracted form not in the tag, to produce a formal style:

It's a fine programme this afternoon, ***is it not****?*

All tag questions have positive/negative bias. If the statement is positive, then a positive answer is expected. If the statement is negative, the question expects the answer *no*. The operator in the tag carries the nuclear tone and may give either rising or falling intonation to the tag, thereby indicating the strength of the positive/negative bias:

A *Wickham Place faced 'north, 'didn't it? ~ I think it did. Am I right?*

B *Wickham Place faced `north, `didn't it? ~ I believed it did. Correct me if I'm wrong.*

A sounds more like a question and needs an answer; B sounds more like a statement and does not necessarily need an answer.

A character in *Howards End* said, 'I ought to introduce myself, oughtn't I? My name is Mrs Munt.' Obviously she used a falling intonation in her tag question, which has no interrogative function at all. Later, when Mrs Munt told her niece, Helen, that the Wilcox family were their new neighbours, Helen blushed.

Mrs Munt was so disconcerted that she exclaimed, 'What, Helen, you don't mind them coming, do you?' and deepened the blush to crimson.
'Of course I don't mind,' said Helen, a little crossly.

This time Mrs Munt's question tag must have carried a rising intonation: she knew very well that Helen had foolishly fallen in love with the younger Wilcox son.

Sometimes we use same-way tags, particularly affirmative tags after affirmative statements, though these are not as common as the contrasting form.

Usually, the tag has a rising intonation and has a patronising and sometimes aggressive implication. Margaret Schlegel says to her social inferior, Leonard Bast:

The mistake arose out of my 'card, 'did it?

The young and arrogant Charles Wilcox bullies a railway station clerk, with

'Sign, 'must I? Why the – should I sign after all this `bother?

In a more modern idiom, we sometimes use positive + positive tag questions with two rising intonation nuclei. Here, the statement makes an informal guess and the tag asks if the guess is correct. For example: *This is 'your car, 'is it?* We can also express sarcasm in the same way: *So you're a brilliant 'linguist, 'are you?* But the corresponding negative + negative question is both rare and menacing: *So I'm not to be `trusted, `aren't I?*

English has no invariant tags – true?

GUIDELINES

Notice that we can use *there* as the subject of a question tag:

__There__ was never a real house called Howards End, was __there__?

When the subject of the statement is *somebody*, *someone*, *anybody*, *anyone*, *nobody*, *no one*, *everybody*, or *everyone*, we use *they* for the pronoun in the question tag:

__Someone__ killed Leonard Bast, didn't __they__?

Similarly, we use the pronoun *it* in the tag when the subject in the statement is *something*, *anything*, *nothing* or *everything*:

__Something__ was wrong with Leonard's heart, wasn't __it__?

Question tags are sometimes added to commands. We usually add *will/won't* to make the command less forceful:

Just lend me your scarf, __will you__?

Won't in the tag, with falling intonation, turns the command into a pressing request or invitation:

You will be careful, ˋ__won't you__?
Ring if you want anything, father, ˋ__won't you__?

Notice the difference in tone between *Sit down, ˊ__will you__?* (possibly) impatient, superior to inferior) and *Sit down, ˋ__won't you__?* (kindly invitation from equal to equal).

There are a few phrases which we use as invariant tags to add to statements, but which do not change their form to match the preceding statement. They usually take a rising intonation. Informally, we can add ***O'K? 'eh? 'what? 'right?*** and ***all 'right?*** to invite our listener to comment on our statement:

I call it a very serious thing, eh?

In the same way, we can add *am I 'right?/'don't you think?/'wouldn't you say?* to our statement.

But Mr Vyse is a wretched weedy man, don't you think?

GUIDELINE

Several languages have invariant question tags, like *n'est pas? verdad?* which make English invariant tags particularly attractive to native speakers of those languages. Several Commonwealth varieties of English use *isn't it?* as a universal tag.

Moreover, the addition of *OK? right?* and even *yes?* or *no?* to statements appears to be increasing in informal speech. The traditional question tag, however, remains an indispensable and irreplaceable feature of the language.

'I think, then, that we should pass a resolution to the effect that peaceful persuasion should be followed by militant conversation. All right?'

V. S. Naipaul, *A House for Mr Biswas*

see
135 Introductory *there*
184 Operator
237 *Yes/no* questions

239

Alternative questions

Like *yes/no* questions, alternative questions ask for a limited answer. They do this by offering two or more alternatives for the listener to choose from:

Do you want me to help you or not?

Notice that we use a rising intonation for each alternative except the last, to which we give a falling intonation. This intonation pattern distinguishes an alternative question from a *yes/no* question. Compare:

Do you play 'tennis or 'badminton? [yes/no question]
No, but I play golf.

Do you play 'tennis or `badminton? [alternative question]
Oh, tennis.

Typical alternative questions use ellipsis, and answers are usually elliptical:

Are you the younger Mr Wilcox or the elder △? The younger △.

Sometimes we use the full form in both halves of the alternative question (but an elliptical reply is still possible):

Shall I say yes, or shall I say no?

And sometimes we are unable to use ellipsis:

Can we be of any use, or shall we go?

Another type of alternative question is a pressing form of yes/no question, and seeks a plain positive or negative answer. Mrs Munt asked Margaret –

'Are you for the rich or for the poor?'

In fact we often use this type of alternative question as a device to limit the choice we are offering, and therefore to impose our opinions or will on someone. In fact, Margaret recognised the trap and avoided it:

'Are you for the rich or for the poor?'
'Too difficult. Ask me another. Am I for poverty or for riches? For riches. Hurrah for riches!'

GUIDELINES

We can change any positive yes/no question into an alternative question by adding *or not?* But in doing so, we are presuming that the whole truth lies in one of the two extreme alternatives and we are aggressively trying to impose this presumption. Compare:

Yes/No Question	**Alternative Question**
Do you love me?	*Do you love me, or not?*
Will you lend me some money?	*Will you lend me some money, or not?*

When we increase the number of alternatives this kind of question becomes less limiting:

Shall we go to a cinema, a theatre, a concert or stay at home?

Least limiting of all is the question in which the final alternative is open:

Shall we call him 'Fido, 'Rover, 'Max?

▶ **see**
88 Ellipsis
237 *Yes/no* questions

240

Exclamatory questions

Exclamatory questions are interrogative in form, but have the function of exclamations. Their structure is the same as *yes/no* questions, but we always give them a falling intonation. There are two types, both with strong positive bias. The commonest type has the form of a negative *yes/no* question: It invites the hearer to agree with the speaker's very strong positive view:

Helen admired a little boy and exclaimed, '\Isn't he \charming?'
'Undoubtedly,' said Margaret.

The less common type of exclamatory question has the form of a positive *yes/no* question, with heavy stress usually on operator and subject and a falling intonation: *'Did 'I \run? 'Was 'he em\barrassed?*

The meaning is equivalent to the parallel exclamation using how:

'How \stupid I am! ~ *'Am 'I \stupid?*

This positive form of exclamatory question is common in American English.

▶ **see**
95 Exclamations
237 *Yes/no* questions

241

Response questions

Response questions, like question tags, consist of two words, operator + personal pronoun subject. The operator is either that repeated from the preceding sentence or a form of *do*: the personal pronoun refers back to the preceding subject:

But I like milk. ***Do you?***

Such response questions do not ask for information, they are our reaction to the earlier statement – acknowledgement, unconcern, surprise, disagreement, anger. We use different intonation to show which.

There are two types of response questions:

Usually we match a positive statement with a positive response question and negative with negative:

'Hello! My new car's been driven!'
***'Has it**, sir?'* [pretended surprise]
'Charles, that reminds me of some poem.'
***'Does it** indeed?'* [impatience]
'Stopping's no good,' drawled Charles. ***'Isn't it**?' said Margaret, and jumped straight out of the car.* [anger]

When we reply to a positive utterance with a negative response question, we are expressing emphatic agreement. This type of response question always has a falling intonation, and is similar in function to an exclamatory question:

'The sword looks well, though . . .'
*'Yes, ˋ**doesn't it**?'*

We occasionally add the answer to the source question:

'Books!' cried Margaret, moved by the holy word.
'Dolly, are you serious? Has she been touching our books?'
*'ˋ**Hasn't she**, though! What used to be the hall's full of them.'*

see
240 Exclamatory questions
184 Operator

242

Declarative questions

Declarative questions are positive or negative statements which we pronounce with a rising intonation. Like tag questions with this intonation, they invite agreement from our listener. Declarative questions all have strong positive/negative bias.

'You won't be ofˊfended?' ~ *Please say you won't be offended.*

Positive statements with questioning intonation have positive bias and invite confirmation:

'Helen, I told you about poor Mrs ˊWilcox; that sad ˊbusiness?' 'Yes.'

Notice how Mr Wilcox, having failed to get an answer with a *wh*-question, used a declarative question with more success:

'What does your ˋbrother say?' 'I forget.'
'Surely he has some oˊpinion?'
'He laughs, if I remember rightly.'

Jacky, desperate for Leonard Bast to marry her, sensed that an emphatic declarative question is more forceful than a *yes/no* question, but found that a falling emphatic tag question was needed to achieve the answer she wanted:

'You ˋdoˇ love me?' [emphatic declarative]
'Jacky, you know that I do. How can you ask such questions?'
'But you do ˋlove me, Len, ˋdon't you?' [emphatic tag]
'Of course I do.'

Negative statements with rising intonation have negative bias and invite the answer *no*:

'Then you don't think I was 'foolish?' he asked . . .
'Heavens, no!' replied Margaret.

Mr Wilcox, having proposed marriage to Margaret Schlegel, could not interpret her silence. He asked:

'You are not of'fended, Miss 'Schlegel?'

His alternative question forms were *Yes/No* question: *Are you of'fended?* (may be answered *Yes*); rising tag question: *You aren't offended, 'are you?* (also may be answered *Yes*); falling tag question: *You aren't of'fended, 'are you?* (the negative bias is too strong for the situation).

The negative declarative question had the right degree of negative bias combined with the uncertainty expressed in the rising intonation. It succeeded:

'You are not of'fended, Miss Schlegel?'
'How could I be offended?'

▶ **see**
238 Tag questions
237 *Yes/no* questions

243

Echo questions

An echo question repeats all or some of an earlier message in order to confirm something, have some part repeated or have something made clearer. There are two types of echo question.

The recapitulatory echo question is like a *yes/no* question; it repeats all or part of an earlier message in order to have confirmation using a rising intonation:

'How did you get on with Tibby?'
'With your 'brother?' *'Yes.'*

'There is nothing to get up for in London.'
'Nothing to get 'up for?' *cried the scandalized Margaret.*

Sometimes we use a *wh-* word (usually *what*) to show what we have not heard or understood. Again we use a rising intonation:

Tibby implored the company generally to look out for the transitional passage on the drum.
'On the 'what, *dear?' 'On the 'drum, Aunt Juley.'*

The explicatory echo question asks for something just said to be made clearer, not just confirmed. It is always a *wh-* question, with the falling intonation nucleus on the *wh-* word:

'Miss Schlegel's got it.' ***'Got 'what?'*** *. . .*
'Howards End.'

'When did you say you paid this call?' 'Call? ***'What call?'*** *said he, staring as if her question had been a foolish one.*

▶ **see**
237 *Yes/no* questions

244
Rhetorical questions

Rhetorical questions have the form of questions but the function of forceful statements. They do not expect an answer. A positive rhetorical question makes a strong negative statement:

Can a body speak plainer? ~ *I can't speak more plainly.*

But the poetry of that kiss, the wonder of it, the magic that there was in life for hours after it – ***who can describe that?*** ~ *No one can describe it.*

Negative rhetorical questions have the effect of strong positive statements:

Helen argued that music and pictures were not very different in their appeal. Margaret passionately argued the opposite: '***Now doesn't it seem absurd to you*** *. . .?*' ~ *Surely you think it's absurd.*
Mr Wilcox excused Margaret's unwifely behaviour to his son by saying: '*She was overwrought,* **as who would not be?**' ~ *as indeed anyone would be in that situation*

▶ **GUIDELINE**

Of the nine types of question, by far the most important are *wh-* questions, *yes/no* questions and tag questions. All of them have inversion of subject and operator, perhaps the main formal feature of questions in English.

245
Reduction

Reduction is a principle of language by which we shorten the grammatical structure of one or more sentences. There are two processes which achieve reduction: substitution and ellipsis.

Substitution is the use of pro-forms as replacements – the most familiar pro-form being pronouns:

Shakespeare was born in Stratford-upon-Avon.
He *also died in Stratford-upon-Avon.*

In the second sentence, *He* replaces *Shakespeare* in the first, and is a pro-form. We can make a further substitution for *in Stratford-upon-Avon*:

Shakespeare was born in Stratford-upon-Avon.
He also died **there**.

Ellipsis is the leaving out of unnecessary words:

Shakespeare was born in 1564 and △ *died in 1616.*
He wrote 'Hamlet' and △ *thirty-five other plays.*

Reduction is both useful and important. Substitution and ellipsis make the message shorter by cutting out needless repetition. This helps us to concentrate on the new information and therefore improves understanding.

GUIDELINES

Reduce whenever you can, and as much as possible. This often means that ellipsis is preferable to substitution as in the following:

Bacon may have written 'Hamlet', but it is unlikely that he did so.
Bacon may have written 'Hamlet', but it is unlikely.

Beware, however, of ambiguity, which can result from thoughtless reduction:

Queen Gertrude, Hamlet's mother, and the King approached.

How many people approached? Two or three? Unless you know the facts, the sentence has become ambiguous because we have omitted *who was* after Gertrude.

Beware, also of using ellipsis which results in unintended humour. Comic writers sometimes use ellipsis for humorous effect:

She arrived in a low-cut dress and high dudgeon.

see
88 Ellipsis
263 Substitution

246

Reflexive pronouns

This *-self* series is a group of personal pronouns (*myself*, etc.) used (as appositive subjects or objects of verbs or prepositions) to refer backwards or forwards to another element in their clause. The complete series is:

myself *herself* *yourselves*
yourself *itself* *themselves*
himself *ourselves* *oneself*

Used reflexively, the series stand as objects of appropriate transitive verbs:

Occasionally you find **yourself** *in an odd situation.*
I could not rid **myself** *of the thought.*

operating as both direct and indirect objects:

'Bengt Danielsson,' said the man, introducing **himself** (D.O.).
I asked **myself** (I.O.) *if we knew when we were doing.*

and complementing prepositions (including the prepositional element of prepositional verbs):

The squid pump sea-water through (prep.) **themselves** *on the rocket principle.*
We couldn't help laughing at (prep. verb) **ourselves**.

In a secondary role we use them emphatically to stress subject or (less commonly) the object:

If only we (s.) **ourselves** *could hold on.*
Heyerdahl visited the **President of Peru** (o.) **himself.**

Emphasising the subject, the pronoun can take mid- or end-position with little change of meaning, though the end-position reflexive is commonest:

The people of Easter Island could ***themselves*** *claim white ancestors.*
I'm willing to build a raft ***myself****.*

GUIDELINES

After third person pronouns for the purpose of generalising, the plural reflexive seems to be favoured, despite an earlier singular form:

Everyone (sing.)/*-body* (sing.), *no one* (sing.)/*-body* (sing.) *allowed themselves* (pl.) *to be persuaded.*

Also we seem to avoid placing next to each other pronouns and reflexives with an identical stem:

The raft ***itself*** *looked bizarre*, but not **It* ***itself*** *looked bizarre.*

One can think about it ***oneself***, but not **One* ***oneself*** *can think about it.*

We prefer not to use a reflexive pronoun in prepositional phrases of place, even though there is reference to the clause subject or object. So:

We had a good laugh at ***ourselves***, but *We had a good view behind* ***us****/a long journey ahead of* ***us****/a huge distance between* ***us***, etc.

Compare, however, the metaphorical use of the same place prepositions, when we select the reflexive pronouns: *behind/ahead of* ***ourselves*** *in our work, in confidence between* ***ourselves****.*

see
37 Apposition
183 Objects
228 Pronouns

247

Relative clauses

These are subordinate finite clauses. They postmodify nouns or noun groups, and are therefore adjectival:

He bought the Jaguar, ***which he had been eyeing in a car showroom****.*

Relative clauses are introduced by relative pronouns which usually refer back to the head of the noun phrase:

... the guest of honour, ***who*** *had rushed back to Cairo*

The choice of pronoun depends upon personal/non-personal reference, whether the reference is subjective, objective or possessive, whether the clause is defining or non-defining and the degree of formality being used:

... the sign that one German driver makes to another ***who*** *has annoyed him* [personal, subjective, defining]

... light music had stopped, replaced by the Funeral March, ***which*** *was evidently all the disc jockey had to hand* [non-personal, non-defining]

... The Jaguar had been sold by a British army officer ***whose*** *wife had grown too pregnant to fit into it.* [personal, possessive, defining]

Contact clauses are always – defining or non-defining?

With defining clauses, a relative pronoun in object position is frequently omitted. This zero pronoun produces a unique relative clause without a relative pronoun – a contact clause:

. . . one of the extravagances △ he permitted himself

In the spoken language, we often omit a relative pronoun and operator, thereby reducing the clause:

. . . a hundred and fifty pages of typewritten script, △ △ apparently banged out on an old machine

. . . The pages . . . bore the unmistakeable tinting of white paper △ △ several years old.

These are reduced relative clauses.

GUIDELINES

In addition to the *wh-* relative pronouns, we also occasionally use *when*, *where* and *why* as relative adverbs, referring back to time and place antecedents. But in both cases, ordinary relative pronouns are alternatives:

It was the afternoon of 11 October, ***when*** *we arrived.*

. . . 200 yards from the house ***where*** *he had his rooftop flat*

see

82, 248 Defining/non-defining
184 Operator
185 Participles
200 Post-modifiers
251 Relative pronouns
261 Subordination
277 Zero forms

248

Relative clauses: defining and non-defining

These are sometimes called restrictive/non-restrictive or identifying/non-identifying. Defining relative clauses define or identify or restrict the preceding noun:

One of them knew two architects ***who would never have worn such a hat.***

Notice there are no commas, because we make no spoken pause after *architects*. The subject knew – not just two architects – but two architects who would not wear a hat like Bosinney's. This is therefore a defining clause: the clause being tightly connected to its preceding noun, and certainly not a loose, additional afterthought.

Non-defining relative clauses simply add additional information about something or someone already defined or identified. This information is separated off by commas in writing, and by pauses and typical intonation patterns in speech:

She was one of those women born to be loved and to love, ***who when not loving are not living.***

Both defining and non-defining relative clauses may refer to personal and non-personal subjects and objects:

The sudden flush **that rose on the young girl's** *face* . . .
[defining relative clause with non-personal subject reference]

He was a very talented architect, **whose professional reputation was . . . at stake.** [non-defining relative clause with personal subject reference]

. . . *the visiting cards in the porcelain bowl* **that stood on the carved oak rug chest** [defining relative clauses with non-personal subject reference]

We use *that* for both people and things in defining clauses only.

GUIDELINES

If you find someone does not understand the difference between defining and non-defining clauses, try them with these two:

His wife, **who works in London,** *is dark-haired.* (He has one wife.)
[non-defining]

His wife **who works in London** *is dark-haired.* (His London wife is dark-haired. But, by implication, he has more than one wife.) [defining]

We use defining relative clauses frequently in both speech and writing, but non-defining are more formal, less common and used more in writing than speech.

'A statesman is a politician who places himself at the service of the nation.
A politician is a statesman who places the nation at his service.'

President Pompidou,
Observer newspaper, 'Sayings of the Year', 1973

---

see
82 Defining/non-defining
247 Relative clauses

249

Relative clauses: sentence relatives

Some *which* clauses refer back, not to an earlier noun/noun phrase, but to the whole sentence: these are sentence relatives and can only be introduced by *which*:

When she entered a room it was felt that something substantial had come in, **which was probably the reason for her unpopularity** . . .

. . . *though looking at Soames he did not seem to see him,* **which gave Soames an unpleasant feeling**.

Which pronoun invariably opens nominal relative clauses?

▸ **see**
247 Relative clauses
257 Sentence adverbials

250

Relative clauses: nominal relatives

What, unlike other relative pronouns, refers both backwards and forwards. In sentences like

This is ***what comes of having no children,***

what behaves like a complement/pronoun – *This is* **what** – and also like a determiner meaning the thing which – *the thing which comes of having no children*. This latter behaves like a noun phrase, in this case a complement. Consider:

What had made her yield *he could never work out.*
It was difficult to see ***what steps could be taken.***
I should like to . . . see ***what you've been doing.***
I have tried to do ***what you want.***

In these examples *what* may be paraphrased as *that which*. It opens a noun phrase in object position (*that*) and acts as a relative pronoun object of the following verb (*which*). We do not use *what* in normal relative clauses, but it has this interesting and unique role in nominal relative clauses.

> *'He knew what's what.'*
>
> Samuel Butler, *Hudibras*

▸ **see**
84 Determiners
156 Nominal clauses
178 Noun phrase
228 Pronouns
247 Relative clauses
274 *Wh-* words

251

Relative pronouns

We use the following *wh-* words as relative pronouns to introduce relative clauses:

who whom whose that which what

The relative pronouns stand first in a clause, except when preceded by a preposition – all can refer to both singular and plural antecedents:

A second shareholder . . . ***whom*** *Soames recognised . . .*
. . . five strong, silent shareholders, with ***whom*** *Soames could sympathise . . .*

Our choice of pronoun depends on whether it refers to a personal or non-personal noun/noun phrase; is the subject or object of its clause; is in a defining or non-defining clause; is in a formal or informal style.

Personal and non-personal reference

Who (subject), *whom* (object) and *whose* (possessive) are normally used to refer to people:

A woman **who** *could make herself a pretty frock had not lost her interest in life.*

... scratched his head ... like the gentleman farmer for **whom** *he loved to be taken*

... a poor devil **whose** *mistress has just been telling him a pretty story ...*

We sometimes use *who* and *whom* for favourite animals, and *whose* for things:

... the dog, Balthazar, **who** *sometimes found a mole*

Old Jolyon disliked silkworms, **whose** *heads and colour reminded him of elephants.*

... on it the first lavender, **whose** *scent filled the room*

Which refers to things:

... a tree **which** *shakes itself free of raindrops*

That can refer to both people and things:

... a poor, thin slip of a shopgirl **that** *passed him*
He opened the Times *with the rich crackle* **that** *drowns all lesser noises.*

GUIDELINES

We use *that* and never *which* after other indefinite pronouns and superlatives:

He had known everything **that** *went on.*
The best **that** *money can buy.*

In these, and in all other uses of relative *that*, we pronounce it weakly, /ðət/

Subject and object relative pronouns

Only the personal pronoun has different forms as subject and object: *who/whom.*

The passer-by **who** *sees them wrapped in ... comfort never suspects ...* [subject]

Soames just talked of the Barbizon school of painters, **whom** *he had just discovered.* [object]

But this is formal, literary English; we often use *who* in object position informally, and especially in speech. The sentence about a gentleman farmer above would more likely appear in today's informal style as: *Like the gentleman farmer he loved to be taken for.*

We tend to be shy of using *whom* if we can avoid it. Many people find correct usage difficult, but are in good company. Here is Shakespeare using *whom* wrongly:

And in these fits I leave them, while I visit
Young Ferdinand, **whom** *they suppose is drowned.*

The Tempest, III. iii. 91–2

Only **which** of the relatives can refer to people and things – true?

Which is used for both non-personal subject and object reference, including use as prepositional object.

. . . *the look on her face* ***which*** *reminded him of his wife* [subject]
. . . *break down the resistance* ***which*** *he had suffered* . . . [object]
. . . *the years of half rations through* ***which*** *he had passed* . . . [obj. of prep.]

That/zero are alternative object pronouns in defining clauses for both personal and non-personal reference:

. . . *one of the first things (****that****) June did . . . all (****that****) he believed in*
. . . *nothing (****that****) she could have done, nothing (****that****) she had done*

In each of these sentences (published 1906) we would most likely today omit *that*, certainly in informal style. This omission is called zero pronoun, and the clause with zero pronoun is a contact clause.

> *'It is very unfair to expect a politician to live in private up to the statements he makes in public.'*
>
> W. Somerset Maugham, *The Circle*

GUIDELINES

Today we prefer the simple, direct and brief style of English, particularly in speech and informal writing. For this reason, contact clauses are favoured: *people we meet*, *the woman I love*, *the man we love to hate*, *the money we earn*, etc. For the same reason, we avoid *whom*, replacing it with *who* or *that* or zero pronoun:

The people ***whom*** *we've invited*
The people ***who*** *we've invited*
The people ***that*** *we've invited*
The people △ we've invited ↓ less formal

Similarly we prefer *that* to *who* or *which*:

The people ***who*** *live next door*
The people ***that*** *live next door* ↓ less formal

The book ***which*** *fell*
The book ***that*** *fell* ↓ less formal

And today we prefer to postpone prepositions to the end of relative clauses:

companies ***of which*** *he was a director*
companies △ he was a director ***of*** ↓ less formal

Bosinney, ***to whom*** *she turned . . .*
Bosinney, ***who*** *she turned to . . .* ↓ less formal

(But notice Galsworthy's *not the sort of thing that she would* ***speak about****.)*

see

247 Contact clauses
82, 248 Defining/non-defining
250 Nominal relative clauses
228 Pronouns
247 Relative clauses
249 Sentence relatives
274 *Wh-* words
277 Zero forms

252

Reporting and thinking verbs

These are verbs of speaking and thinking which we use to introduce direct speech:

Eustace **asked**, *'Was it dark in church?'*
'I've told you,' she **added**, *'it really wasn't so sad.'*
'Well,' **exclaimed** *Minney.*

Notice that the reporting verb with its subject may take front-, mid- or end-position. Also, though never in front-position, subject and reporting verb can be inverted, though normally only when the subject is not a pronoun, and when the verb is in the present simple or past simple tenses.

'I shall never go that way again,' **thought Eustace**.

The commonest reporting and thinking verbs used with direct and indirect speech include:

add	*confess*	*order*	*shout*
admit	*cry*	*promise*	*state*
agree	*declare*	*protest*	*tell*
announce	*exclaim*	*remark*	*think*
answer	*explain*	*repeat*	*warn*
argue	*insist*	*reply*	*whisper*
ask	*object*	*report*	*wonder*
claim	*observe*	*say*	*write*

Most reporting and thinking verbs can have a *that*- clause as object:

He **felt** *that there was still something he wanted to ask her.*

but we often omit *that* (zero *that*):

Who would have **thought** △ *the old lady had all that money.*

Some verbs have a compulsory indirect object before the *that*- clause:

She **informed** *him that Dick had been there.*

The commonest of these verbs are:

assure *convince* *inform* *notify* *persuade* *remind* *tell*

Many reporting and thinking verbs are followed by a *wh*- clause:

You may **say** *what you like, Alfred.*

The commonest include:

argue	*discuss*	*imagine*	*remember*
arrange	*explain*	*know*	*say*
ask	*find out*	*learn*	*see*
choose	*forget*	*notice*	*show*
decide	*guess*	*observe*	*tell*
discover	*hear*	*realise*	*think*

A few of these verbs require an indirect object in this pattern:

Minney **told** *him what had happened.*

These verbs include:

advise inform instruct show teach tell

Some reporting and thinking verbs are in catenative use with *to*-infinitive, others may be followed by an indirect object + *to*-infinitive.

One group of verbs we can follow with the pro-form *so*:

Well, some people might ***think*** *so.*

This group includes:

assume	*guess*	*notice*	*suppose*
believe	*hear*	*prefer*	*suspect*
expect	*hope*	*promise*	*think*
fear	*imagine*	*say*	*understand*
gather	*maintain*	*suggest*	

▶ **see**

53, 57	Catenative use	136	Inversion
85, 110	Direct/indirect speech	277	Zero forms

253

Sentences, simple, compound and complex

In speech we separate sentences by pauses and mark them with typical intonation patterns: in writing we start each sentence with a capital letter and end it with a full stop, question mark or exclamation mark. Sentences are made up of one or more clauses, which are the basic units of grammar. The simplest sentence consists of one finite clause, having a subject and a finite verb, for example: *She* (S.) *fell* (V.).

Sentences are either simple, compound or complex. A simple sentence has one subject (S.) and one finite verb (V.). It may also have a direct object (D.O.), a complement (C.), an indirect object (I.O.) and a direct object, or a direct object and a complement, according to the kind of verb. A simple sentence may also have an adverbial (adv.).

All of the following are simple sentences:

S. V. D.O.
'The wife of a friend of mine has had an accident.

S. V. S.V. Adv. V.
She fell. I'm just going over.'

V. S. V. Adv. S. V. C.
'Shall I come too ? I might be useful.

Adv. S.V. Adv. C. Adv.
After all, I'm still a doctor in the eyes of God.'

S. V. D.O.
We got a taxi.

A compound sentence has two or more clauses which are equally important and usually joined by a coordinating conjunction like *and*, *but* and *or*; sometimes by being one after the other with zero coordinator.

For example:

Arnold jumped up **and** *made for the door,* **but** *I stopped him.*

I've never been myself **or** *lived my own life at all.*

A complex sentence has one main clause (M.C.) and one or more subclauses (S.C.). These are frequently introduced by a subordinator like *because*, *if*, *when* and *who*. For example:

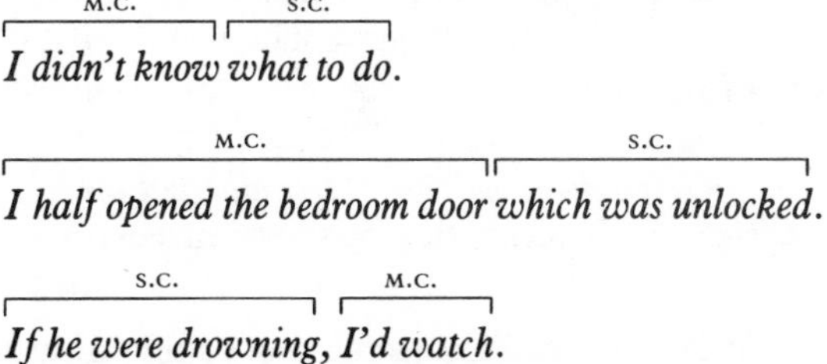

There are also compound-complex sentences which have two or more main clauses and one or more subclauses. For example:

M.C.

There was a darkening reddish bruise under one eye and

M.C. S.C.

the eye was narrowed, though this was hard to see

S.C.

because the eyelids . . . were red and swollen with weeping.

S.C. M.C.

And even when I went to get some water she jumped up and

M.C.

ran upstairs to the bedroom and locked herself in.

see

61 Clauses
76 Conjunctions
77 Coordination
96 Finite/non-finite
183 Objects
261 Subordination
262 Subordinator
272 Verb types
277 Zero forms

254

Sentence form and function

There are four types of sentence: declaratives, interrogatives, imperatives and exclamations. Each has a typical form, which helps us recognise it; we know that *He is brave* is a declarative. *Is he brave?* is an interrogative. *Be brave* is an imperative and *How brave!* is an exclamation.

Traditional grammar has suggested that the work, or the function of a declarative is to make a statement, that the function of an interrogative is to ask a question, that of imperatives to give commands and that the function of exclamations is to exclaim. Each of these is true – sometimes. But each of the four sentence types can do several different jobs, can fulfil several functions. One particular sentence form is not tied to one sentence meaning.

The following sentences all have the form of declaratives. But their function in Iris Murdoch's *The Black Prince*, taking into account the situation, the speaker and his audience, is that suggested in brackets:

Julian said, 'Bradley, I wonder if I could buy this off you?' ~ *'Bradley, can I buy this . . .'* [question by statement, a request]

You can just shut up, you're leaving here in three minutes . . . ~ *Shut up and get ready to go.* [command by statement, a warning]

Roger and that young girl, God, it sickens me! ~ *Roger and that young girl. How the idea sickens me!* [exclamation by statement, expressing disgust]

Other examples show how declaratives can fulfil a range of communicative functions:

'This is Marigold. She is my mistress.' [introducing someone]
'He'll send everything on.' [making a promise]
'I think I really must go.' [saying goodbye]
'You've got to forgive us.' [apologising]
'I'd go to bed if I were you.' [giving advice]

The following sentences have the formal features of interrogatives, but the first three are not asking questions:

If I was settling abroad, why send (the letter) anyway? ~ *It would be pointless to send it, if . . .* [statement by interrogative expressing a contradiction]

'Could you deal with this?' ~ *'Deal with this (please).'* [command by interrogative, a request]

'Oh, why was I such a fool?' ~ *'Oh, what a fool I was.'* [exclamation by interrogative, expressing remorse]

Further examples show how the interrogative form covers other pragmatic categories:

'Is it too early for a drink?' [making a request]
'Won't you drink?' [making an invitation]
'Did you want me to fight him?' [making an offer]
'I'll pack them, shall I?' [making a suggestion]

Similarly the following sentences have the form of imperatives but the first three are not giving commands:

'Don't think I'm the devil incarnate, Bradley, old man.' ~ *'I'm not the devil incarnate . . .'* [statement by imperative, persuasion]

'Oh you should be ashamed, look at you both.' ~ *'Doesn't your appearance make you ashamed?'* [question by imperative, expressing disapproval]

'Oh, go to hell!' ~ *'How infuriating you are!'* [exclamation by imperative, expressing anger]

Here the imperative form covers other pragmatic categories:

Have some more chocolate. [offering]
Do something for me. [making a request]
Let me come with you. [pleading]

Even sentences which have the grammatical form of exclamations may have non-exclamatory functions:

How heavy (my heart) is, like a great stone in my breast. ~ *My heart is so heavy, like . . .* [statement by exclamation, expressing sorrow]
How nice. How kind. [expressing thanks]
What a schoolboy you are. [expressing affection]

Notice, however, that when Iris Murdoch's precious hero-author indulges in an excess of exclamations, the style becomes embarrassingly rhetorical:

'How can one describe oneself? With what an air of false coy humility, with what an assumed confiding simplicity one sets about it! "I am a puritan," and so on. Faugh! How can these statements not be false? Even "I am tall" has a context. How the angels must laugh and sigh.'

GUIDELINES

Think of sentence types as people. Perhaps you are a tax inspector, but in several situations you play other roles: a parent to your children, a customer to a shopkeeper, a passenger to a taxi-driver. Yet you still look the same, you haven't changed your shape. In the same way, a declarative – without changing its form – can ask a question, give an order, show emotion, say hallo or goodbye and fulfil many other functions, according to the situation. Remember, also, that any sentence form can have a questioning or an exclamatory function if it is taken up by a second speaker.

CAPTAIN: *Though 'Bother it' I may*
Occasionally say, I never use a big, big D.
CHORUS : *What, never?*
CAPTAIN: *No, never!*
CHORUS : *What, never?*
CAPTAIN: *Well, hardly ever!*

W. S. Gilbert, *HMS Pinafore*

---

see
95 Exclamations
109 Imperatives
132 Interrogatives

255

Sentences: four kinds identified by form

A simple sentence may be a declarative, an interrogative, an imperative or an exclamation.

Which of the four kinds of sentence usually has no subject?

Declaratives are the commonest kind of sentence. Their regular function is to give information and the subject usually comes before the verb – s. + v.

She's (s.v.) *all right!*
She (s.) *wants* (v.) *to see you.*

Interrogatives are usually used when we want information. We recognise interrogatives because one or more of the following features is present:

they start with a *wh-* word
***What** happened?* ***Where** are the scissors?*

the operator is placed before the subject
Are (op.) *you* (s.) *all right?*
Shall (op.) *I* (s.) *get you some tea?*

the sentence is spoken with rising intonation
Have you called a 'doctor? *She 'fell?*

Notice that all written questions end with a question mark.

Imperatives are used not only to give orders or instructions but to make suggestions and requests. An imperative uses the base form of the verb, and usually has no stated subject:

***Go** in and look at her.*
***Don't** be angry . . .*
Well, you (s.) ***stay** here, I said.*

Exclamations show surprise or other strong emotion. They start with either *how* + adjective/adverb, or *what* (+ adjective) + noun, followed by subject and verb.

***How** fortunate we are to have English as our native tongue!*
***What** a schoolboy you are!*

Written exclamations usually end with an exclamation mark.

Some utterances which may be confused with exclamations are fixed phrases, like *Goodness me! Oh dear!* But these do not have sentence structure (nor can we claim that they are elliptical).

It is worth repeating that sentences which have declarative forms can also be used to ask questions or give commands, just as interrogative forms often function as statements, requests and commands.

▶ **see**
88 Ellipsis
95 Exclamations
109 Imperatives
131 Interjections
136 Inversion
184 Operator
235 Questions
254 Sentence form and function
274 *Wh-* words

256

Sentence parts

Traditional grammar divides a sentence into subject (the person or thing we are talking about) and predicate (what is said about the subject). These meanings still have a limited usefulness, though throughout this book *subject* means grammatical subject of a verb. We use the terms topic or theme for the initial subject matter of a sentence – which may or may not be the grammatical subject. What is said about the topic is called the comment.

Compare these two sentences:

S. Pred.

I turned my head.

Topic Comment

P. S. P.

What was she thinking?

Topic Comment

The predicate in complete sentences always contains a verb phrase (V.P.) and according to the verb may have a complement (C.) or a direct object (D.O.) and an indirect object (I.O.) and sometimes an adverbial (Adv.).

see

23 Adverbials
97 Focus
183 Objects
184 Operator and predication
259 Subject and predicate
266 Topic and comment
272 Verb types and sentence patterns

257

Sentence adverbials

When an adverbial relates to a whole sentence rather than another element, it is a sentence adverbial. It may consist of a single adverb: *honestly*; a prepositional phrase: *in all honesty*; an infinitive clause: *to speak honestly*; an *-ing* participle clause: *honestly speaking*; an *-en* participle clause: *honestly put*; or even a finite verb clause: *If I may speak honestly*, etc.

Most sentence adverbials take front-position. Most sentence adverbs end in *-ly* and are used elsewhere as manner adverbs. One type of sentence adverbial tells how the speaker feels he is speaking:

Personally*, I thought it was . . . too short.*

Other adverbs like *personally* are:

frankly honestly seriously truly

With another type of sentence adverbial, the speaker comments on the sentence content:

Obviously*, it was surprise time for Cable again.*

Other adverbs include:

actually	*clearly*	*indeed*	*obviously*
certainly	*evidently*	*inevitably*	*really*

Other adverbials include:

in fact to my annoyance to my regret as I had feared

See also Comment clauses (63).

A third type of sentence adverbial gives the speaker's emotional reaction to the sentence:

__Unexpectedly__, the rather studious features dissolved into a grin.
__Curiously__, everything seemed to get very quiet.

Other adverbs include:

annoyingly	*naturally*	*surprisingly*
fortunately	*rightly*	*understandably*
hopefully	*strangely*	*wrongly*
luckily		

Other sentence adverbials include:

to my annoyance	*as seemed natural*	*to my surprise*
as I had hoped	*rightly speaking*	*as I found understandable*
by luck	*strange as it may seem*	*in my view wrongly*

▶ GUIDELINE

Sentence adverbs which prefer mid-position include *definitely*, *possibly and probably*.

▶ **see**

12	Adverbs	120	Infinitive clauses
63	Comment clauses	129, 185	*-ing* participle clauses
96	Finite verb clauses	18	Manner adverbs
		218	Preposition phrases

258

Some-any-no- series

The title of this entry is a shorthand way of saying that *some*, *any* and *no* are not only determiners in their own right but when added to *-thing*, *-body* and *-one* form three groups of indefinite pronouns (*something/somebody/someone*, etc.). Added to *-where*, they also form a parallel group of adverbs (*somewhere*, etc.).

Traditional grammar taught that *some-* words were used in positive statements and *any-* words in negative and interrogative sentences. But it was then bound to note exceptions in order to explain sentences like –

May I get you __something__? [*some-* with interrogative]
He sang Schubert better than __any__ . . . [*any-* with positive]

The concept of assertion/non-assertion gives a better account of accepted use.

Assertive forms – positive statements and questions with positive bias take *some-* words, also *any-* words in their 'identification' meaning.

I lost __some__ money in the theatre. [positive statement]
May I get you __something__? [positive bias question]
They swarmed out in __anything__ that would float. [identifying *any-*]

Non-assertive forms – statements with unspecific identity, questions without positive bias, comparative clauses, putative *should* clauses, conditional clauses and their negatives take *any-* words:

Apart from ***anything*** *else, I don't know where to go.*	[unspecific]
Does ***anyone*** *wish to say* ***anything*** *more?*	[open question]
People take life more seriously than ***any*** *of you imagine.*	[comparative]
Should ***anyone*** *call . . .*	[putative *should*]
If there was ***anything*** *more he needed . . .*	[conditional]
She never took ***anything*** *seriously.*	[negative]

We use *no-* words to make assertive forms negative and *not* applied to the operator to negate non-assertive forms:

Nothing *and* ***no one*** *appeared.*	[assertive]
Apparently she did not suspect ***anything.***	[non-assertive]

▶ GUIDELINES

With personal pronouns in the *some-* series (including *every-* words) we use singular verbs – *somebody has brought him.* Yet see how we use third person plural pronouns with the series:

Somebody ***has*** *brought* ***their*** *brother.*
Everybody ***has their*** *own ideas.*
Nobody *knows, do* ***they****?*

▶ **see**

46	Assertion/non-assertion	228	Pronouns
27	Comparative clauses	150	*Should* clauses
29	Conditional clauses	231	*Some/any* quantifiers
84	Determiners		

259

Subject and predicate

Traditionally a simple sentence consists of a subject (s.) and a predicate (pred.). In simple statements, the subject usually comes first. In these cases, it is the theme of the sentence – what the sentence is about (information which may have been mentioned before). The predicate is what is being said about the subject, and more likely to be new information:

I (s.) *am not hungry* (pred.).
The fire (s.) *was out* (pred.).
His head (s.) *had fallen on his chest* (pred.).

The subject controls the form of the following verb, if there is a choice – *I* (s.) *am, The fire* (s.) *was . . .*

The subject changes position when a statement forms a *yes/no* question:
'Is my uncle (s.) *not liked?'*
'Is something (s.) *the matter?'*

In negative sentences, the negation is usually part of the predicate:

The man would **not** *commit himself. 'I do***n't** *want to make trouble,' he repeated, 'and I do***n't** *know anything . . . Respectable folk do***n't** *go to Jamaica any more.'*

In some kinds of elliptical sentences, the nature of the subject is so obvious, that we omit it completely, leaving only the predicate:

'△Didn't think to see me, did you?' he said.
'△Thought I was down on the shore . . .'

Alternatively, we sometimes omit the predicate leaving only the subject to represent the elliptical sentence:

'Come now. Did not the landlord's brother take you to Launceston Fair?'
'. . . the landlord's brother△?' she repeated, playing for time.

This echo question selects the subject of the earlier sentence as carrying the most important information and therefore omits the predicate (though it is still understood) which normally carries greater focus.

Sentence predicates are often replaced by *do* pro-forms:

'I know I deserve black looks for speaking to you as I **did***, but if you knew my brother as well as I* **do** *you'd understand . . .'*
'No,' said Mary steadily, 'he never comes here.'
'Oh, he **doesn't***?'*

More often the pro-form replaces the predication.

GUIDELINE

The subject is much more easily identified than the predicate, which can be of any length and complexity. Modern grammar prefers to divide sentences into subject, operator and predication.

see

243 Echo questions
97 Focus
89 Initial ellipsis
155 Negative sentences
184 Operator and predication
263 Substitution

260

Subjunctive mood

The subjunctive is very rare in modern British English. Some other languages have a regular subjunctive form to express possibility, uncertainty or hypothetical conditions, but we usually use modal verbs.

There are three areas in which we regularly use the subjunctive: the *were* patterns for hypothetical situations; the so-called mandative use, when we are trying to get something done; and a small number of fixed formulas and phrases.

The *were* subjunctive is often used after *if*, *as if*, *as though* and *wish*.

It would be different if he **were** *a member of our religion.*
Mr March began to grumble, almost as though he **were** *parodying himself.*
'I wish it **were** *not so,' said Charles.*

In informal and conversational use, we use *was* instead of *were*.

Very occasionally we use inversion instead of *if* (+ *were*) as with other *if* patterns:

If she were really happy ... ~ ***Were** she really happy ...*

but this is a very literary style, when *was* would be impossible for the inversion.

Notice If I were you (~ *If I were in your place ...*) is a common fixed phrase in which we do not use *was*.

The mandative subjunctive is used in subordinate *that*- clauses, and consists of the base form of the verb. The *that*- clause follows demands, proposals, recommendations etc.

*They demanded that Sir Philip **resign** his position.*

*It was imperative that Ann **stop** giving information.*

This subjunctive use occurs in *that*- clauses following:

verbs like
decide demand insist order prefer propose require suggest

adjectives like
advisable desirable essential fitting imperative necessary vital

nouns like
decision demand insistence order resolution requirement

In every case, however, this use is highly formal and pedantic. Most people would say, and even prefer to write, *should* in the *that*- clause.

*that Sir Philip **resign*** ~ *that Sir Philip **should resign***

(See *Should* in subordinate clauses.)

The commonest formulas using the subjunctive are:

Heaven forbid Long live the King God be praised

The fixed phrases in which we use the subjunctive in everyday language include:

as it were ~ *as you might say*
be it x or be it y ~ *whether it is x or y*
be that as it may ~ *that may be true or not*
if need be ~ *if there is a necessity*
and *so be it* ~ *I accept/agree*

'Fee, fi, fo, fum,
I smell the blood of an Englishman,
Be he alive, or be he dead,
I'll grind his bones to make my bread.'

Nursery Rhyme

▸ see
136 Inversion
143 Modal verbs
150 *Should* in subordinate clauses

261
Subordination

This is the joining of a clause to a main clause in such a way that we know that the clause is dependent – subordinate. Usually we do this by starting the subordinate clause with a subordinating conjunction.

__While__ Maria sets the table for breakfast, he hums a little tune to himself.

. . . black sloe-shaped eyes __which__ seem to have had all the good humour worn out of them

There are four kinds of subordinate clauses: adverbial, relative, nominal and comment clauses. We show the subordinate status of adverbial clauses by starting them with a subordinating conjunction:

__Where__ possible, she reserved judgement.

Nominal clauses are subordinated by initial *wh-* words, *that* or zero.

I do not know __what__ they pay him for it.

Relative clauses are subordinated by *as*, *that*, relative adverbs, relative pronouns and zero pronoun.

All __who__ refused to bear arms had been expelled.

. . . a journey __which__ would put us within striking distance of Rhodes

We do not always need to use a subordinator. Non-finite and verbless clauses are subordinate by definition. They have no finite verb, whereas the main clause has. Their form has already downgraded them in relation to the main clause:

(here) an old shepherd kept his sheep, __standing under the great tree which crowns the amphitheatre__.

Subordination is also occasionally marked by inversion in some conditional and comparative clauses:

. . . if you see someone afflicted ~ ***should you** see someone afflicted*

. . . __so great__ is the hum of the crowd that the priests remain as yet beyond earshot.

▶ GUIDELINES

When the subjects of two coordinate clauses are the same noun phrase we have a choice of repeating the noun phrase or using a pro-form in one clause:

Your brother brought it and __your brother/he__ can take it back.

But with subordination we have no such choice, one clause must have the pro-form:

Since your brother brought it, he can take it back.
Since he brought it, your brother can take it back.

▶ **see**

24 Adverbial clauses
27 Comparative clauses
29 Conditional clauses
63 Comment clauses
136 Inversion
156 Nominal clauses
157 Non-finite clauses
247 Relative clauses
76 Subordinating conjunctions
277 Zero forms

262

Subordinators

These are the conjunctions and other words which join a subordinate (dependent) clause to a main clause. We subordinate adverbial clauses by introducing them with subordinating conjunctions or correlatives:

***Rather than** give me the telegram . . . she tore it up and put it down the lavatory.*

***When** an idea struck him, it was his habit to slam on the brakes.*

But subordinate nominal clauses and relative clauses are subordinated by *as*, *that* and some *wh-* words which may be relative adverbs or pronouns:

*I have not been able to discover **whether** he visited Rhodes.*

*. . . comes from the story **that** the Great Turk had a bird that laid an egg with a puppy in it*

*. . . this sunlit landscape **whose** wine and fruit could only lead a man to laziness*

These subordinators are different from subordinating conjunctions because they are an essential part of their subordinate clauses. By contrast, conjunctions join complete clauses.

GUIDELINE

In addition to obvious subordinators like conjunctions and relatives, we occasionally use noun phrases which function as adverbials of time:

Each time we had fun. Each time ~ whenever.

Other similar noun phrases include: *every time/occasion*; *the second/minute/day/year*.

see
76 Conjunctions
79 Correlatives
156 Nominal clauses
247 Relative clauses
261 Subordination

263

Substitution

We reduce the length of sentences – reduction – by two processes. One is ellipsis, in which we omit unnecessary items, the other is substitution. In this process, we replace items which are too long or too well-known to be repeated. Substitute words of this kind are called pro-forms, the most common of which is the group of noun-substitutes we call pronouns. Substitution is most commonly found in the noun phrase and in the verb phrase and occasionally as a replacement for adverbials.

Is he deaf or dumb? Both – what does **both** substitute for?

Substitutes for nouns and noun phrases

Nouns and noun phrases are perhaps the commonest carriers of information, as subjects, objects and complements. So it is not surprising that we use a wide range of pronouns as substitutes in those positions.

Personal pronouns, *I* and *you*, usually refer directly to someone in the situation, but outside the text. Substitution is most often made by third person pronouns.

Looking up, she caught David Ollerenshaw's eye.
***He** was sitting almost directly opposite.*

In this example, the pronoun *he* is preferred to a second use of David Ollerenshaw. Similarly, *it* can substitute for a noun phrase:

*The sight of his wet jacket filled her with despair. She could not endure **it**.*

Notice an important difference between coordinate and subordinate clauses. With coordinate clauses (or where the reference backwards is to another sentence) we can choose between repetition, substitution or omission:

*It was Giles who suffered from hubris, and it was **Giles** who ought to have a heart attack.* (*Giles* is repeated, but *he* could be substituted.)

But Giles had wanted those last few properties, and △ had bought them, and △ borrowed for them. (*he* is omitted.)

In a subordinate clause, however, we do not repeat the noun phrase and we do not omit it: a pronoun substitute is necessary:

*Giles . . . let them think what they chose . . . for **he** wanted to make his mark in other fields.*

Other common pronouns include: *one(s)*, *another*, *both*, *this/that/these/those*, *the same* and *the former/latter* as illustrated in the following:

*She wrote a real postcard to her children: that **one**, she would post. And **another** to her parents . . .*

*David had leapt around in a most uninhibited fashion, all by himself. She liked **that** . . .*

*All in all it had been quite an enjoyable day. **The same** could not be said for Stephen's funeral.*

*Had he driven her away, or had she departed? **The latter**, surely.*

In the last three examples the pronouns replace main clauses, which have become subjects and objects of their following sentences.

Substitutes for predication

We use *do* to substitute for an earlier predication in the simple tenses:

*'I always hope people won't really read that kind of rubbish. I never **do**.'*

We also use *do so* as a substitute for a predication:

*When (journalists) descended on her with cameras and tape recorders and notebooks, she gave them the freedom of her house, as though she were contracted to **do so**.*

*Sometimes she dignified it with the name of Despair – had usually **done so**, in fact, as a child.*

Notice that *do* in this use is a main verb and not an auxiliary – we also use *do it* and *do that* as predication substitutes:

> *. . . she had married, had given birth cheerfully, and produced as it seemed cheerful children. Maybe she shouldn't have* ***done it****?*

We use *so* to substitute for a predication when we are confirming a statement.

> *'She'll be delighted,' said her husband . . . and* **so** *indeed she seemed to be.*
>
> *Frances would have thought it beneath her dignity and his, but evidently this was not* **so***.*

Notice that *so* may not be a pro-form when it means *too*, that is, when new information is added after *so*. In this case we reverse the order of subject/auxiliary.

> *'You have a lucky nature.' '***So** *have you.'*
> *He found all this very amusing and* **so** *did they.*

The corresponding negative forms are *neither/nor*:

> *'You haven't any time to waste on Mrs Mayfield.'*
> *'***Nor** *has anybody else.'*

GUIDELINE

We stress the initial *so/nor* and also the final word of these phrases: ***So*** *they are* (confirming); ***So*** *are they* (adding new information).

Both structures use pronouns, but proper nouns are only acceptable in the final stressed position.

> *I wanted to take my clothes off.* **So** *did Len. (= Len did too)*

Substitutes for clauses

So is a substitute for an affirmative *that*-clause after certain verbs:

appear	*fear*	*presume*	*think*
assume	*guess*	*say*	*trust*
believe	*hope*	*suppose*	*understand*
expect	*imagine*	*tell*	*be afraid*

Not is a substitute for a negative *that*- clause after the same verbs. These are, in fact, noun clauses which are the objects of the above verbs, reported statements.

> *She had to do it, the recipe said* **so.**
>
> *'Do you mean one can inherit a landscape?' 'Yes, I think* **so***.'*
>
> *'A hot-water bottle?' she asked. 'I'm afraid* **not,***' he said.*

Sometimes we place the *so* at the beginning of a response utterance: *So it seems*, *So it appears*, *So they say*.

> *Ted hated the way Kate let her cat walk about the kitchen table, lick plates, sleep in beds. Or* **so** *he told Evelyn.*

Initial *so* is also common before verbs of perception: *hear*, *notice*, *observe*, *perceive*, *see*.

> *'When I saw you, I nearly died of shock.'*
> *'***So** *I saw,' he said.*

Notice that *believe*, *expect*, *imagine*, *suppose* and *think* have two negative structures which have no difference in meaning:

one with *so* *'I don't suppose* ***so,*** *' said Janet.*
one with *not* *'I suppose* ***not,*** *' Frances said.*

In conditional clauses starting with *if*, *so* or *not* substitute for a whole preceding clause:

Perhaps Hunter's line was simply a more sophisticated version . . . If ***so,*** *she preferred it to the other.*

To show (un)certainty or (im)possibility in a response utterance, we can use *so* (after *maybe*, *perhaps*, *possibly*) or *not* (after *apparently*, *certainly*, *perhaps*, *probably*, *surely* and *of course*) as a substitute for a preceding clause:

Perhaps ***so,*** *thought Anthony, but then – perhaps* ***not.***

'It's those aeroplanes,' he said. 'They take them out specially in this weather. To test them.' 'Surely ***not.***'

It, *this* and *that* are often used as clause substitutes.

She wondered why she had ever got married . . . Could she possibly have done ***it*** *because her younger sister had just done* ***it*** *before her?*

*'I don't get in anybody's way.' (****This*** *was a thought that would arise in his mind in the most remote places.)*

'Bob's terribly ill. Seriously ill. He didn't tell you ***that,*** *did he?'*

Substitutes for adverbs expressions of place and time
Here and *there*, *now* and *then* are useful pro-forms for longer adverbial expressions which have already been stated:

Further south she had felt like a prophet, a wanderer (which in a sense she was). Perhaps that had made it better. She had felt a purpose ***there. Here*** *she had none.*

GUIDELINE

The use of pro-forms is one grammatical feature that binds sentences together into discourse and makes it more coherent. As with the related feature of ellipsis, the golden rule is: substitute wherever possible, provided you do not lose meaning.

'Never speak disrespectfully of Society, Algernon. Only people who can't get into it do that.'
Oscar Wilde, *The Importance of Being Ernest*

see

29 Conditional clauses
77 Coordination
86 *Do*
88 Ellipsis
110 Indirect speech
136 Inversion
228 Pronouns
245 Reduction
261 Subordination

264

Tenses

Traditional grammar was based on the grammar of Latin, a language which – like modern French, Italian and Spanish – had inflections of the verb to mark present, past and future meaning and express these in present, past and future tenses. Therefore verb forms were equated with meanings of time.

Modern grammar argues that modern English, a relatively uninflected language, has present and past tenses, (i.e. verb forms which reflect these meanings of time) but no future tense.

We recognise the 3rd person *-s* inflexion as the marker of the tense which typically refers to present time. Even more clearly we recognise the *-ed* tense form which typically refers to past time. But there is no parallel marker of a tense which we typically use to talk about future time. Clearly we are able to think and talk about future events, but we do so by using a number of dissimilar devices and these are brought together in 99 under the heading 'Future time.' Each of the present and past tense families has four members, a simple tense and three complex tenses, using auxiliaries and marked for aspect. These are illustrated below:

Present		**Past**
She plays	Simple	*She played*
She is playing	Progressive	*She was playing*
She has played	Perfect	*She had played*
She has been playing	Perf. Prog.	*She had been playing*

To appreciate the complexity of time-relationships available from only three past tenses, let us take one sentence from Richard Adams' classic children's novel about rabbits, *Watership Down.*

> *We learned* (past simple) *later that some time after we'd been brought* (past perfect passive) *in . . . a runner arrived* (past simple) *from a Wide Patrol to say that they'd picked* (past perfect) *up the track of three or four rabbits (who had been) coming* (past perfect progressive) *. . . from the north; and were* (past simple) *there any orders?*

The time-relationships of the events of the six finite verbs bear little relationship to their order of appearance in the sentence. But we can decode the sequence of events, largely from the interplay of simple and complex tense forms:

Rabbits approaching from north
Rabbits brought in: patrol picks up tracks
Patrol runner arrives to report
Runner requests orders
Rabbits learn all this

↓ TIME

English verbs, then, usually have two simple tenses and six complex tenses. Additionally every transitive verb has eight corresponding passive tenses. Modals combine to form four active modal tenses:

she ***must*** *play*	***must*** *have played*
must *be playing*	***must*** *have been playing*

and four passive counterparts:

it ***must*** *be played* ***must*** *have been played*
must *be being played* ***must*** *have been being played*

Among these modal tenses are the forms (*she* ***will*** *play*, etc.) traditionally called future. This constitutes the system of English tenses. In the entries on each tense we concentrate on the active forms of the present and past tenses and ways of talking about the future.

▸ **see**
45 Aspect 143 Modal verbs
99 Future time 265 Tense and time

265

Tense and time

English verbs have a system of tenses, simple and complex. This system is a grammatical device which we use to indicate amongst other things the timing of the event to which the verb refers. Time is not a grammatical device, but a common concept in the physical world. Many languages use verb forms for talking about events in past time, present time and future time. We also sometimes need to express verbal meanings which are not associated with any particular one. When Lingard tells Willems:

Life ***is*** *very long,*

for instance, his thought is of future and past time no less than the present. Yet we identify it as being in the simple present tense. Lingard uses the same tense to identify a patently future action when he says:

I ***sail*** *tonight.*

Here is the crux of much confusion about the English tense system. We have the concepts of time; past present and future. We also use *past*, *present* and *future* to talk about tenses and thereby encourage the false assumption that the present tenses refer only to the present time, and the past tenses refer only to the past time etc. This, of course, is not so – witness ***I sail*** *tonight*, ***I am sailing*** *tomorrow*.

Modern grammar partly simplifies the traditional confusion between time and tense. It recognises only present and past tenses in English, arguing that *shall* and *will* patterns are more like modal patterns than the simple present and past forms. It also argues that *shall* and *will* are only one way of talking about the future and that we use these forms with other meanings too:

That ***will*** *do!* ~ Stop!

▸ **see**
264 Tenses

266

Topic and comment

The first main word of a sentence or clause is often the topic. It is usually the second most important part of the sentence/clause after the focus (normally at the end). We give maximum prominence to the focus, because it is the most important part of the message. By contrast, the opening topic is often known or familiar, setting the scene for the rest of the sentence and linking it with what has preceded it. The topic is often the subject of the sentence, and the rest of the sentence – what we say about the topic – is the comment.

topic — comment

These people are just playing at village life.

Sometimes topic and focus are identical, particularly when omission or substitution results in a short clause with a single information point:

He ***fattens*** *them.* [topic = focus]

The process of fronting often brings into topic position parts of the sentence/clause other than the subject:

Anything unusual I write down. [topic = object]
How surprised they must have been. [topic = complement]
Back they came. [topic = adverbial]

Cleft sentences similarly shuffle sentence elements about in order to switch emphasis. See how their use gives end-focus to an original topic.

The beginning of the shepherd's year *is the autumn.*

It's the autumn that's ***the beginning of the shepherd's year.***

I ***like*** *breeding pedigree animals.*

Breeding pedigree animals is ***what I like.***

GUIDELINE

In the unmarked sentence the topic and grammatical subject coincide. Where these are not identical, the sentence is marked in some way:

(T.) (S.)
Never have I seen such a play. [Marked for negation]

(T.) (S.)
What did you do? [Marked for question]

(T.) (S.)
Great, that idea of yours. [Marked for emphasis]

(T.) (S.)
What splendid ideas you have! [Marked for exclamation]

see

62 Cleft sentences
98 Fronting
142 Marked/unmarked

267

Transitive verbs: monotransitive

These are the large number of verbs which are followed by an obligatory noun phrase as direct object.

I | *lost* | *my ticket.*
transitive verb — direct object

The typical direct object of a transitive verb becomes the subject of the corresponding passive:

(o.)
I lost my ticket. [active]

(s.)
My ticket was lost. [passive]

Among the many thousands of verbs taking a single object, many can also be intransitive, like *begin*, *close*, *shine*. Others like *catch*, *buy* and *look at* are only transitive. Included among these are a number of phrasal verbs, (which naturally have a passive form).

I brushed off the leaves. → *The leaves were brushed off.*
I put on my bandages again. → *My bandages were put on again.*

However, some verbs which take a single object are not found in the passive. The reflexive pronouns of reflexive verbs are direct objects, as in

I must bury ***myself*** *in some farm,* or *He described* ***himself*** *as a hiker.*

But we never use such verbs in the passive voice. An even commoner transitive verb is *to have*, as in

(D.O.)
He ***has*** *perfect self-possession.*

But a passive transformation is unthinkable! *To have* is one of a small number of stative verbs which we call middle verbs. Middle verbs are not usually found in the passive, nor used in a progressive tense. Examples are:
become (= suit) *belong to* *consist of* *equal* *fit* *have* *lack* *measure* *possess* *resemble* *suit*

Consider:

Fortunately I ***had*** *a couple of pound notes.*
Who ***belongs to*** *Class X?*
I couldn't guess which pair would best ***fit*** *me.*

The object-like complementation of middle verbs is seen in the last example above, reminding us that they are followed by the objective case, and are therefore classed as transitive verbs.

GUIDELINE

A number of rather predictable direct objects may be dropped and are felt to be understood in the intransitive phrase – *He drinks too much* (alcohol) =

(understood object). But most direct objects are obligatory, and ellipsis is impossible when the verb and its direct object are as close as most transitive verbs and their objects. For example:

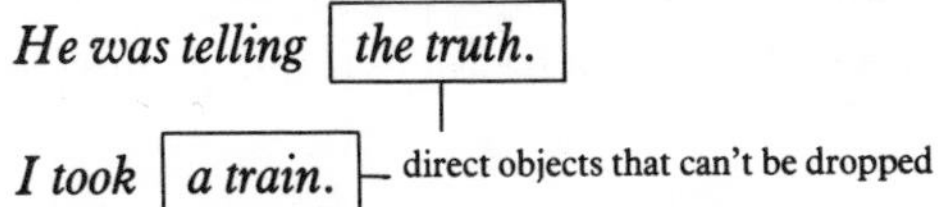

One unusual transitive verb is *to put*. It is not only followed by a direct object but by an obligatory adverbial.

It puts him *under suspicion.*
adverbial cannot be dropped

Many phrasal verbs are transitive. Unless the direct object is a pronoun or lengthy, we may place the particle before or after the direct object:

I put on my bandages again. ~ *I put my bandages on again.*
I brushed off the leaves. ~ *I brushed the leaves off.*
I had never taken off my gloves. ~ *I had never taken my gloves off.*

In the case of a longer direct object, it is less clumsy to place the particle in mid-position:

He seemed to be summing up *me and the bargain.*
lengthier object

Pronoun objects take mid-position between the phrasal verb and its particle:

I took *it* *apart.*
compulsory mid-position for pronoun object

Prepositional verbs and phrasal-prepositional verbs are by definition transitive, their direct object being a prepositional object, which always follows its preposition in the active voice:

. . . a gate that led into (prep. v.) *another open field*
It accounts for (prep. v.) *my folly*
The farm and its dogs woke up to (phrasal-prep. v.) *the fact . . .*

Phrasal verbs and prepositional verbs sometimes have a passive use:

I felt as if I'd been knocked down (phrasal v.) *by a railway engine.*
I had been prepared for (prep. v.) *it.*

But phrasal-prepositional verbs are rarely used in the passive voice.

GUIDELINES

The alternative positions of particle and direct object of transitive phrasal verbs are not quite the same. *To take off one's gloves* is more formal than *to take one's gloves off*. In *Rogue Male*, Geoffrey Household consistently places the particle in mid-position. This is part of the carefully formal style appropriate for his author/hero, a well-educated 'gentleman' writing in

1939. A modern writer of adventure stories would choose the less formal pattern (which we invariably use in speech) placing the particle last. The same sense of formality taught that sentences should not end in a preposition. Household's hero cannot avoid sentences like:

I knew what he was looking for.

But he chooses to write:

I couldn't see myself of what they consisted.

A sentence amusingly shaped for stylistic reasons, but not to be copied.

▶ **see**

3	Active/passive	196	Phrasal prepositional verbs
87	Dynamic/stative use	221, 222	Prepositional verbs
133	Intransitive verbs	246	Reflexive pronouns
183	Objects	270	Transitivity
194, 195	Phrasal verbs	272	Verb types and sentence patterns

268

Transitive verbs: complex transitive

Verbs followed by object and complement are called complex transitives. In this pattern the complement refers back to the object and may be either nominal or adjectival:

I called him a damned **fool.** [noun complement]

His delicate movements made the reason perfectly **clear.** [adjectival complement]

In both cases the verbs may have current or resulting meaning. Verbs commonly followed by object and noun complement are as follows. (Notice that current verbs are usually stative and resulting verbs dynamic.)

Current		**Resulting**	
believe	*leave*	*appoint*	*make*
call	*presume*	*certify*	*name*
confess	*profess*	*choose*	*proclaim*
consider	*pronounce*	*declare*	*prove*
find	*rate*	*elect*	*vote*
hold	*reckon*		
imagine	*suppose*		
judge	*think*		
keep			

I ***considered it ample*** *for my purpose.* [current]

Let me ***make the position perfectly clear.*** [resulting]

Notice that with both forms of complement, we can use introductory *it* as object:

. . . make [*it*] [*a lot easier*] *for both of us if you . . .*

intro. *it* as o. — adj. complement

▶ GUIDELINE

This pattern, s.v.o.c., is clearly close to patterns where the complementation is one of the non-finites. Compare:

We imagined him foolish.
We imagined him to be foolish.

Verbs complemented with non-finites are dealt with under catenative verbs.

▶ **see**

51 Catenative verbs
87 Dynamic/stative use
134 Introductory *it*
157 Non-finites
270 Transitivity
272 Verb types and sentence patterns

269

Transitive verbs: di-transitive

These are verbs with two objects, and they normally have:

a noun phrase as indirect object (i.o.) which is animate and follows the verb, and

a noun phrase as direct object (d.o.) which follows the indirect object. For example:

(i.o.) (d.o.)

Sell [*him*] [*the punt.*]

The s.+v.+i.o.+d.o. pattern includes *that-* clauses and *wh-* clauses as direct object (see reporting and thinking verbs).

that- clause as d.o.

I also told him [*that I was a rich man.*]

Many verbs which we use in this pattern can also be used in the related pattern s.+v.+d.o.+to/for+i.o.; for example: *Sell the punt to him.*

The choice between *for* and *to* is not an open one; certain verbs are followed by *for* and others by *to*. The following lists show common verbs which we can use in both patterns grouped according to the *for/to* selection:

s. + v. + d.o. + for + i.o.		s. + v. + d.o. + to + i.o.		
buy	*find*	*bring*	*owe*	*send*
call	*get*	*fetch*	*pass*	*show*
choose	*keep*	*give*	*pay*	*talk*
cook	*leave*	*hand*	*post*	*teach*
do	*make*	*leave*	*promise*	*tell*
fetch	*save*	*lend*	*read*	*throw*
		offer	*sell*	*write*

We tend to use the S.+V.+I.O.+D.O. pattern with short and/or known indirect objects.

She showed me the punt.
. . . to bring him luck

When the indirect object is longer and needs end-focus because it is new information, we use the pattern with *for* or *to*. This is also the preferred pattern when both objects are pronouns:

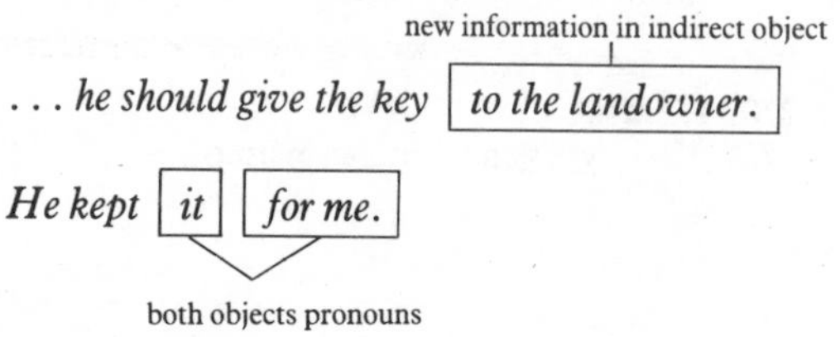

In some cases we can omit one of the objects with no change of meaning. But this is impossible with certain reporting verbs, like *tell*, which have a compulsory indirect object before the objective clause:

I told *him* *he certainly could.*

unavoidable I.O.

GUIDELINE

The verb *to give* is unusual; it can take inanimate indirect objects. In this case we cannot use the *for/to* pattern:

Give your shoes a good clean. Give the account a closer examination.

see
97 Focus
183 Objects
252 Reporting verbs
270 Transitivity
272 Verb types and sentence patterns

270

Transitivity

Finite verbs are central to the meaning of their sentences. We can classify verbs and sentence patterns according to the relationship between the verb and the following parts of its sentence. Verbs often have a following object – these verbs are transitive. At other times, verbs have no objects, though they may have a following adjective or noun phrase as a complement. Verbs used with no object are intransitive. Those intransitive verbs used with a complement are linking verbs.

Transitive verbs have one object, the direct object; this is the person or thing affected by the action of the verb:

direct object, person affected by hurting

You hurt *me.*

Sometimes transitive verbs have two objects, the direct and indirect object. The indirect object usually refers to a person or thing that receives the direct object.

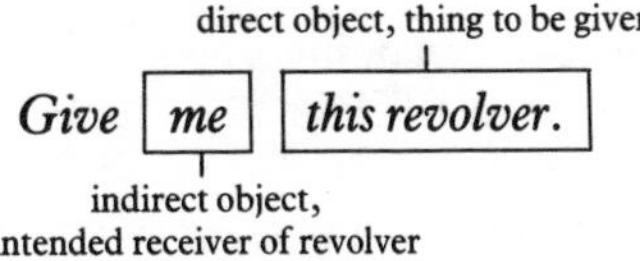

Intransitive verbs often need nothing after them to complete a sentence:

A troop of long-tailed monkeys appeared.

Or they may have an adverbial as modifier:

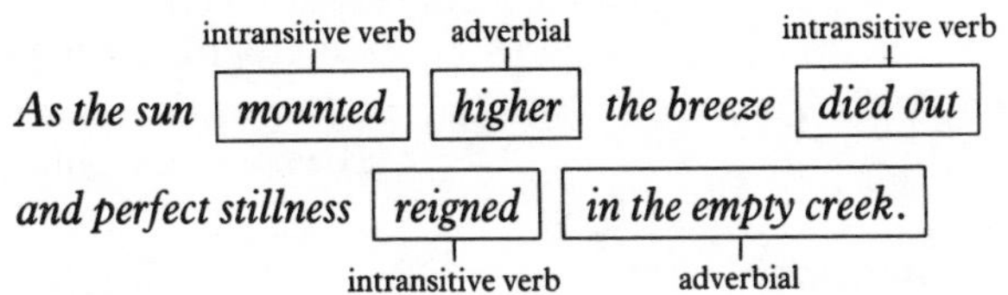

Compared with objects, which are usually essential components, adverbials are dispensable optional extras: in the sentence above, Conrad could have omitted at least the second adverbial, if not both.

Linking verbs, or copular verbs are intransitive, and link their subject to its complement which is usually an adjective or noun: though sometimes it is an adverbial. In every case, subject and complement refer to the same thing – they are co-referential:

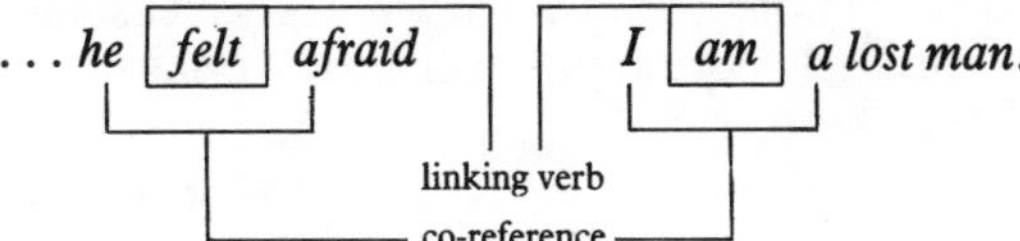

GUIDELINE

Serious modern dictionaries use symbols to show transitive/intransitive/ linking use (T.) (I.) (L.). Verbs like *arrive* and *depart* are always intransitive. Verbs like *inhabit*, *look at* and *use* are always transitive. But we use many verbs both transitively and intransitively: *He closed his eyes* (trans.). *His eyes closed* (intrans.). *Conrad lived a full life* (trans.). *Conrad lived in London* (intrans.). We even use some verbs transitively, intransitively and in linking use:

*She's **growing** roses* (trans.). *She's **growing*** (intrans.).
*She's **growing** old* (linking).

Since we use many verbs in more than one pattern (transitive, intransitive, linking) it is more accurate to talk about verbs in transitive use than transitive verbs, etc.

see

23 Adverbials
268 Complex transitives
269 Di-transitives
133 Intransitive verbs
141 Linking verbs
183 Objects
272 Verb types and sentence patterns

271

Verbs: general

We define verbs from both their form and function. In doing so we identify two kinds of verbs: lexical verbs, a major word class, and auxiliary verbs, a minor word class.

Lexical verbs, like *look*, *run* and *sell*, carry full meaning and are the key to all sentences.

Auxiliary verbs, like *can*, *be* and *must* carry less meaning than lexical verbs, and are used in combination with lexical verbs in verb phrases to form tenses and to express modality (possibility, permission, etc.).

I ***was standing*** *at the window.* [auxiliary *was* + lexical verb in *-ing* > past progressive tense]

By craning out, I **could** *see Hymettus.* [modal auxiliary *could* + lexical verb expressing ability]

Some characteristics of verbs

The verb, or the verb phrase is often heavily packed with meaning. This is because we build into it a number of concepts and devices. Some of these apply to all verbs, others more selectively. We use verbs to talk and think about activities, or states:

The hills became even barer. [activity]
The island was so beautiful. [state]

These are rather different kinds of happenings and call for two kinds of verb use – dynamic and stative. The activities described happen at some time or other, and verbs accordingly have a system of tenses to show when their actions take place.

Do you like *my house?* [present simple]
I ***designed*** *and* ***built*** *it myself.* [past simple]

The tense forms also often carry a feature which marks them for aspect: this indicates whether the action of the verb is ongoing, or occurring before-now/before-then: progressive and perfective aspect.

A moment later, I ***was standing*** *alone.* [past progressive tense – action ongoing]

When I looked back . . . he ***had disappeared***. [past perfect tense – action occurring before-then]

Lexical verbs also have both active and passive forms (voice) which we use for different communicative purposes. Compare:

She ***was watching*** *me.* [active – subject important]
We're ***being watched***. [passive – subject unknown, subject unstated]

The forms of verbs are either finite or non-finite. Finite verbs have a subject, e.g. *He* (s.) *shrugged* (v.), whereas non-finites like the infinitive (*to see*) or the *-ing* form (*seeing*) usually appear only in combination with finite verbs:

I had been ***swimming*** *a long time.*
I tried ***to make up*** *my mind about Colchis.*

Verb types

We build sentences with verbs in four basic ways: the verb may be in transitive, intransitive, linking or catenative use. When a verb is transitive, it has one or two objects which receive the verbal action of the subject.

I.O. D.O.

He gave me a swift look.

When verbs are intransitive they have no object.

I smiled.

Linking verbs are intransitive but have a complement or adverbial to complete their meaning:

C.

He seemed surprised.

When we follow an ordinary lexical verb with a non-finite form, it is in catenative use:

V. non-finite

Meanwhile, he had started weaving his web again . . .

V. non-finite

I am trying to describe what happened to me.

These four basic ways of patterning verbs, with their sub-categories, account for all the different kinds of sentences of English.

▶ **see**

3	Active/passive voice	139	Lexical verbs
45	Aspect	141	Linking verbs
48	Auxiliary verbs	265	Tense and time
51	Catenative verbs	264	Tenses
87	Dynamic/stative use	270	Transitivity
96	Finite/non-finite	272	Verb types and sentence patterns

272

Verb types and sentence patterns

We can classify types of verbs by the way they are complemented, or followed. These regular groupings allow us to identify a small number of common sentence patterns.

Intransitive verbs – may have adverbials only [S.+V.(+adv.)]
Linking verbs – take a complement [S.+V.+C.]
Mono-transitive verbs – take single direct objects [S.+V.+O.]
Di-transitive verbs – take direct and indirect objects [S.+V.+I.O.+D.O.]
Complex transitive verbs – take objects and complements [S.+V.+O.+C./S.+V.+O.+adv.]

Catenative verbs – take non-finite forms [S.+V.+ infin., etc.]

Several verbs are restricted to one pattern, but many verbs are used in more than one.

see

51	Catenative verbs	141	Linking verbs
268	Complex transitive verbs	267	Mono-transitive verbs
269	Di-transitive verbs	270	Transitivity
133	Intransitive verbs		

273

Wh- clauses

Wh- clauses are clauses introduced by a *wh-* word (*how, what, when, where, whether, which, who, whom, whose, why*). As main clauses, they form *wh-* questions:

What is it you want?

As subordinate clauses (with or without a finite verb) they are in wide use as –

adverbial clauses

When he spoke*, there was in his voice a mingling of quietness and animation.*

While he sat on his bed*... his mind returned to the mystery.*

indirect questions

They asked Lewis ***whether he would help****.*

Why you should shut yourself away*, I don't know.*

nominal clauses

Lewis knew ***what bitterness was in Herriot's mind****.*

It's a question of ***how to attain it****.*

and relative clauses

He was no older than his brother, ***who had been killed at his side****.*

Separated from their men, ***with whom they had been living****... they were being taken to closer imprisonment.*

'I keep six serving-men
(they taught me all I knew)
Their names are What and Why and When
And How and Where and Who.'

Rudyard Kipling, *Just-So Stories*

---

see

24	Adverbial clauses	247	Relative clauses
110	Indirect speech	236	*Wh-* questions
156	Nominal clauses		

274

Wh- words as determiners and pronouns

A number of *wh-* words, along with *such*, are used as pronouns and determiners of various kinds. Several are used as both pronouns and determiners, two as pronouns only, and one as determiner only:

Pronouns only	*who(ever)* *whom*
Pronouns and determiners	*whose* *what(ever)* *which(ever)*
Determiner only	*whatsoever*

Pronouns only

The interrogative pronouns *who* and *whom* refer to people only:

***Who** is that girl with yellow hair and dark eyes?* [personal subject]
***Who** do you mean?* [informal personal object]
***Whom** do you think I passed today in Richmond Park?* [formal personal object]

In today's spoken English we prefer *who* to *whom*, which is very rare. Even in written English we often write *who* when the reference is to a personal object: ***Who** do you think I passed . . .?*

Pronouns and determiners

Whose, *what* and *which* as determiners may refer to both count nouns, singular and plural, and non-count nouns. *What(ever)* as pronoun refers to things and, less commonly, people:

***What** is it, my darling?* [non-personal subject]
***What'**s he going to give her?* [non-personal object]
***What** did Soames want to go into the country for?* [non-personal prepositional object]

But *what(ever)* as determiner can refer to personal and non-personal subject and objects:

***What** other reason was there?* [non-personal object]
***What** name shall I say, sir?* [non-personal subject]
***What** other ladies were there?* [personal subject]
***What** person did you hear it from?* [personal object]

Interrogative *what* is a chameleon word taking on the meaning/colour of its surrounding context. The following examples all come from *A Man of Property* by John Galsworthy.

***What** was her father?* ~ occupation
*inquired **what** he had given for it.* ~ money
***What's** the name of your doctor?* ~ name
***What** do you say, Mr Bosinney?* ~ opinion
*Remarkable for **what**?* ~ quality
***What** if Irene were to leave Soames?* ~ result
***What** was the world coming to?* ~ state
***What** can they expect?* ~ affliction
*. . . and all for **what**?* ~ benefit
*. . . and **what**!* ~ incredulity

Which (det. and pron.) refers to a limited set of things or people, i.e. personal/non-personal subjects/objects:

Which (det.) *marriage failed? Which* (pron.) *of the dogs was Young Jolyon's?* [non-personal subject]
Which (det.) *Forsyte loved paintings? Which* (pron.) *was an artist?* [personal subject]
Which (det.) *house did Soames build? Which* (pron.) *did Phil design?* [non-personal object]
Which (det.) *man did Irene love? Which* (pron.) *did she marry?* [personal object]

In modern English we distinguish between limited and unlimited reference, sometimes called definite and indefinite reference. We use *which* (det. and pron.) for limited reference and *what* (det. and pron.) for unlimited reference. Compare:

***What** novels do you like? **Which** Galsworthy novels do you like?*
***What** will you have to drink? **Which** will you have, red wine or white?*

Whose (det. and pron.) has personal reference only (sing. and plural) and indicates possession:

Whose (det.) *daughter was Fleur? Whose* (det.) *children were Jolly and Holly? And whose* (pron.) *were Val and Imogen?*

Determiner only

The old-fashioned determiner, *whatsoever*, remains only in fossilised legal language:

*. . . my property of **whatsoever** kind*

GUIDELINE

Notice the word-order in questions starting with *wh-* interrogatives. When *what/which/who/whose* are the subject of questions with verbs other than to be, we have the normal statement order: *Wh-* subject + verb + object. When the *wh*-interrogative is the object we have interrogative order: *wh*-object (+ operator) + subject + verb. Compare:

Who (s.) *married* (v.) *Soames? Who(m)* (o.) *did* (op.) *Soames* (s.) *marry* (v.)*?*
Which Forsyte (s.) *left* (v.) *money to Timothy? Which Forsyte* (o.) *did* (op.) *Irene* (s.) *inherit* (v.) *from?*

Such and *what* as determiners and pronouns

What and *such* as pre-determiner intensifiers stand before the indefinite article with singular count nouns, and with zero article with plural count nouns and non-count nouns. They can both open sentences of exclamation, though *what* does so more often.

We often use *such* to show admiration or disappointment:

***What** a feeling of weariness.*
***What** atoms men were.* ***What** traffic!*
*To think of a Forsyte living in **such** a place!*
***Such** a horrid sight.*

The noun phrase with *what* often stands alone. Noun phrases with *such* are usually subject, complement or object of a verb:

__Such__ thoughts were inconceivable. [subject]
There are __such__ things. [complement]
Most people would consider __such__ a marriage . . . fairly successful. [object]

Such as a determiner can follow *all*, *any*, *many*, *no*, *some*, etc. and is usually anaphoric (backwards pointing):

Nonsense! I couldn't have sworn any __such__ thing!

At the most a flirtation, ending, as all __such__ attachments should, at the proper time.

Such as can signal post-modification of a noun:

The look on her face, __such as__ he had never seen there before, __such as__ she had always hidden from him, was full of secret resentments . . .

Similarly *such . . . as* and *what* (dets.) are used in split structures:

But it could not be __such__ knowledge __as__ this he was seeking . . .

Some thistledown came on __what__ little air there was . . .

Such (pron.) is anaphoric when we use it alone:

Forsyte girls had become engaged to __such__ before, and had actually married them.

And __such__, as everyone knows, is fit accompaniment for a perambulating Forsyte.

but cataphoric when followed by *that/as to* in a result clause:

(he) had __such__ a taste in his mouth that he was prepared to drink anything.

GUIDELINE

Roald Dahl's short story 'The Great Automatic Grammatizator' describes a computer which wrote novels, designed by a man who 'was struck by a powerful and simple little truth, and it was this: that English grammar is governed by rules that are almost mathematical in their strictness!' That was fiction! We have seen among the *wh-* words how shady are the frontiers between pronouns and determiners, how some are interchangeable and others take on meaning from their context. Categories like determiner, quantifier and contact clause do not appear in older grammars. Perhaps we are nearer today to satisfactory accounts of how language works, but shady areas, like *wh-* words, remain.

> *'In this noble country of ours there is no such thing as summer weather or summer clothing. There are simply different kinds of temperatures and different kinds of garments appropriate to them.'*
>
> *The Times*

I'm hoping not but never **I'm wishing not** – explain.

see

84	Determiners	251	Relative pronouns
95	Exclamations	33	Result clauses
130	Intensifiers	273	*Wh-* clauses
200	Postmodification	236	*Wh-* questions
84	Predeterminers	274	*Wh-* words
228	Pronouns		

275

Wishing

We use two common ways to express our wishes: with the verb *to wish* and using the exclamation *if only*. In both cases the following verbs are back-shifted like the tenses in indirect speech and hypothetical conditional sentences. So in wishing about the present, we use the simple past tense of the verb:

Oh God, I wish this **was** *over.*
I wish they **wouldn't** *concentrate on me.*

In wishes about the future, we use *could* and *would* and other forms of modals:

I wish I **could** *stop it.*
If only you **would** *eat something . . .*
If only I **didn't** *have to go to court.*

Notice that we use *would* in future wishes, only for habits, willingness or insistence. When we are talking of the pure future, as in *Perhaps it* **will** *be fine tomorrow*, the corresponding wish can only be expressed by *hope – I* **hope** *it will be fine tomorrow* and not **I wish it would be fine tomorrow.*

In wishes about the past, we use the past perfect tense:

Patrick wished the trial **had finished.**
Marlene wished she **hadn't been** *so hard on Tim.*

As with conditional clauses, we use subjunctive *were* for all persons in making more formal wishes:

I wish it **were** *over.*	[present]
He wished it **were** *over.*	[past]
If only she **were** *able to come tomorrow.*	[hypothetical future]

But in all cases, we hear *was* increasingly often.

GUIDELINES

To wish is a stative verb and therefore we do not normally use it with the progressive. So, never **I am wishing that* – nor do we use it with *so/not. I hope so* but not **I wish so.*

Although its main use is to express wishes, we use it for other functions:

I wish you **would** *stop that.*	[annoyance/command]
I wish I **knew** *how to find it.*	[indirect request for help]
I wish I **hadn't said** *that.*	[regret]
I wish I **could** *help.*	[polite refusal]

I wish I **could** *believe you.* [polite disbelief]
I could have wished you **had done** *better.* [understated disappointment]
I do wish you **would** *be more punctual.* [reprimand]

'I wish I loved the Human Race;
I wish I loved its silly face;
I wish I liked the way it walks;
I wish I liked the way it talks;
And when I'm introduced to one
I wish I thought What Jolly Fun!'

Sir Walter Raleigh (1861–1922), *Laughter from a Cloud*

▶ **see**
49 Back-shift
87 Dynamic/stative use
74 Hypothetical conditions
111 Indirect speech
260 Subjunctive

276

Word classes (parts of speech)

In his *English Grammar* in 1817, the admirable William Cobbett wrote: *There are nine parts of speech.* Modern grammarians distinguish ten word classes, having divided Cobbett's *verbs* into two and replaced the traditional class articles by determiners.

There is no one way of identifying all words as members of a particular word class. Cobbett used the traditional, notional, definition: *a word which stands for any thing that has an existence is a noun.* We are probably safer to classify words by their position or function in a sentence – in *The car's *wim the shop*, **wim* is probably a preposition.

Form is another good guide for those classes of words which have typical inflections – **widgeful* must be an adjective; **widged* is likely to be a past participle. Using sentence position, word-form and sometimes meaning, modern grammarians identify major word classes and minor word classes.

Major word classes

These carry most of the meaning of sentences. They are:

Nouns	*book decision furniture*
Lexical verbs	*sing decide furnish*
Adjectives	*big quick contemporary*
Adverbs	*quickly tomorrow at home*

These four major word classes are often described as open in the sense that their membership is open-ended. New members are constantly being added to them and we could never write a complete list of them with any certainty.

In what sense are minor word classes **closed**?

Minor word classes
These have a more structural function in sentences.
They are:

Pronouns	*you her one*
Auxiliary verbs	*can must has*
Determiners	*the some such*
Prepositions	*on through behind*
Conjunctions	*and but although*
Interjections	*oh ouch*

The minor word classes are closed, in the sense that their membership does not change from one decade to another.

GUIDELINES

Think of word classes as jobs that words do. The open classes, in particular, are abstract grammatical categories to which we can allot words doing a particular job. Words are not of their essence nouns, verbs or adjectives, etc. but are commonly used as these. Although for the sake of brevity we say that *little* is a determiner, a pronoun, an adjective or an adverb, it is more accurate to speak of *little* in use as a determiner, etc. Most words in English can be used as nouns, verbs and adjectives – even structure words:

> *'Nay, but me no buts.'*
> Sir Walter Scott, echoing
> *'Grace me no grace, nor uncle me no uncle.'*
> William Shakespeare, *Richard II*

see

4–11	Adjectives	139	Lexical verbs
12–22	Adverbs	158–77	Nouns
48	Auxiliary verbs	205–17	Prepositions
76	Conjunctions	228	Pronouns
84	Determiners	271, 272	Verbs
131	Interjections		

277

Zero forms

Zero is a term used in modern grammar to indicate the absence of a feature. We talk about zero article, zero determiner, zero plural, zero pronoun, zero subordinator and zero coordinator. The three ways in which the term zero is used are best illustrated with reference to plural nouns. We say that nouns like *sheep* have zero plural. In this sense zero means non-existent in form. But we also say that words like *dozen* have both zero and regular plural usage. For example:

dozens of eggs – regular plural for vague numbers
two ***dozen*** eggs – zero plural for precise numbers

In this sense, zero does not mean non-existent, but an alternative form unmarked for plural which is compulsory in certain situations. The third meaning of zero plural is for the unmarked form which is a freely optional alternative. *Eskimo*, we can say, takes either *-s* or zero plural – *Eskimo(s)*.

Zero article is found with non-count nouns and plural count nouns in certain meanings:

△ *Petrol is cheaper.* △ *Bus fares aren't.*

Zero coordinator is a choice of style as in:

I came, I saw, I conquered.

Zero determiner is required in phrases consisting of two or more nouns which are notionally a single unit:

a man and △ *woman*
Put on your coat and △ *hat.*
Have some cheese and △ *biscuits.*

Zero pronoun is an optional feature of defining object relative clauses, where the relative pronoun may be dropped, so forming a contact clause:

*. . . people (**that**) we meet*
*someone (**whom**) they're fond of*

Zero subordinator is used to account for the compulsory omission of *if* in the alternative form of hypothetical conditions which use inversion of subject and operator:

If you should think so . . .
Should you think so . . .

But zero subordinator is also used for the optional omission of that introducing subject and object nominal clauses:

*It's only right (**that**) he's punished.*
*I believe (**that**) he's guilty.*

▶ **see**

40–44	Zero article	173	Zero plural
78	Zero coordinator	247, 251	Zero pronoun
84	Zero determiner	74, 156	Zero subordinator

Literary sources

References to and quotations from the following works are made in the entries.

Index

Bold numbers indicate major entries.